D1487774

WITHDRAWN

HOT TOPICS

Everything You Ever Wanted to Know
About the Fifty Major Controversies
Everyone Pretends to Know All About

DANIEL STARER

A TOUCHSTONE BOOK
Published by Simon & Schuster
New York   London   Toronto
Sydney   Tokyo   Singapore

TOUCHSTONE
Rockefeller Center
1230 Avenue of the Americas
New York, New York 10020

Copyright © 1995 by Daniel Starer

TOUCHSTONE and colophon are registered
trademarks of Simon & Schuster Inc.

Designed by Deirdre C. Amthor

Manufactured in the United States of America

1   3   5   7   9   10   8   6   4   2

Library of Congress Cataloging-in-Publication Data
is available
ISBN 0-671-88708-4

To Paul Plumer and Mike Abrams, with thanks
for twenty years of friendship and wilderness canoe trips.

Contents

Medicine and Morals 57

Money Matters 95

Schools and Rules 113

Combat Fatigue

Culture Wars

Governing the Government

Nature Versus Nurture

Being Green 215

Foreign Despairs 225

Bibliography 235

Acknowledgments

My thanks to Lauren Petit and my wife, Maggie Meehan, for their editorial assistance. I also appreciate the help from many experts at associations and political action committees who helped clarify their positions on a variety of issues over the telephone.

Special thanks to my superb editor, Mitch Horowitz. His keen intellect, knowledge of current issues, and evenhanded criticisms were invaluable.

Introduction

Do you sometimes find yourself defending a dearly held belief without having the facts at your fingertips?

Every day the media bombard us with sound bites about the issues and moral dilemmas that divide America. But the media often neglect to clarify the competing arguments that could help us really understand these controversies. In *Hot Topics* I've tried to write a book that clearly, concisely, and evenhandedly debates both sides of fifty key issues. Knowing both sides helps you understand current events, form or bolster your positions, debate politics more effectively, and even play devil's advocate.

Hot Topics is a crash course in current events. After presenting the pro and con arguments, I summarize the history, current status, and likely future of each controversy. The book covers all the perennial hot issues—such as abortion, the death penalty, and school prayer—as well as the newer debates likely to heat up in the next few years—such as "three strikes" prison sentences and government funding levels for AIDS research. *Hot Topics* includes social, political, economic, health, defense, legal, educational, and cultural controversies. Besides the obvious "big" issues you'll find smaller, cutting-edge disputes that also serve as battlegrounds for liberals and conservatives, rich and poor, men and women, hawks and doves, generation X and retirees. Some of the basic, ethical dilemmas in this book transcend politics and affect the lives of every person.

In writing *Hot Topics* I hunted for the strongest arguments to help me debate contrary viewpoints with equal vigor. I found these opinions in a wide range of books, editorials, newspaper and magazine articles, and from interviewing representatives of political action committees, special interest groups, and various associations that focus on these issues.

I particularly enjoyed researching and then paraphrasing points of view I strongly disagree with. Only by learning your opponent's arguments can you completely understand your own. Now, I believe I can sit down at the dinner table and defend my beliefs effectively. Reading *Hot Topics* will give *you* the same ammunition to understand and argue both sides. And perhaps you, as I did, will surprise yourself by changing sides on a dearly held belief or two.

Daniel Starer
New York, NY
November 1994

CRIME
AND
PUNISHMENT

1. Will "Three-Strikes-and-You're-Out" Laws Reduce Violent Crime?

YES

A three-strikes law protects society. So-called three strikes legislation incarcerates violent three-time felony offenders for life, ensuring that they cannot harm society again. Criminals who cannot mend their ways after two convictions should not get another chance. They clearly demonstrate incorrigibility and deserve severe punishment.

Seven percent of young men with substantial arrest records commit *two-thirds* of all violent crime. Eighty percent of criminals who commit three violent crimes go on to commit a fourth. Three strikes laws protect the public by permanently taking these repeat, violent offenders out of circulation.

Today's criminal justice system coddles criminals. Three out of four convicted criminals avoid incarceration. Fewer than 10 percent of all serious crimes result in jail time. Not only are prison sentences too short, but the combination of parole and time off for good behavior can allow some criminals to serve only one-sixth of their sentence. The current system fails to protect the innocent.

Three strikes will deter some young offenders. Not all young violent offenders are destined to spend their life in crime. The serious nature of three strikes sentences will scare some criminals into turning their life around.

Life imprisonment programs are worth the cost. According to former-Attorney General Edwin Meese, society's financial cost of allowing a violent criminal to roam free is two to five times greater than imprisoning him. That does not even include the immeasurable human costs of violent crimes.

Three strikes laws help create a more fair, objective legal system. Standardized sentencing guidelines preclude a judge's giving out different sentences for the same crime or letting prosecutors use discretion to let criminals get off easily. Three strikes laws ensure that all criminals receive impartial, honest, and equal treatment under the law.

N O

Why fill our prisons with docile old men? Studies show that most violent criminals "burn out" and outgrow their brutal tendencies in middle age. Why should we operate geriatric prisons for aging criminals whose days of actual crime are behind them? These men will take up valuable prison space that should go to imprison young, still-violent criminals.

Three strikes laws will cost a fortune. To accommodate the crush of three strikes prisoners, the California Department of Corrections predicts it must build twenty additional prisons at a cost of about $500 million each, adding to the twenty-eight state prisons existing today. In addition, taxpayers will have to spend at least $600,000 to support each harmless prisoner from age fifty until death.

Increased incarceration does not reduce crime. According to the Justice Department, from 1980 to 1992 the American state and federal prison population soared nearly 150 percent, from 139 to 344 jailed for every 100,000 of total population—the Western world's highest ratio. In the same period, however, violent crime per capita has remained essentially steady, with some measures rising or falling slightly. Over the past decade no one has proven that mandatory life sentences reduce violent crime.

Automatic sentencing reduces flexibility. An automatic life sentence ignores the circumstances of a crime, prohibiting judges and prosecutors from examining cases individually. It precludes judges from considering extenuating or mitigating circumstances.

Court backlogs will multiply. Automatic sentencing discourages plea bargaining because criminals would rather take their chances with a trial than plead guilty to a crime that would count as a final strike. The influx of criminals seeking a trial will clog the overburdened court system and further strain already overworked public defenders.

Racial inequality will grow. Since the United States fails to address the social and economic factors that contribute to crime, a three strikes law would significantly increase the number of black and Hispanic prisoners. Instead, shouldn't we divert the $20,000 to $30,000 a year it costs to incarcerate each prisoner and spend it on job-training and substance-abuse programs?

Background

The idea of abolishing parole, although not new, has gained enormous popular support because of crimes like the 1993 murder of twelve-year-old Polly Klaas in Petaluma, California. When a career criminal, recently paroled from a previous kidnapping conviction, abducted and killed the girl, commentators argued she would be alive today if her killer had remained behind bars, where he belonged.

Although some states already had habitual offender laws, the Sentencing Reform Act of 1984 first crystallized the idea for the nation as a whole. The act allows for no parole and limits time off for good behavior to 15 percent of the sentence. Congress wanted to base punishments on the *crime,* not on a judge's *opinion* of the criminal. It established the Federal Sentencing Commission, which constructed a point system for sentencing. Since November 1987 federal judges have had to consider seven factors regarding the crime and eleven regarding the criminal. The judge tallies the points and finds the appropriate punishment on a table.

Some judges adhered to the new law, others did not. The dissenters declared the law unconstitutional since only Congress can directly set rules that bind judges. The Supreme Court, foreseeing chaos in this situation, heard a test case and in 1989 upheld the federal sentencing rules, putting to rest any question of legality.

Behind the Sentencing Reform Act and similar state laws exists a simple premise: prison is to punish, not to rehabilitate. Such laws limit flexibility in sentencing based on the possibility of rehabilitation. Previously, parole guidelines could reduce a sentence by as much as two-thirds.

By 1993, thirty-one states enacted life-without-parole laws for the most serious felonies. A federal version passed in the Senate, but not in the House. In November 1993, 77 percent of Washington State voters approved a referendum for a new type of repeat offender law which was popularly titled "Three-Strikes-and-You're-Out." It encompasses forty different crimes that, repeated three times, will result in life imprisonment. The law excludes juvenile offenders and allows adult criminals to erase "strikes" after a certain amount of time as a reward for not committing another offense. Class A crimes, such as murder, rape, and felony sex offenses, remain a strike regardless of elapsed time. As soon as a criminal accumulates a third strike, or conviction, by committing any one of the forty qualifying crimes, life in prison without parole is automatic. An estimated seventy-five criminals per year will be sentenced under the new law.

In March 1994, California became the second state to pass a three strikes law, though one that does not call for life imprisonment. Under the California law, second-time felony offenders receive double the usual penalty, plus five years extra prison time. Third-time felons receive a minimum of twenty-five years in prison, with no chance of parole.

A February 1994 nationwide *Los Angeles Times* poll found that 74 percent of Americans favor three strikes laws even if their state has to raise taxes or take money from other programs to build new prisons.

Outlook

As crime has become a hot political issue at both the federal and state levels, criminal justice policy is increasingly determined by voters and the politicians eager to please them. The tough anti-crime stances of Republican candidates helped many of them win congressional and gubernatorial elections in November 1994. The citizens of Georgia voted for one of the nation's toughest laws, mandating life in prison after *two* violent felonies.

In 1993, Virginians elected George Allen governor in part because of his promise to abolish parole. New York, Maryland, and eight other states have bills under consideration that also would abolish parole. A total of thirty states are expected to consider three strikes laws in the next few years. President Bill Clinton has also voiced support for such laws. The comprehensive crime bill he signed into law in September 1994 requires life imprisonment without parole for anyone convicted in federal court of a third violent crime.

The National Rifle Association (NRA), which substantially bankrolled the Washington State campaign, has vowed to spend $3 million to pass three strikes laws elsewhere. Given the tough anticrime mood nationwide, chances are they will succeed. However, no one can predict if violent crime will really decline as a result.

2. Should Hate Crimes Receive Harsher Sentences?

YES

Hate crimes are different. The perpetrator of a hate crime verbally or physically attacks another person solely because of his or her immutable characteristics, such as being a Jew or a black. Since hate crimes are committed for no material gain, they represent an especially heinous form of lawlessness.

Hate crimes threaten society as a whole. A hate crime not only injures an individual or destroys property, but also causes great emotional trauma. A hate crime intends to intimidate—attacking one black person for being black threatens *all* blacks. Such crimes increase tension within a community, incite copycat crimes, and provoke retaliation.

The number and severity of hate crimes are rising. Desecrations of synagogues and Jewish cemeteries have risen dramatically in recent years. Violent attacks against homosexuals rose 161 percent between 1988 and 1991. Victims of hate crimes are hospitalized four times more often than victims of other crimes.

The punishment must fit the crime. Enhanced sentencing is not without precedent. The murderer of a police officer, for example, receives a stiffer sentence than do other killers. Sentencing has always taken motivation into consideration. Stealing to satisfy one's greed is far more reprehensible than stealing to feed one's family. Greed in turn is less destructive than naked hate. The special evil of hate attacks demands special punishment.

Harsher sentences do not conflict with First Amendment rights. Even before the advent of enhanced sentencing for hate crimes, the Supreme Court had ruled on the expression of antisocial ideas. "Fighting words," defined in a 1942 case, threaten the peace and are thus punishable. In 1993, Chief Justice William Rehnquist, speaking for the Court's majority, declared that physical assault is not expressive conduct requiring First Amendment protection. Sentencing for hate crimes punishes not one's thoughts, but one's behavior—behavior already defined by law as criminal.

N O

Don't punish thoughts. Criminal acts motivated by bigotry may inspire fear and sorrow, but so do certain rallies, speeches, and books, which receive First Amendment protection. Tying punishment for criminal behavior to punishment for odious opinions violates the Constitution. Hate crime laws threaten freedom of expression by punishing the *ideas* behind a crime. In 1972, Supreme Court Justice Thurgood Marshall wrote that the key principle of the First Amendment is to prevent government restrictions on any expression no matter what idea, message, or subject matter it contains.

Hate laws can lead to police abuse. Laws written to protect a specific minority can be turned against them. In Florida, a black man being arrested by a white police officer was charged under a bias crime law for calling the officer a "cracker." Although the charges were dropped for lack of evidence, the potential for abuse is clear.

Hate-filled acts are punishable under existing criminal laws. Prosecutors do not need hate crime laws to gain fair sentences. For example, in the well-publicized cases of a Vietnamese student who was killed in Florida and a Hasidic Jew who was murdered in New York's Crown Heights, prosecutors found the murder charges adequate without relying on hate crime laws.

Hate crime laws violate equal protection and due process. Different levels of punishment for the same crime mean that victims and perpetrators receive unequal treatment under the law. The viciously battered victims of domestic or random violence suffer no less than victims of hate crimes. All victims have equal value and the same right to vindication.

Furthermore, in some states, sentencing that takes into consideration hate as a motive occurs *after* the trial. These special sentencing hearings sometimes allow hearsay and omit cross-examination of the accuser.

Background

Minorities have suffered violence and discrimination throughout American history. First came the enslavement of African-Americans and the rampant disregard of their rights after the Civil War. Later discrimination plagued the Irish, Jews, Asians, Mexicans, and homosexuals on up to the present time.

The most sweeping legislation to protect minorities arrived only in 1964 with the passage of the Civil Rights Act. The act forbids discrimination in the workplace, in public accommodations, and in federal funding on the basis of race, creed, or national origin. Although the act requires the Justice Department to enforce and protect civil rights, it does not require increased punishments for hate crimes.

Special punishments for hate crimes first gained popularity on university campuses, where our society's racial disharmony is often enacted in microcosm and reacted to with deep sensitivity. In 1975 a Yale University commission had rejected a proposal to regulate speech because it restricted freedom of expression. However, through the 1980s, in what was perceived as a response to hate-inspired graffiti, speech, and behavior, nearly three hundred colleges and universities adopted speech codes. When challenged in court, these policies were found to be too broad and too vague in their wording, and thus unconstitutional. Speech codes, courts ruled, hampered academic freedom and the spirit of free inquiry. Traditionalists felt such codes imposed an unfair liberal bias on controversial issues. Today, although some universities still enforce speech codes, many are now using general student conduct codes that encompass what administrations define as offensive behavior to comply with court rulings.

Off campus, racially motivated crime continued to escalate. In 1982, Vincent Chin, a Chinese American, was beaten to death by two Detroit automobile workers who, assuming he was Japanese, blamed him for job losses. In 1986 a gang of white youths in Howard Beach, New York, chased a young black man onto a highway where he was struck and killed by an oncoming car. In 1991 a young Jewish scholar was stabbed to death during an anti-Jewish riot in Brooklyn.

In 1990, President George Bush signed into law the Hate Crime Statistics Act, assigning the Federal Bureau of Investigation the difficult task of compiling annual figures on hate crimes. While hate crime statistics are difficult to gather, the majority of such crimes apparently go unprosecuted. In 1991 in Los Angeles County, of the 670 hate crimes reported, only twenty-one went to court.

During the 1990s two major cases have helped define hate crimes and the legality of enhanced sentencing. In *R.A.V.* v. *St. Paul* a white youth burned a cross on the lawn of a black family. He received an increased sentence for violating St. Paul's hate crime ordinance, which forbade the display of any symbol known to cause "anger, alarm, or resentment." In 1992 the Supreme Court struck down the ordinance because it in essence regulated a point of view. The rejection of the ordinance left local governments in a quandary as to how to punish bias-motivated crime.

However, on June 11, 1993, the Court, in *Wisconsin* v. *Mitchell,* allowed states to increase sentencing for bias-motivated crimes. In 1989 black youths incited by a nineteen-year-old following a discussion of the movie *Mississippi Burning* brutally beat a fourteen-year-old white boy into a coma. The majority opinion stated that the Wisconsin law differed from the St. Paul ordinance because it simply enhanced jail terms and fines for crimes already on the books, rather than created a new crime directly punishing thought. Chief Justice William Rehnquist wrote that a physical assault is not protected by the First Amendment and that the motives of defendants have long influenced convictions and sentences.

Outlook

Although the Supreme Court most recently ruled in favor of enhanced sentencing for hate crimes, the battle will continue as new challenges are brought in lower federal and state courts to test the limits of hate crime laws. The Supreme Court is not expected to hear other such cases anytime soon.

3. Should the Death Penalty Be Allowed?

YES

Some crimes are so reprehensible that death is the only suitable penalty. Since premeditated murder is so much more heinous a crime than most other offenses, the punishment for murder must reflect its magnitude. Life is our most precious possession. Cold-blooded murder tears at the basic fabric of our society. Only by putting a murderer to death can we appropriately express our outrage. Not putting this criminal to death cheapens life itself.

The American people yearn for renewed confidence in their criminal justice system. For some crimes even life imprisonment without the possibility of parole imposes an insufficient penalty. Americans need to know that punishments are proportionate and just.

Capital punishment is a deterrent to murder. One famous statistical analysis found that for each murderer executed, eight potential victims are spared. Can we risk the chance that execution *does not* save the lives of potential victims?

Logically, capital punishment sends a message to all murderers that if you commit an inhuman crime you may forfeit your own life. We owe nothing to a convicted killer, but don't we owe future victims of premeditated murder as much protection as possible?

Capital punishment serves as a deterrent even in crimes of passion. Someone who, during a heated argument, contemplates killing a spouse or friend has been taught that he will pay for murder with his own life. We internalize this knowledge and resist the impulse to kill because we know the price.

Capital punishment helps define and protect the moral order. Since the United States does not have an official religious code to define right and wrong, we must rely on our criminal laws. Laws viewed as arbitrary, soft, and easily changeable offend the public and tempt the criminal. Strict and just laws provide an important measure of society's values and mores.

N O

The death penalty is barbaric and morally wrong. Does the biblical injunction "an eye for an eye" suit our modern world? Not if we hope to advance our civilization. It makes no sense to kill someone as an example that killing itself is wrong.

Innocent people die. Between 1900 and 1985 a total of twenty-three innocent people were executed in the United States, including the wrongly accused pair Sacco and Vanzetti. Some of the 2,700 prisoners on death row today will also die unjustly. Mistaken executions are statistically unavoidable in our huge, imperfect criminal justice system.

No government or state should be allowed to kill its subjects. Americans must safeguard their democratic principles and protect themselves from government tyranny. State-sanctioned killing can easily descend into governmental abuse of its power over the people.

The death penalty constitutes cruel and unusual punishment. Dying by electrocution, which can take four minutes, induces terrible pain as you are internally burned to death. The gas chamber causes sharp pain and a strangling sensation for several minutes. Execution violates our constitutional prohibition against cruel and unusual punishment.

The poor do not receive adequate counsel. More than 90 percent of death row inmates cannot afford to hire a private attorney. Most states lack a structured public-defender system, leaving the poor to accept court-appointed attorneys who are frequently inexperienced and underpaid, and can make serious mistakes.

The death penalty discriminates against African-Americans. Statistics show that murderers of whites incur the death penalty four times more often than do murderers of blacks. A 1990 General Accounting Office report found a pattern of racial discrimination in the charging, sentencing, and imposition of the death penalty.

The death penalty does not deter. No study has conclusively shown that those who kill in the heat of passion or with premeditation are deterred by the consequences.

Background

America has sanctioned the death penalty during most of its history. Prior to the 1840s you could be executed for up to fourteen crimes, including idolatry and adultery. From then until the 1960s anti–death penalty activists succeeded in banning capital punishment in a handful of states and in limiting the crimes for which you could die. In 1967 a variety of these groups sued California and Florida, the states with the largest death row populations, arguing the death penalty was unconstitutional.

In 1972 a narrowly divided Supreme Court reached a 5–4 decision in *Furman* v. *Georgia,* ruling that "as the statutes are administered . . . the imposition and carrying out of the death penalty [is] cruel and unusual punishment in violation of the Eighth and Fourteenth Amendments." The majority opinion objected to the wide discretion given to juries and judges in determining which prisoners would die and which would be imprisoned. The unfair administration of the death penalty, they held, means "it is the sick, the ignorant, the powerless, and the hated who are executed. . . ."

To meet Court objections, Georgia and other states quickly rewrote their capital punishment laws. The new laws instructed juries to consider mitigating circumstances before recommending a sentence, allow defendants automatic appeals to the state supreme court, and include other safeguards to increase fairness.

In 1976 the Supreme Court ruled 7–2 in *Gregg* v. *Georgia* that, as administered under these new laws, the death penalty no longer violated the Constitution. The following year Gary Gilmore was executed in Utah, the first state-ordered death in ten years. Forty-two percent of the death sentences imposed by state courts since 1976 have been reversed on appeal, most often because of violations of the defendant's constitutional rights.

Since the late 1980s federal courts have become much less supportive of defendants' rights. In 1987 the Supreme Court declined to reverse the death sentence of a black Georgia inmate who maintained his harsh sentence was imposed because his victim was white. The Court's majority agreed that statistics show those who killed whites were more likely to receive the death sentence than those who killed blacks. But, the Court ruled, these statistics did not prove *intentional* discrimination. In 1991 the Court further reduced the chances for death-row appeals by dramatically reducing the circumstances under which state prisoners could appeal violations of constitutional rights before federal courts.

More than 20,000 murders are committed in the United States each year. Approximately 2,700 people wait on death row today, a larger number than ever in our history. Only forty of these are women. Since 1976 more than 240 men and one woman have been executed. According to the Death Penalty Information Center, forty-five men who had been sentenced to death were found innocent and released since 1976. Currently, thirty-seven states have statutes permitting capital punishment. Most death-row inmates are eventually executed for murder.

Aside from the United States, more than a hundred other countries permit capital punishment. However, none of the European Community nations use execution and none are even close to bringing it back. Most Latin American countries also shun capital punishment. China, Iran, and the republics of the former Soviet Union conduct most of the more than two thousand executions yearly reported by the human rights group Amnesty International. The United States ranks fourth in capital punishment executions. The methods legally permitted here today include electrocution, the gas chamber, lethal injection, a firing squad, and hanging. The last two methods have fallen out of favor.

Outlook

Each year the Supreme Court is asked to consider new challenges to the death penalty. Typically, cases involve arguments around racism, mitigating circumstances in the defendant's life, and inadequate instructions to juries that vote for execution.

Upon his announced retirement in 1994, eighty-five-year-old Supreme Court Justice Harry Blackmun—a former death penalty advocate—declared that the death penalty was an experiment that had failed. However, his change of heart is unlikely to sway the solid majority of Supreme Court justices who generally support capital punishment. A change of attitude is also unlikely from President Clinton, who permitted several executions while he was governor of Arkansas. Although considered liberal, Clinton, like other politicians, finds it politically impossible to be seen as soft on crime.

4. Should Recreational Drugs Be Legalized?

YES

The war against drugs is not worth the cost. Catching, trying, and imprisoning drug offenders divert vital tax dollars from other forms of law enforcement as well as from health care and education. In some locales, police resources are so strained that officers can no longer properly investigate burglaries, robberies, and even rapes. Approximately 20 to 25 percent of the one million prisoners in federal and state jails are imprisoned for drug offenses. The war against drugs costs a crushing $20 billion to $30 billion per year.

Clogging our courts and prisons with nonviolent drug offenders costs not only money but also lives. Violent criminals—who *really* belong in jail—sometimes go free because so many drug offenders occupy cells.

Illegal drugs cause street violence and other crimes. Just as in the 1920s, when the prohibition against alcohol led to mob warfare among gangs, rival gangs today create a war zone of poor neighborhoods, putting innocent people at risk. Since illegal drugs are so expensive, addicts steal frequently to support their habit. Illegal drugs are also at the heart of inner-city police corruption.

Legalized drugs would pose fewer dangers. Today prohibition creates dangers for the public. Amateur drug dealers frequently concoct hazardous products, even diluting their drugs with poisons like strychnine. Intravenous drug users, unable to buy their drug paraphernalia, share needles and spread AIDS much more quickly.

People should have free choice. When abusing drugs, a person harms only him- or herself. If abused, alcohol and cigarettes are also dangerous substances. In a free society people are permitted to take their own risks.

Drug prohibition only enriches criminal organizations. The government should tax and regulate drugs, as it does alcohol and tobacco, rather than let the Mafia and other crime organizations grow wealthy and powerful.

N O

Legalizing drugs will be more costly. Today 57 million Americans are addicted to cigarettes, draining society of many billions in annual health-related costs. Eighteen million are addicted to alcohol, at a cost of $600 million a year for health and productivity losses. Even without legalization, one million Americans are presently addicted to heroin and another million to cocaine, at a cost of $40 million. If the number of drug users rises as a result of legalization, the cost to society will be enormous.

Legalizing drugs increases their use. The use of alcohol and the rate of liver disease dropped significantly in the 1920s during Prohibition. When the Eighteenth Amendment was repealed, ending Prohibition, the number of drinkers in the United States rose by 60 percent. A similar increase is inevitable if hard drugs become legal. Opium sold in large quantities in nineteenth-century China created a social disaster. In Thailand today, where drugs are cheap and easily available, addiction rates soared above those in the rest of the world.

Legalizing drugs will not reduce crime. Legalization advocates claim that some crime caused by addicts trying to obtain drugs might decrease. However, violent crime overall will rise since more people will grow addicted to drugs like crack which induce violent behavior. Drugs and alcohol are already involved in up to 80 percent of violent crime and 50 to 75 percent of suicides.

Decriminalizing drugs has failed in Europe. When a park was opened to addicts in Zurich, Switzerland, and they were provided with clean syringes and health care, the experiment failed miserably. Addicts from elsewhere in Europe descended on Zurich, crime rose, and emergency rooms were inundated with overdose cases.

Drug use among children will increase. Teenagers have always been among the most eager drug users. Although the government would forbid selling legalized drugs to minors, they would obtain drugs just as easily as alcohol and cigarettes are gotten today.

Background

U.S. crackdowns on drug use, which have fluctuated throughout this century, grew out of racial animosities. Beginning late in the nineteenth century, the Chinese were imprisoned for their use of opium; blacks were targeted for cocaine use starting around 1900; and Mexicans for using marijuana during the depression.

In 1972, President Richard Nixon first championed a modern war against drugs. Years later President George Bush earnestly engaged in this battle by appointing rigorous drug enforcement officials and spending a fortune to imprison drug pushers in the United States and stop foreign traffickers. By one estimate, the United States spent a total of $100 billion fighting drugs in the 1980s. Most experts agree these efforts failed miserably. Cocaine prices and availability remain little changed since 1989. The number of cocaine addicts dropped slightly to one million. The small drop in overall cocaine use results more probably from treatment and educational programs, and the increase of heroin abuse, not from law enforcement efforts. U.S.-grown marijuana has essentially replaced the contraband confiscated from importers.

As a result of the drug war's failure, prominent Americans advocating the controlled legalization or decriminalization of drugs have included Nobel Prize–winning economist Milton Friedman, former U.S. Secretary of State George Shultz, author William Buckley, and Kurt Schmoke, the mayor of Baltimore. Other advocates include civil libertarians, some clergy, and even police officials. Not surprisingly, cancer sufferers, who would use marijuana to relieve the symptoms of chemotherapy, and members of the Native American Church, who use other drugs in religious rituals, also advocate legalizing drugs.

More than 75 million Americans aged twelve or over have tried an illicit drug at least once in their life. That represents one-third of the U.S. population. An estimated 20,000 Americans die each year from illegal drugs, compared to 400,000 deaths attributed to tobacco use and 100,000 deaths from alcohol consumption. Approximately one-third of all Americans convicted of robbery or burglary commit crimes for drug money.

In this era when politicians rarely risk being seen as soft on crime, few have suggested legalizing drugs. But policy analysts suggest a variety of scenarios to implement legalization, ranging from a virtual end of all government restrictions to extremely limited decriminalization. Most proposals call for the government to control the quality and distribution of drugs, much as it does tobacco and alcohol today. Drugs would be regulated through licensing, strict policing, no advertising, high taxation, and substantial penalties for sales to children. Equipment operators, bus drivers, pilots, and others would be prohibited from using drugs. The billions collected through taxes on drugs could be spent on drug treatment and education programs.

Outlook

Decriminalization is most likely for drugs possessing medicinal value. Morphine is used medically, as is the active ingredient in marijuana, THC, sold as Marinol in pill form. Marijuana can be used effectively to treat glaucoma (which causes blindness), help AIDS patients regain weight, and relieve pain and nausea for cancer patients. In 1988 a federal judge recommended to the Drug Enforcement Administration (DEA) that marijuana be reclassified by no longer being lumped together with heroin and LSD. After a lengthy review the DEA declined in March 1992, finding the drug offered few beneficial effects and could be dangerous. The U.S. Public Health Service reached the same conclusion at the same time, curtailing its "compassionate use" program that allowed thirteen patients to receive marijuana cigarettes. Some communities, however, quietly accept the medical use of marijuana. The San Francisco Police announced they would not arrest the sick who use marijuana.

On a larger scale, the most important government official advocating serious discussion of drug legalization is U.S. Surgeon General Dr. Joycelyn Elders. In December 1993, Dr. Elders said that legalization of drugs could lead to a major reduction in crime and should be studied. The Clinton administration promptly disavowed her statements. But Dr. Elders has suggested that if the government does not cooperate, she will pursue a national debate by approaching private universities and foundations to sponsor new research on drug legalization.

5. Should Jury Awards Be Capped?

YES

Awards are totally out of proportion to damages. In Alabama alone, juries have awarded half a billion dollars in punitive damages over the last five years. A company that caused $19,000 of actual damages by unfairly denying oil-drilling profits to another firm was charged with $10 million in punitive damages as a punishment and a deterrent to future misconduct. In February 1993, in a Georgia case against the General Motors Corporation, a jury awarded $105.2 million to the parents of a teenager who had died in a pickup truck that exploded when hit—$101 million of it was in punitive damages. Such awards bear little relationship to the defendants' conduct.

We all pay for outrageous awards. As liability insurance rates soar, American consumers pay more for everyday products. Product liability insurance costs fifteen times more in the United States than in Japan, and twenty times more than in Europe. Soaring jury awards also drive our health-care costs upward. Fearing lawsuits, doctors order unneeded and expensive tests. Ever-increasing medical malpractice insurance gets passed on to all of us.

Excessive jury awards harm U.S. competitiveness. American business pays more than $100 billion in product liability judgments each year. That puts us at a severe competitive disadvantage in developing low-cost goods to market worldwide.

Punitive damage awards are often repetitive. When the defendant is guilty, juries usually award plaintiffs *compensatory* damages to pay for the actual harm suffered. But when juries also award many different plaintiffs *punitive* damages in the same case, the defendant is unfairly punished over and over again.

Lawyers, instead of their clients, often get rich. Too much award money often goes to court costs, expert witnesses, and especially the contingency-fee lawyers who typically take a third of all money received.

Frivolous suits clog the courts. Jury awards have become so attractive that many people—with the help of eager lawyers—bring frivolous or nuisance suits based on flimsy evidence.

N O

Damage awards are much rarer than many people realize.
The vast majority of liability cases do not result in large jury awards. In most cases, negotiation or mediation arrives at a reasonable payment for the specific injuries or suffering caused. Only the most outrageous cases of malpractice, fraud, or negligence require large awards—which, in turn, receive the most publicity.

Most jury awards get dramatically reduced. In June 1994 a Georgia appeals court overturned the $105.2 million verdict against General Motors. Most other awards are later overturned or reduced by trial or appellate courts.

High awards are a necessary punishment and deterrent. Damage awards motivate companies to create safer products, employers to prevent accidents, and doctors to take greater care to avoid mistakes. A cap on damages would send companies the message that they can risk the lives of consumers or employees. If someone gets hurt or killed, the cost becomes predictable and acceptable.

Caps unfairly punish victims who have suffered the most. The typical cap proposed on noneconomic damages, usually for pain and suffering, ranges from $100,000 to $500,000. That amount inadequately compensates a victim for massive life-altering injuries such as crushed limbs, brain damage, or paralysis.

Award caps interfere with jury trials. Caps are by definition arbitrary. Capping denies your right for a jury to determine appropriate damages. Each injury, wrongful death, or other loss is different. Rules cannot put a price on every injury; only a fair jury trial can determine the proper level of compensation.

Jury awards give everyone a chance at justice. Capped awards leave few individuals the means to pay the legal fees necessary to win justice against a large wealthy defendant. Only the fee-contingency system affords *any* person, no matter what income level, the high-quality legal representation he deserves. Jury awards give everyone her day in court.

Background

The controversy over jury awards involves civil lawsuits, called tort cases, in which individuals sue to recover money for injuries and death usually caused by medical malpractice, defective products or pharmaceutical drugs, or catastrophic accidents, such as airplane crashes. Companies and other organizations also sue under tort law. Of the one million tort suits filed annually, the vast majority are settled out of court. Those that go to trial can sometimes result in the massive jury awards that make front-page news. The battle to cap these awards has pitted manufacturers, local governments, and doctors, often represented by the American Tort Reform Association, against consumer groups and contingency-fee lawyers, often represented by the American Trial Lawyers Association.

Most juries that find for the plaintiff award them compensatory damages, which typically include hospital bills, rehabilitation, and lost wages. In addition, juries may award the plaintiff noneconomic damages, usually called pain and suffering, for reasons such as emotional distress or loss of a child or spouse. Another hot area of contention in tort reform is jury awards for punitive damages, which seek to punish defendants for outrageously neglectful or wrongful actions and deter them from harming others in the future.

The movement toward capping awards for pain and suffering grew in popularity starting in 1975, when the California legislature passed the Medical Injury Compensation Reform Act (MICRA), a model for most future medical malpractice reforms. One of MICRA's key provisions capped damages for pain and suffering at $250,000. Some state legislatures have since established such caps, while elsewhere state supreme courts have found these caps unconstitutional.

Awards for punitive damages gained ground in the late 1970s with a series of lawsuits against the Ford Motor Company, whose Pinto model exploded upon rear-end collision. Many famous cases followed against the manufacturers of pharmaceuticals, asbestos, pesticides, and contraceptives.

During the Bush presidency tort reformers found a champion in Vice President Dan Quayle. As head of the Council on Competitiveness, Quayle worked to change a variety of tort laws—including unlimited jury awards—which he considered harmful to American competitiveness. Although Congress declined to vote for nationwide changes, twenty-nine states have instituted some form of tort reform. These reforms include caps on jury awards, a higher standard of evidence and proof for awards of punitive damages, and paying a portion of awards to the state rather than to the plaintiff. Another reform restricts the use of "joint and several liability," which allows plaintiffs to collect the entire amount from the wealthiest defendant, even if that company or government was only remotely at fault.

Jury award cap cases have reached the Supreme Court four times. Most recently, in 1993, the Court refused to cap jury awards by arguing that it cannot "draw a mathematical bright line between the constitutionally acceptable and the constitutionally unacceptable that would fit every case." In the case of *TXO Production Corp.* v. *Alliance Resources Corp,* TXO employed malicious tactics to deprive Alliance of its royalties from oil and gas development rights. Although actual damages were $19,000, the Court upheld a $10 million punitive damage award against TXO Production Corporation, arguing that many intangible factors affected this case.

Outlook

As of 1994, the Clinton administration has shown no sign of making tort reform a major issue. But the President's health reform package does include medical malpractice reform. A health-care reform compromise worked out by Congress may limit jury awards in pharmaceutical and medical device cases. The medical and insurance lobbyists are fighting the plaintiff attorneys on Capitol Hill, with jury award caps a key issue.

The battle to limit punitive damages is being fought mainly at the state level. Proposals to reform damage awards include limiting punitive awards to five times compensatory awards, letting judges determine the amount, or dismissing awards in cases where the company complied with all laws and safety regulations, and did not conceal information. Tort reformers argue that the hodgepodge of state laws still makes punitive damages much too high, inconsistent, and unpredictable. They hope the Supreme Court or Congress will cap damages at the federal level. But the plaintiff lawyers' lobby argues that the states have already gone too far in limiting jury awards.

6. Should We Repeal Mandatory Prison Sentences for First-Time Drug Offenders?

YES

Nonviolent criminals congest precious prison space. In some overcrowded prison systems, violent criminals gain early release to make room for new, nonviolent drug offenders. On average, a convicted murderer today receives a six-and-one-half-year sentence. The federal mandatory minimum sentence for possession of seven hundred marijuana plants is eight years. Since murderers can be paroled—except for those sentenced to a mandatory minimum—violent criminals sometimes get returned to the streets more quickly.

We must reduce our spending on prisons. In the 1980s, U.S. per capita incarceration rates surpassed those of the Soviet Union and South Africa to become the world's highest. Our jail population doubled to a million in just one decade. More than half of new prisoners get jailed for drug offenses. Our criminal justice system costs $61 billion per year. At a time of massive deficits, we simply cannot afford to keep imprisoning nonviolent, first-time offenders.

Mandatory sentences do not act as a deterrent. Since most criminals do not think they will be caught, the fear of imprisonment rarely deters them from crime. According to one study, 67 percent of state prison inmates knew nothing about mandatory sentences before they were arrested.

The cycle of drug addiction and crime remains. So much money is spent imprisoning people, little is available for drug rehabilitation. Nationwide, only 20 percent of state prison inmates needing drug treatment receive it. In New York State, it costs $58,000 per year to jail someone, $14,000 per year for residential drug treatment, but only $5,000 per year for outpatient drug treatment.

Mandatory sentences favor drug kingpins. These laws were supposed to ensure that major drug dealers received harsh sentences. But current sentencing guidelines allow criminals to reduce jail time by providing incriminating evidence against other traffickers. As a result, low-level couriers and others with little information to trade can be jailed for five to twenty years, while the masterminds get off with much less.

N O

Swift, severe, and certain punishment works as a deterrence. In the 1960s and 1970s many criminals, particularly drug dealers, stood a good chance of evading punishment. In 1980 only 77 percent of convicted traffickers served time in prison. By 1990, the rate had risen to 90 percent. While we continue to imprison drug dealers in ever higher numbers, the "business" will grow less attractive to newcomers.

Mandatory minimums are fair. Drugs cause terrible destruction in our communities. Mandatory sentences fairly punish those who cause the most destruction, especially dealers selling to minors or near a school.

While some judges may complain about their lost power to consider extenuating circumstances, it was the same broad use of judicial discretion that initially created the need for mandatory sentences. Before minimum sentencing guidelines, punishments for the same crime varied widely in different jurisdictions. Mandatory minimums set nationwide, evenhanded standards.

Mandatory sentences make our neighborhoods and nation safer. Most of the drug dealers in prison today belong there. We can feel sorry for some because of their impoverished backgrounds, but mitigating circumstances do not make them any less dangerous to society. The public deserves protection from anyone who tries to sell drugs to our children. Drive-by shootings, crack wars, and the tragedy of crack babies are real consequences of the drug trade. Everyone's life improves by keeping dealers off the streets.

Crime costs more than prisons. According to some studies, for every dollar we save by releasing an inmate, we must later pay $2 to $4 for new criminal activity. We pay for lenient sentences in the form of burglarized homes, higher insurance rates, and even physical violence. In the long run, we must pay something to curb crime. Prisons are our best alternative.

Background

The U.S. Congress imposed mandatory prison sentences from the 1950s through the early 1970s, after which criminal rehabilitation programs became popular. But the Reagan administration, responding to public despair about the crack cocaine epidemic, advocated a "zero tolerance" policy in the war against drugs. Congress complied by passing the 1984 Sentencing Reform Act and the 1986 Anti–Drug Abuse Act, which eliminated federal parole in drug cases and called for tough mandatory sentences.

Under these laws any defendant convicted of possession of five grams of crack (worth about $500) with intent to sell receives a five-year sentence. Other minimums include five years for a hundred grams of heroin, a hundred kilograms of marijuana, or one gram of LSD. If caught with fifty grams of crack, the sentence is ten years. These sentences double if the defendant has prior felony drug convictions. Since 1984 median prison terms have climbed from twelve months served out of a thirty-six-month sentence to fifty-six months served out of a sixty-six-month sentence.

In the last two decades Congress has passed sixty mandatory sentencing statutes that cover drug dealing and a variety of other crimes. Today four of these statutes, all concerning drugs, account for 94 percent of the mandatory sentences meted out. Some of the judges who must impose these sentences are their most vocal critics. In 1990, San Diego Judge J. Lawrence Irving, a Reagan appointee, quit the bench, protesting that minimums had destroyed judicial discretion and were grossly unfair to first-time offenders.

In June 1991 the Supreme Court upheld the nation's toughest mandatory sentence. A Michigan man, caught with one and a half pounds of pure cocaine, was sentenced to life imprisonment, as required by Michigan state laws. The Court held 5–4 that while mandatory sentences might seem cruel, they do not violate the Constitution because Eighth Amendment protection from cruel and unusual punishment refers to torture, not length of prison terms.

Some judges continue to challenge the constitutionality of mandatory minimums. In April 1993, U.S. District Judge Harold H. Greene refused to impose the mandatory thirty-year sentence on a twenty-five-year-old repeat drug offender who was caught with eight grams of heroin and cocaine. The judge's twenty-one-page opinion declared the minimum sentence totally out of proportion to the crimes since the dealer's previous two convictions involved small amounts of drugs. Greene argued the mandatory sentencing guidelines violate both the

Eighth Amendment protection against cruel and unusual punishment and the due process clause of the Fifth Amendment. He sentenced the man to ten years. This sentence, and those of other judges who ignore minimums, can be overturned on appeal by prosecutors.

Outlook

In February 1993, Congressman Don Edwards (D-California) introduced legislation calling for an end to mandatory minimums. It failed to pass Congress. Organizations opposing minimums include the U.S. Sentencing Commission, the twelve Federal Judicial Conferences, the American Bar Association, and the Federal Courts Study Commission. FBI Director Louis Freeh opposes minimums, arguing that while violent criminals must be "neutralized," we need to attack poverty and other root causes of crime, not build more prisons. But such a politically volatile issue makes change difficult.

Some believe a compromise may get through Congress within a few years. The new laws might continue harsh minimums for repeat drug kingpins, but provide a safety valve for first-time nonviolent offenders whose involvement is minimal. In the meantime, judges will continue to test the laws. Several senior federal judges, who can choose their cases, now refuse to accept those involving drugs. U.S. District Judge Jack B. Weinstein of Brooklyn, New York, announced his decision by writing "I simply cannot sentence another impoverished person whose destruction has no discernible effect on the drug trade."

Although Attorney General Janet Reno opposes minimums and ordered the Justice Department to examine current practices in 1993, she has not actively pursued the issue. The White House has probably silenced Reno on the issue, which means any repeal of mandatory minimums must wait till politicians no longer fear it will make them look soft on crime.

7. Should Gun Control Be Further Tightened?

YES

The numbers speak for themselves. Each year nearly 30,000 Americans die from guns; the 40,000 other gun-related injuries cost America $4 billion in medical and related expenses. Every ten seconds a gun leaves the factory; every eleven seconds one is imported. Gun violence in our society is rampant, which is why numerous associations of police chiefs and sheriffs support gun control.

The "right to bear arms" does not imply every citizen's right to own a gun. The authors of the Bill of Rights, understandably fearing the power of a standing army, ensured a *state's* right to protect itself by forming a militia. The right was designed for states, *not* private citizens.

Guns victimize even their owners. A handgun at home is six times more likely to kill a family member than an intruder. There is no convincing evidence that guns deter burglary, mugging, or rape. Far too often a criminal overpowers the victim and uses the gun against him.

Gun control today applies only to handguns and semiautomatic weapons. Hunters and other sports users will not be deprived of their rifles, but they do not need a MAC-10 converted to a semiautomatic handgun, which fires thirty bullets in seconds, or other weapons that fire armor-piercing bullets. What private citizen needs such guns? A ban on handguns would prevent many murders. According to a 1990 Justice Department report, 44 percent of all homicides from 1979 to 1987 were committed with handguns.

Stiffer sentencing alone is no solution. Longer sentences and steeper fines do not deter crimes of passion—and they come too late for the victim. Since 1984 many gun-related crimes have received lengthy sentences, yet gun-related violence has not decreased. More prisons, increased sentences, and additional police are not a substitute for reducing the supply of guns on our streets.

N O

Innocent citizens need guns for protection. Law-abiding citizens buy handguns when the government and police cannot protect them. After the Los Angeles riots many felt their survival depended on their ability to fight back. While handguns figure in nearly 580,000 crimes each year, about 645,000 times in that same period innocent people use guns to *defend* themselves against criminals.

Gun control punishes only the law abiding. Ninety-nine percent of those legally owning firearms never commit crimes with them. Tighter gun-control laws, if enforceable, would simply disarm law-abiding citizens, not the criminals we fear.

Waiting periods do not stop criminals from purchasing guns. Criminals wanting guns will get them easily on the black market. Didn't anyone wanting liquor during Prohibition get it? Waiting periods strain already overburdened law-enforcement organizations. Furthermore, although waiting-period databases track criminal history, databases tracking psychiatric evaluations are rare and often illegal.

No evidence clearly links gun availability with gun violence. It is not true that the more guns owned by the public, the higher the gun-related violence. Even as the ratio of handguns to total population has remained constant over the last century, gun-related violence has continued to rise. Only strong law enforcement can put a dent in gun-related violence.

The Constitution guarantees our *individual* right to bear arms. The right of each American to keep weapons is deeply rooted in common law and constitutional history. The interpretation that the Second Amendment in the Bill of Rights applies to arming militias appeared only in the twentieth century. Writings by members of the First Congress prove the right to keep arms applied to each citizen.

We need criminal control, not gun control. Far better than ineffective gun control is to punish the violent criminal. We need a greater police presence, tougher sentencing, more prisons, and a crackdown on drug crimes.

Background

On November 30, 1993, President Clinton signed the Brady bill into law. The law imposes a five-day waiting period on gun buyers. This provides a cooling-off time for a buyer who in the heat of passion intends to do harm, and time for a check of criminal records by law enforcement agencies.

Many gun-control activists view the Brady bill as merely a first step toward an outright ban on gun ownership by private citizens. This is the worst nightmare of the National Rifle Association (NRA), the leading pro-gun lobby. The debate between the two sides centers both on the government's right to regulate firearms and on how much and what kinds of regulation.

Through the early 1900s it was commonplace for citizens to carry handguns. An urban explosion between 1820 and 1860, outpacing law enforcement efforts, had left the individual feeling pressed to fend for himself.

The NRA, formed in 1871, was originally a sporting organization to promote shooting proficiency and safety. Then, in 1911, New York City passed the Sullivan Law, enacting handgun controls. Gun control was promulgated as an expression of America's status as a civilized nation, shedding its violent frontier past.

The assassinations of Martin Luther King Jr. and Robert Kennedy spurred Congress to pass the Gun Control Act of 1968. The act prohibits mail-order gun sales and regulates interstate transportation of guns and ammunition.

Through the 1960s and 1970s the NRA shifted its focus toward political action. Exercising considerable clout by the 1980s, it convinced Congress to reduce penalties against gun dealers for records violations. However, the lower courts rejected the challenge by gun owners of a handgun ban in Morton Grove, Illinois, and the Supreme Court refused to hear the case. The courts have never interpreted the Second Amendment to prohibit most gun control.

In 1989, after a California man bearing a large assault rifle sprayed 106 bullets into a schoolyard full of children, killing five and wounding thirty, President Bush banned the import of assault rifles. Four years later another deranged Californian killed eight people in a San Francisco law firm with a semiautomatic weapon manufactured in China. In response, President Clinton halted the import of semiautomatic assault weapons. The comprehensive crime bill signed by President Clinton in September 1994 bans the manufacture, sale, and possession of nineteen types of semiautomatic weapons.

The current controversy, however, focuses on the handgun—a small, easily concealed weapon. Various polls revealed that 40 percent of Americans favor a ban on private possession of handguns; one in six favors a ban on *any* gun ownership. However, half of American households own at least one gun. Still, 70 percent support some form of gun control. The NRA, however, believes that no matter how limited the present controls, they will inexorably lead to a total prohibition of any private possession of firearms.

Gun-control activists claim Americans are increasingly uncomfortable with the easy availability of guns. In February 1994, Wal-Mart, the country's largest retailer, discontinued its over-the-counter sale of handguns. Gun supporters allege the decision was precipitated by fear of lawsuits brought by victims of gun violence.

Outlook

The current phase of the gun-control debate began in December 1993, when gunman Colin Ferguson killed six people and wounded seventeen on a Long Island Rail Road commuter train with a 9-mm pistol purchased legally in California. A flurry of new proposals followed, including a complete ban on assault weapons (which passed), gun registration, a firearms-fatality reporting system, and a 30 percent sales tax on handguns, assault weapons, and ammunition. President Clinton instructed the Justice Department to review the possibility of establishing a national regulation and licensing system.

During the 1993 Christmas season a New York carpet-store owner inaugurated a toys-for-weapons exchange program. The swap proved far more effective than previous buyback programs to collect guns and is being copied around the nation.

The Clinton administration would like to fight the next gun-control battle over rules for licensing gun dealers. But a Republican-controlled Congress may put an end to gun control legislation for the next few years.

8. Should a Battered Woman Who Murders Her Husband Be Granted Clemency?

YES

Abused women often have no other way to defend themselves. "Battered-woman syndrome" describes a cycle of violence and intimidation that leaves women with no self-esteem and so fearful for their life that they sometimes believe they have no choice but to kill their husband. The syndrome often makes women feel so isolated and anxious that it affects how they think and act. When battered women kill they do so to protect themselves and often their children. Every year between 3 and 4 million women are beaten by their husbands and boyfriends. Of these women, approximately 1,500 are killed annually.

Why can't these women just leave? Many abused women *do leave*— some lack the money and support network of friends or family that make departing possible. Few communities have enough room in their shelters. Some women receive tremendous religious pressure to remain in their marriage. Most women believe with good reason that if they leave, their husband will find and beat them more severely. These women have in effect become brainwashed into staying until the instinct for self-preservation forces them into killing.

In many states, battered women cannot expect a fair trial. Judges in thirty-seven states are not required to consider evidence of battered-woman syndrome or wife abuse during a trial. In many cases the jury never hears the reasons that drove the women to murder. Juries do not learn about the horrible beatings, spousal rapes, and humiliations that would drive anyone to action. The only way these abused women can receive justice is through a governor's pardon or a reduced sentence.

Battered women need counseling, not prison. These women often experience post-trauma disorders similar to those suffered by hostages. Abused women are victims that our justice system victimizes a second time. In the few cases where governors have released battered women, they have already served four to ten years in prison.

N O

No one should be granted a license to kill. Large-scale pardons set a dangerous precedent. Our laws and punishments are necessarily harsh to deter murder. If we send women the message that it is all right to kill their husband rather than leave the home, get divorced, or improve their marriage, then people may even die unnecessarily. Others in society will be sent a dangerous message that some types of murder are both morally and legally pardonable.

Governors should not substitute their judgment for that of judges and juries. Many judges have discretion to consider evidence of wife abuse. In most cases judges and juries know much more about individual cases than governors. If a jury of one's peers finds the defendant guilty and if appellate review is available, a governor should not interfere with the judicial process.

Some *unabused* women have petitioned for pardon. In several states, women hoping to gain their release from prison claim they were battered. By granting clemency, governors create a loophole for killers trying to avoid a just punishment.

The clemency review process has failed. In 1992, Governor William Schaefer of Maryland granted clemency to eight battered women who killed their mate. One of the women, Bernadette Barnes, had hired someone to kill her husband so that she would receive life insurance benefits. These circumstances make her pardon highly questionable.

Another inmate released by Governor Schaefer, Virginia Johnson, claimed abuse but could provide no corroborating evidence that she was abused the night of the killing or at any other time. Neighbors reported there was no disturbance, Johnson showed no signs of injury, and the victim was stabbed through the heart at the wheel of his car. A few months after her pardon, Johnson was arrested for attempting to stab a potential trial witness with a knife.

Background

Of the millions of women battered in the United States, between 800 and 1,000 kill their abuser each year. Since fewer than one-third of these women gain acquittal, an advocacy movement has grown to improve their chances in the legal system.

In many states, the police are notoriously ineffective in protecting battered women. A study in Texas found that police ignore a third of the calls from battered women. Court restraining orders rarely prevent a determined batterer from attacking his victim. Only in half the states do laws mandate that police arrest and charge batterers.

Prior to 1989 only a few battered women were granted clemency in a handful of states. So far two governors have taken this controversial step to a large scale. In December 1989, two weeks before his term expired, Governor Richard Celeste of Ohio granted clemency to twenty-five women, including one on death row. Two months later, Governor William Schaefer of Maryland granted clemency to eight women who killed or attacked their partner. Both states had denied the women an opportunity to present evidence at trial of their history of abuse or of battered-woman syndrome. The governors cited this denial as their main reason for granting mass clemencies.

Both governors took dangerous political risks by their actions. As expected, they received a torrent of criticism from newspaper editorial writers, prosecutors, and others in the criminal justice system.

Today clemency advocates in more than twenty states fight to free more convicts. Their three-pronged effort includes lobbying prosecutors and judges about battered-woman syndrome, convincing state legislators to change laws that prohibit introducing evidence of prior abuse at trial, and directly petitioning governors for clemency in certain cases.

Lobbying prosecutors and judges about domestic violence against women proceeds slowly. In many cases where battered women kill, any evidence is purely circumstantial. Typically, the husband and wife were home alone with no witnesses. In some cases the man was sleeping when his wife killed him. Prosecutors often ignore the battered-woman syndrome when prosecuting women, but embrace aspects of the syndrome when trying to convict batterers themselves. Clemency advocates take care not to alienate prosecutors who are their allies on some cases.

Outlook

The largest gains for abused women who kill are likely to come from convincing state legislatures to routinely admit evidence of domestic violence into trials. Advocates believe that only when juries view such evidence as an integral part of the proceedings will abused women receive fair trials. In October 1992 the House of Representatives passed House Concurrent Resolution 89, a nonbinding resolution that urges the states to consider battered-woman syndrome during jury trials. This was the first time Congress considered the issue.

For abused women already in jail, gubernatorial clemency is the only hope. In addition to Maryland and Ohio, several other states are considering the idea. Florida's Board of Executive Clemency adopted rules allowing for a case-by-case review of the sentences of abused killers—both women and men. Upon review of the records of its prison inmates, Texas invited 102 women to file applications for a clemency review.

The California state legislature, often a harbinger of change, has passed laws permitting evidence of abuse in court. Now advocates are trying to pass a law allowing evidence of brutal domestic violence as an accepted defense in murder cases. With the help of advocacy groups, lawyers in prominent California law firms are offering free legal services to battered women in jail. Governor Pete Wilson is reviewing several dozen cases for possible clemency.

The 1994 trial of Lorena Bobbitt for cutting off her husband's penis increased the public's awareness of women who strike back at abusive husbands. In the widely publicized trial, she was found not guilty by reason of insanity after her lawyers convinced the jury she suffered a long history of spousal abuse and rape. Bobbitt's acquittal, perhaps more than any other recent event, may create a public acceptance of clemency for battered wives who kill or maim their husband. The murder of Nicole Simpson, who allegedly suffered beatings at the hand of her ex-husband, O. J. Simpson, has also put a spotlight on battered women.

9. Should the Insanity Defense Be Allowed?

YES

The truly insane cannot distinguish right from wrong. Our legal system is based on certain premises. We expect people to stay within the bounds of acceptable behavior. And because they can freely make rational and voluntary choices, we hold people accountable for their actions. If a person's mental disability hinders the capacity for rational and voluntary action, however, then he can no longer be held accountable for his acts. Incapable of complying with the law, he must be treated differently by the courts.

The insanity plea is the mark of a civilized, merciful society. Throughout history many societies have protected those who are not responsible for their actions. Just as we do not hold young children accountable for certain actions, so we have refused to punish the insane as ordinary criminals. The insanity defense underscores the moral authority of our criminal laws.

The criminally insane are deeply ill. Just as any person has a basic right to medical help, the insane need psychiatric assistance. Our society gains moral stature by our compassionate treatment of the insane.

Deterrence means nothing to the mentally incompetent. A major purpose of punishing criminals is to deter them from future crimes. But since the insane do not comprehend their own actions or the warnings society sends them, conventional punishment becomes useless in preventing crime.

Most of those using the insanity defense today truly are mentally ill. Some people claim that the insanity defense provides malicious but sane criminals with an easy alternative to prison. According to major studies, most of those pleading insanity really do suffer serious mental incapacity. Most mental hospitals, while helpful to the deranged, are hardly more pleasant than prison. Some of those committed to mental hospitals stay there much longer than they would in prison.

N O

Insanity is irrelevant to the criminal process. A court of criminal justice has only two purposes: to decide if the defendant committed the crime and, if so, to determine the punishment. Courts are not qualified to decide the sanity of the accused and juries should not have to choose between competing psychiatrists arguing for the defense and the prosecution.

Psychiatry is not an exact science. Who can really say if a criminal had control over his actions, if he understood right from wrong? Who can decide if mental illness or temporary insanity really motivated the criminal? Human beings exhibit a broad range of behavior, from total self-control to uncontrolled evil. Psychiatrists cannot objectively measure self-control or the ability to resist criminal impulses.

Those found not guilty by reason of insanity are treated much too leniently. Allowing defendants to successfully use the insanity defense unfairly discharges them from any responsibility for their actions. When John Hinckley shot President Reagan in 1981, he planned his crime carefully. He wanted the President dead and knew he was breaking the law. Why should he receive preferential treatment by being sent to a mental hospital rather than prison? Our insanity laws result in overly gentle treatment for some of our most heinous criminals.

The insanity plea dilutes the power of deterrence. Criminals and their attorneys try to use the insanity plea as an escape. By allowing the insanity plea, we give violent criminals a potential escape hatch. We send all criminals the message that punishment is not necessarily inevitable.

The insanity plea favors elites. Only wealthy, usually white, defendants can afford the stiff fees required by the best psychiatrists. According to one state study, 64 percent of those found not guilty on grounds of insanity were white, though only 31 percent of all prisoners were white.

Background

Despite the public perception that the insanity defense is used widely and indiscriminately, only one percent of all felons and 10 percent of mass and serial killers actually plead insanity. The plea has, however, been used with varying degrees of success during some recent cases, including the trial of Dan White, who murdered San Francisco Mayor George Moscone and Supervisor Harvey Milk; John Hinckley, who shot at President Ronald Reagan; Jeffrey Dahmer, a serial murderer and cannibal; and Lorena Bobbitt, who cut off her husband's penis.

The legal code of ancient Rome distinguished between the insane, who were deemed not responsible, and the sane. Eighteenth-century English law found innocent the defendant who "doth not know what he is doing no more than a wild beast."

In England in 1843, Daniel M'Naghten, a Scottish woodcutter, assassinated a secretary to the prime minister. M'Naghten, blaming the prime minister for his personal misfortunes, mistakenly killed the wrong man. During M'Naghten's trial medical experts described him as extremely paranoid and delusional. He was found not guilty and committed to a mental institution. In response to the ensuing uproar, the House of Lords reviewed existing law to establish a standard for criminal responsibility of the insane. Under the new law a person could not be convicted only if, at the time the crime occurred, he or she suffered a "disease of the mind" preventing an understanding of the act or an awareness that it was wrong.

The "M'Naghten rules" served as U.S. law until 1954, when the District of Columbia Circuit Court overruled M'Naghten in *Durham* v. *United States*. The Durham rule, acknowledging an increasing acceptance of psychiatry, considers only mental illness with no associated incapacitating or debilitating condition, as in most other tests of criminal responsibility.

In 1962, after a nine-year study, the American Law Institute (ALI) introduced a Model Penal Code test of criminal responsibility. As in M'Naghten, the ALI test incorporates cognitive and volitional standards. The test incorporates a broader understanding of mental disease, explicitly recognizing degrees of incapacity. By 1972, all but one federal circuit had adopted the ALI test.

In 1981, John Hinckley attempted to assassinate President Reagan. His acquittal by reason of insanity created an uproar similar to that of the M'Naghten acquittal. Many decried the pervasive presence of psychiatry and psychobabble in the courtroom.

In 1984, Congress enacted the Insanity Defense Reform Act, shifting to the defense the burden of proof of insanity with "clear and convincing evidence." The act also allows juries to find a defendant insane but still guilty and eligible for prison. Today an insanity defense cannot be based on a defendant's inability to conform his conduct to the law. The heinousness of a crime, as with Jeffrey Dahmer's cannibalism, cannot be used as a defense in itself. Cruelty is a proof of evil, not of madness.

A November 1993 ABC News/*Washington Post* poll revealed that 65 percent of Americans believe accused murderers should not be allowed to use the insanity defense, 23 percent would allow the plea, and 12 percent are not sure.

Currently, only Montana, Idaho, and Utah prohibit defendants from using the insanity plea. In February 1994 the U.S. Supreme Court let stand a ruling by the Montana Supreme Court that said abolishing the insanity defense is constitutional, violating neither the due process nor the cruel-and-unusual-punishment clause. Montana legislators enacted the law because they believe too many criminals exaggerate their mental illness. However, Montana protects mentally incompetent defendants in other ways, including pretrial psychiatric evaluation.

Outlook

Additional states will probably follow Montana in abolishing the insanity defense. The defense rarely works in today's courtrooms. Rapid advances by neurobiologists who study the effects of brain damage on behavior, however, may one day prove conclusively which defendants really suffer an incapacity to judge right from wrong.

10. Should Laws Against Prostitution Be Relaxed?

YES

Prostitution today is a victimless act between consenting adults. Except in rare cases, no one forces either the prostitute or the customer. If she gets paid and he is satisfied, how has anyone been hurt? Many prostitutes, who do not feel victimized by their chosen profession, resent infringements on their freedom of choice.

The state should not legislate private morality. Restrictions on prostitution violate our right to privacy and autonomy.

Curbing prostitution does not work and costs a fortune. Most police departments admit that arresting, fining, and jailing prostitutes rarely take them off the streets for very long. It only wastes scarce law-enforcement resources that should focus on violent crimes instead. According to one Los Angeles official, his city spends more than $100 million per year on enforcement and court costs involving prostitutes.

The government loses income tax revenue. Studies have shown that were prostitution government-regulated rather than forced underground, the federal government might collect $3 billion per year in income taxes on this $20 billion-a-year industry.

Decriminalizing prostitution would decrease crime and disease. Certain Nevada counties with legal, government-regulated brothels have virtually eliminated many problems associated with prostitution. Violent pimps have been replaced by more respectable business owners, and the robbing of customers has greatly declined.

As a result of careful screening by doctors, virtually *none* of the brothel prostitutes carry the HIV virus. In comparison, an estimated half of prostitutes working the streets in major cities are HIV-positive. Legalized prostitution would help curb the spread of AIDS.

Antiprostitution laws frequently discriminate against poor women. For some poor women prostitution is the only way they can draw a decent wage. Earning the minimum wage working at a fast-food restaurant will not let them pay for an apartment in a decent neighborhood. The government has no right to deprive them of a lucrative income.

N O

Prostitution destroys the lives of women and children.
Prostitution is nothing less than trafficking in human beings. This exploitation hurts the weakest members of society—poor women, young teenagers, and children. Our governments *should* put up as many hindrances as possible to protect these victims of the sex industry.

Many prostitutes do not voluntarily choose this demeaning life. An abusive home life forces most prostitutes to start selling themselves at an average age of fourteen. On the streets they suffer from drug and alcohol addiction, rape, and beatings. They are the castaways of our society, suffering humiliation and degradation. We cannot sanction the legal destruction of their lives.

Prostitutes in Nevada are no better off. While legalized brothels may relieve the worst abuses of street life, the women still endure miserable lives. The rules protect only the brothel owners and their customers. Prostitutes rarely choose when they work or whom they must take to bed. These women become isolated, living in a sexual ghetto. Legalization condemns a certain percentage of our daughters to this life forever.

Prostitution harms legitimate businesses. Wherever prostitutes gather, crime and drug trafficking follow. The police must keep this street life out of residential and business districts or local businesses and real estate values will suffer. Tough laws against soliciting minimize the criminal culture that attaches to and feeds off this public nuisance.

The government must uphold community standards. Our laws reflect the commonly held view that prostitution is ethically wrong. The vast majority of our communities persist in choosing to criminalize it. Can you imagine a world in which we introduce prostitution to our daughters as just another legitimate career choice? Our government cannot legitimize the exploitation and dehumanization of women.

Background

Attempts to wipe out "the world's oldest profession" have never fully succeeded. At present, up to 500,000 prostitutes work in the United States. About 18 percent of American men have visited one in the last five years. According to the FBI, 86,988 arrests were made for prostitution and commercial sex in 1992. The majority of customers are white, middle-class, middle-aged, married men. Only 10 to 20 percent of prostitution takes place at the street level. The vast majority of America's sex trade is found in massage parlors, strip bars, private clubs, and escort services.

Prostitution is legal in seven countries. The sex trade in foreign countries dwarfs that in the United States. Thailand alone has more than 2 million prostitutes. Throughout Europe the huge influx of poor refugees from former Soviet bloc countries has doubled or tripled the number of brothels in many towns and created new zones for streetwalkers. Many European and Asian countries do not actively prevent prostitution within unofficially sanctioned areas.

In the United States, efforts to ban prostitution have traditionally come from the religious and women's rights sectors. But in recent years several associations of prostitutes have formed to argue both for and against legalized prostitution. The 1962 Supreme Court decision in *Robinson* v. *California* held that people may not be convicted merely for their status as a prostitute, drug addict, or homosexual. The sexual revolution of the 1960s went further in relaxing America's sexual mores and reducing the crackdowns on prostitutes.

Today American police respond to prostitution in many ways, depending on the level of public outcry. In some California communities, the police ignore streetwalkers who register themselves and meet certain health requirements. On the other hand, in Portland, Oregon, and other cities, police decoys confiscate the cars of cruising customers. Elsewhere, antiprostitution groups have published the names and photographs of customers. But even the toughest crackdowns on streetwalkers and their clients fail to eradicate prostitution. Most simply take their services to another nearby community.

Proposals to change U.S. laws involve either legalization or decriminalization. Legalization usually entails governmental zoning and supervision of brothels. With decriminalization the police ignore private sex transactions between individuals, but still crack down on pimps, on crimes associated with prostitution, and on established brothels.

In the United States, only Nevada allows brothels in a handful of rural counties. Nevada's prostitution laws were established in 1971 to induce tourists to visit its poorer areas. In the thirty-six Nevada brothels currently operating, doctors check prostitutes regularly, require customers to use condoms, and prohibit certain sexual practices, including sodomy. To date, no prostitute in a legal Nevada brothel has tested positive for the HIV virus. Legalized brothels reduce, but do not eliminate, local streetwalking. Some clients continue to prefer the seamier side of the streets, the prohibited sexual practices, or the greater anonymity.

Outlook

The likelihood of full legalization in other states—where brothels would operate under government license—seems remote. Very few politicians and police chiefs dare support such a move. The American sense of morality makes legalization too risky. But San Francisco, always a leader in the sexual revolution, has appointed a twenty-member commission to consider establishing a legal brothel. Officials hope to reduce the street trade that currently infringes upon residential neighborhoods.

Elsewhere in the United States, decriminalization stands a better chance. As more people realize that our patchwork of inconsistent enforcement is ineffective and as the costs of enforcement continue to rise, more communities will practice decriminalization by default.

The future of U.S. decriminalization also depends on whether the public and law enforcement officials come to see it as a way to prevent the spread of HIV. In some cities, such as Newark, New Jersey, over 60 percent of prostitutes test HIV-positive. More than half the states now require or allow health officials to test all arrested prostitutes for HIV. Decriminalization becomes more likely if it widens HIV testing, which in turn curtails transmission rates by prostitutes.

Medicine and
Morals

11. Should Physician-Assisted Suicide Be Legalized?

YES

We own our bodies. No government or doctor can tell us what to do with it. If patients wish to refuse life-sustaining medical treatment, that is their business. If patients wish to commit suicide or ask a physician to end their life, that is their right, too. Rational, mentally competent patients have a fundamental and constitutional right to self-determination, to choose their time of death.

We deserve a merciful death. In their last weeks some terminally ill patients suffer agonizing pain that modern medicine cannot relieve. Why can't these people enjoy the same humane treatment given to dying animals? We should not use medical technology to postpone an inevitable death that brings release from pain.

We deserve dignity when dying. Most patients facing death care more about their quality of life than its length. They want to live pain-free and be treated with respect. Fifty years ago most of us died in a dignified atmosphere, at home among loved ones. Today we often die in hospitals hooked up to invasive machines. Controlling our death, like controlling our life, is one of the things that makes us human.

Patients in comas divert precious medical funds. We should help people live out their natural life span, but not beyond. Approximately 10,000 patients in the United States will never wake from a coma. Money used to unnaturally extend these lives should go to reducing the infant mortality rate and to caring for the 37 million Americans with no health insurance.

Passive euthanasia is secretly practiced all the time. According to the American Hospital Association and other sources, up to 70 percent of hospital deaths involve a secret decision to withhold medical care. Since this passive form of euthanasia is already practiced, why not actively help those who wish to die?

N O

Human life is sacred. Each person's life is fundamentally valuable and sacred, even if she is old and care is costly, inconvenient, or unpleasant. Killing someone is morally wrong even if he asks to die.

Who dies next? Legalized physician-assisted suicide requires doctors and families to judge the value of other people's lives. If we do not protect the terminally ill, who comes next? Will it become legal to kill the chronically ill? The mentally retarded or senile? The handicapped? The Nazis used pro-euthanasia arguments to justify killing the elderly, homosexuals, and Jews. We, too, could descend this "slippery slope" of devaluing life.

Medical miracles may disappear. Some of the 10,000 coma patients *will* suddenly wake up. Some "terminally ill" patients *will* survive. How can we condemn these people to death? Most doctors can describe cases in which the body suddenly reversed its course, letting a patient live on. Euthanasia makes such recoveries impossible.

Abuses will occur. Patients may be killed prematurely if their medical insurance runs out or if they have no family to fight for their rights. The poor already receive second-rate medical care, if any. With legalized euthanasia the poor will die in much greater numbers.

Physicians cannot be killers. When taking the Hippocratic oath, doctors promise: "I will give no deadly medicine to anyone if asked, nor suggest any such counsel. . . ." How can we force doctors to reject their solemn vow and their training?

Euthanasia puts unfair pressure on patients. Many patients feel enormous guilt about financial and other burdens they impose on family members. Euthanasia gives patients an easy way to relieve guilt even if they do not wish to die. By giving patients "the right to die" aren't we really encouraging them to take "the responsibility to die"?

Background

The euthanasia question is important because each of us may need to make life-and-death medical decisions for our loved ones someday. We may also need to make decisions about our own death or empower others to do so. In some ways the battle over euthanasia resembles the one over abortion. At the heart of each controversy lies the sanctity of life versus the individual's right of choice.

Euthanasia, meaning literally "a good death," has been practiced and argued about for thousands of years. Only in recent decades, as medical technology has increased our ability to extend life and medical costs have soared, has the issue become so urgent. The debate will escalate as the percentage of older people in our society increases and as the number of AIDS cases rises.

In 1991 euthanasia became an explicitly political issue. The electorate of Washington State narrowly rejected a ballot proposal making physician-assisted suicide legal for a person with a life expectancy of less than half a year. California narrowly rejected a similar ballot proposal in 1992.

In November 1994, Oregon voters narrowly approved the Death with Dignity Act, which legalizes assisted suicide according to stringent rules. An Oregon resident with a maximum life expectancy of six months, living in excruciating pain, must request death three times, once in writing. There must be witnesses to the requests who are not members of the patient's family, a second doctor must verify the patient's condition, and the patient must receive a last-minute opportunity to choose hospice care or an increased dosage of painkillers. Only then can the physician write a prescription for a lethal dose of drugs. A key point distinguishing Oregon's law from the ballot proposals that failed in Washington State and California is that the patient must self-administer the drug.

The Supreme Court recognized in 1990 (*Cruzan* v. *Missouri*) that a person's right to reject unwanted medical treatment is protected under the Constitution. Since then, the number of people writing living wills has soared. These wills instruct physicians about what medical measures can be taken should a patient become unable to make decisions. Living wills also can designate another person to make such decisions if needed.

The most visible champion of physician-assisted suicide today is Dr. Jack Kevorkian, a sixty-five-year-old Michigan pathologist-physician who assembles suicide machines and has assisted in the deaths of twenty patients since 1990. Most of them died after inhaling carbon monoxide gas through a gas mask. After Dr. Kevorkian, sometimes called Dr. Death, helped seven to die between January and February 1993, the Michigan legislature hurriedly enacted a law specifically to stop him. Dr. Kevorkian has been brought to trial and, as of late 1994, acquitted for the suicides he facilitated since Michigan passed this law. A number of county judges have declared the law unconstitutional on several grounds, including its violation of the right to self-determination. Dr. Kevorkian, an American folk hero to some, has been jailed and subjected himself to a seventeen-day hunger strike to publicize his cause.

According to a November 1993 Harris poll, 58 percent of Americans approve of Dr. Kevorkian assisting the terminally ill wishing to commit suicide, 38 percent disapprove, and 4 percent are not sure.

Euthanasia is openly practiced in only one foreign country. Since 1973 courts in the Netherlands have not prosecuted physicians who assisted terminally ill patients to die under certain conditions. The patient must be rational and must explicitly and repeatedly request to die. The patient's physical or mental suffering must be acute and irreversible. Also, two physicians must agree that the request is reasonable.

Although euthanasia is technically a criminal offense in the Netherlands, physicians who follow these guidelines are not prosecuted. The estimated number of deaths from physician-assisted suicide in the Netherlands ranges from 2,000 to 10,000 a year.

Outlook

In the United States, the euthanasia battle is expected to heat up in the next few years. The electorates in more states will be asked to vote on euthanasia referenda. Pro-euthanasia forces will rewrite the referenda defeated in Washington State and California to satisfy voter objections. Dr. Kevorkian may also succeed in gathering the 250,000 petition signatures needed to put a constitutional amendment on the Michigan ballot. Conversely, Michigan's law against assisted suicide will be tested if Dr. Kevorkian goes to trial for breaking it.

12. Should Abortion Remain Legal?

YES

Life begins at birth. Most doctors and scientists believe a fetus becomes a person only at birth, or when it can survive outside the womb. Survival occurs at approximately twenty-four weeks, the point up until which the Supreme Court sanctioned abortion in its *Roe* v. *Wade* decision in 1973.

Although the zygote created when a sperm fertilizes an egg contains all forty-six human chromosomes, that hardly constitutes a person. Most of the individual cells in our body contain those same forty-six chromosomes. An embryo is simply a mass of cells.

Just as human life ends with brain death, human life begins with the consciousness of a well-developed brain. At four months, hemisphere formation of the brain of a human fetus resembles that of a reptile. Even into the sixth month the brain resembles that of a lower mammal, such as an opossum.

The claim that life begins at conception cannot be made on medical grounds.

Women must retain control over their own body. Conservatives and the religious right cannot justify forcing their beliefs on women. Forcing a woman to unwillingly carry a fetus to term is nothing less than a form of legalized rape.

Abortion restrictions discriminate against poor women. The poor are least able to afford an unplanned or unwanted child. Yet restrictions on abortion place the greatest financial burdens on them, while antiabortion forces are loath to increase social spending that might make such births easier.

Legal abortions save women's lives. Of the 1.6 million legal abortions in the United States each year, an average of only six women die from the procedure. In Mexico, where about the same number of *illegal* abortions takes place, thousands of women die from the procedure.

We must never return to the days of quacks—or the women themselves—performing abortions with coat hangers or knitting needles, or by douching with turpentine.

N O

Life begins at conception. At the moment of conception a baby contains all forty-six chromosomes—all the inherited characteristics needed to form a new human being. In terms of hormones, genetics, and other organic characteristics, the child is totally distinct and separate from the mother. The fetus requires only nourishment. The baby's heart starts beating at eighteen days and has brain waves at forty days.

Abortion is murder. In first trimester abortions, a powerful suction machine rips the fetus from the womb. In late second and third trimester abortions, the child, too big to fit through the cervix, is dismembered and pulled out piece by piece with medical pliers. How can we condone such treatment of a fellow human being?

Killing a defenseless child—particularly your own—becomes a monstrous crime against the sanctity of life. It distorts our whole moral order. That abortionists collectively earn hundreds of millions of dollars each year renders the crime even more despicable.

Protecting the reproductive rights of women cannot justify killing innocent human beings. The inconvenience of disrupting the work, career, or home life of a pregnant woman does not warrant murder.

"Accidental" children have every right to live. Who can say accidental or unwanted children are less valuable, can contribute less to the world, or will live less happily than planned-for children? Most parents who consider but reject abortion fall in love with their new babies. Most children saved from abortion lead happy, productive lives.

Abortion teaches that children are expendable. No wonder child abuse runs rampant in our society. Abortion teaches us that children can be kept or thrown away on a whim.

Abortion has hurt women's health. After the *Roe* v. *Wade* decision in 1973, the number of abortions soared. Today well over 100,000 women a year suffer complications from abortion, such as excessive bleeding or infection.

Background

Not since slavery and the Civil War has an issue so divided the United States. On one side are conservatives, Roman Catholics, and evangelical Protestants whose moral vision considers abortion murder. On the other side are feminists, liberals, and civil libertarians who believe in a woman's right to privacy and control over her own body.

In ancient Rome, abortion was used to control family size, but Christian theologians later condemned abortion. Widespread criminal sanctions began only in the nineteenth century. By the middle of this century, most U.S. states passed laws forbidding abortion. But in 1973 the U.S. Supreme Court ruled in *Roe* v. *Wade* that such restrictive state laws were unconstitutional. In effect this landmark decision permitted abortion on demand during the first three months of pregnancy.

During the Reagan-Bush years antiabortionists gained on several fronts. Demonstrations and bombings against abortion clinics and their doctors reduced the number of physicians willing to perform abortions. State legislatures passed new restrictions, including requirements for parental and spousal permission, and waiting periods. The increasingly conservative Supreme Court upheld certain state restrictions in 1989 and 1992. Many expected the Court to overturn *Roe* v. *Wade* during the Bush presidency. The election of President Clinton turned the tide in favor of pro-choice forces.

Clinton has overturned some federal regulations from the Reagan-Bush years, making abortion easier to obtain. In the most dramatic change, the Clinton administration pushed through the Freedom of Access to Clinic Entrances Act, which punishes protestors for using force or the threat of force, or physically obstructing women seeking abortions.

Estimates for the number of abortions performed worldwide each year range from 30 to 55 million. In the United States, approximately 2,500 clinics or doctor's offices perform 1.6 million abortions annually—totaling one-fourth of all U.S. pregnancies—at an average cost of $251.

Today abortion is unavailable in 83 percent of U.S. counties, although most women who can afford an abortion are able to obtain one. Cities are well served by clinics, though many rural women must travel great distances. In South Dakota, for example, only one doctor performs abortions. Although surveys indicate a large majority of obstetricians and gynecologists consider themselves pro-choice, many refuse to perform abortions because they feel the work is low-paying and distasteful, or because they fear harassment from right-to-lifers. Only one-quarter of U.S. medical schools require abortion training for ob/gyn students.

Outlook

The Clinton administration will continue its pro-choice policies and the courts will continue to uphold abortion rights. The Republican-dominated Congress will attempt to chip away at abortion rights. Pro-abortion and antiabortion forces will continue battling each other directly and trying to influence public opinion. Pro-life forces may have to find more ingenious methods to defy the Freedom of Access to Clinic Entrances Act. Additional physicians may be killed by zealous activists.

The number of properly trained doctors willing to perform abortions is declining. However, the American College of Obstetricians and Gynecologists has proposed training nonphysicians to perform first trimester abortions—a simple procedure routinely performed in outplacement clinics. Such a program could alleviate the shortage of abortionists.

The arrival of RU-486 could also dramatically change the U.S. abortion scene. This effective and safe French abortion drug blocks the action of the hormone progesterone, triggering the onset of the menstrual cycle and flushing out the fertilized egg. Taken in pill form, it could be prescribed anonymously by thousands of doctors nationwide. The antiabortionists, lacking abortion clinics to target, would probably focus their anger on the pharmaceutical company distributing the drug. The French company that owns the RU-486 patent has turned over the U.S. rights to the Population Council, a New York–based nonprofit group. The drug could become available in 1996 if it passes Food and Drug Administration test standards for safety and efficacy and if a U.S. firm agrees to manufacture the drug.

13. Should Experiments on Animals Be Banned?

YES

Animal experimentation is morally wrong. Animals such as monkeys are living, valuable creatures who have as much right to life as humans. Since we can not justify lethal experiments on humans, how can we for animals? Some contend that humans are superior because we possess rational thought and advanced language. But a chimpanzee is superior in one or both of these ways to the insane, the severely retarded, and the senile. How can we condone doing to chimps what would be unthinkable doing to impaired people?

If civilized people oppose racism and sexism, why is the torment of animals acceptable?

We must protect helpless creatures—human or animal. Contentions of human superiority or inferiority aside, we must protect animals from exploitation just as we protect human infants and the retarded. We are morally obligated to safeguard all living creatures entrusted to our care.

Many animal studies can be replaced. Taxpayers support a large industry of scientists and researchers who thrive on animal experiments. But new techniques for cell and tissue testing in test tubes can now supplant animal toxicology studies. Sophisticated computer models can also replace some live experiments.

Many animal studies offer little value. Many animals die in cruel, pointless studies to prove the obvious. How can you justify experiments that isolate animals in tiny cages devoid of all stimuli, just to prove they become depressed? How can you justify blinding thousands of rabbits each year simply to protect cosmetics companies from product liability?

Results from animal tests are often ambiguous. Typically, tests on mice to determine the cancer-causing potential of a chemical agree only 70 percent of the time with comparable tests on rats. If two rodent species provide widely different results nearly one-third of the time, can we trust these tests to predict the cancer risk of chemicals in a species as different as humans?

NO

Medical progress relies on animal research. Almost everyone alive today benefits from animal experimentation. Vaccines for infectious diseases such as polio, measles, rubella, and smallpox were developed in animals. Medications we take for diabetes, ulcers, asthma, arthritis, and hypertension exist because of animal tests. Most advances in surgery were first tried and perfected in animals. Finding a cure for the AIDS virus will depend heavily on animal research.

Veterinary medicine also benefits. Experiments on animals even led to cat and dog vaccines for rabies, distemper, and other life-threatening diseases. Horses, cattle, and other livestock can be immunized against various diseases and treated for worms and parasites only because of research using other animals.

Few alternative methods work. Computer models, tissue cultures, and cell cultures can and do supplement some animal experiments. But since animals resemble humans in their intricate organs and physiological complexity, only animal studies can more closely predict how humans will react to drugs and chemicals.

Few trivial experiments get funded. Much of our biomedical research is supported by the National Institutes of Health. Since only a third of worthwhile proposals receive funding, wasteful projects that abuse animals rarely get under way.

Only a small percentage of research animals suffer pain. According to a Department of Agriculture survey, nearly two-thirds of research animals suffer no pain. Of the remaining third, most receive anesthesia or pain-killing drugs. The 6 percent that experience pain do so because of the objective of the experiment. For example, the most effective way to research pain control in humans is by testing animals.

Future patients will die without animal testing. If the radical minority succeeds in ending or even limiting animal experiments, many new drugs and surgical techniques will languish undiscovered. Are we really willing to cripple cancer and AIDS research or reduce our longevity?

Background

Of all animal rights issues, experimentation on animals may be the most divisive. On one side stand activists who feel theirs is a moral crusade to protect innocent animals from human exploitation. On the other side are scientists who resent being painted as animal torturers motivated by profit rather than by compassion for humanity.

No issue raises more hackles than research on primates. Because chimpanzees and other monkeys physiologically resemble humans, they make the best experimental subjects. Because of this resemblance, their suffering stirs activists the most.

Only twenty years ago most animal activism was confined to well-known humane societies. Since then pro-animal groups have grown explosively. Today thousands of local and national groups exist. The most powerful is People for the Ethical Treatment of Animals (PETA), whose 400,000 members provide it with an $8 million annual budget. Its founder infiltrated a Maryland research laboratory in 1981 and filmed seventeen caged monkeys living in terrible conditions. As a result of publicity from this incident, Congress passed amendments to the Animal Welfare Act in 1985 which govern the treatment of laboratory animals. Although the Department of Agriculture has been slow in implementing these animal protection rules, many laboratories adopted them on their own. Specifically, most research facilities receiving funds from the National Institutes of Health set up committees that review all research involving animals.

According to the Department of Agriculture, American laboratories used approximately 554,000 rabbits, 539,000 guinea pigs, 416,000 hamsters, 180,000 dogs, 61,000 primates, and 50,000 cats in 1987. Perhaps another 20 million mice and rats were also used.

Antivivisection activists have tried both legal and illegal methods to spread their message. Their tactics include laboratory break-ins, vandalism, sit-ins, lawsuits, letter-writing campaigns, and product boycotts. Only the antiabortion lobby is better known for such guerrilla tactics.

Over the last twenty years Americans have become more concerned about experimentation on animals. An August 1993 National Opinion Research Center poll shows that 64 percent of Americans agree strongly or moderately that we should allow animal testing if it saves human lives; 19 percent disagree strongly or moderately. A February 1992 Gallup poll revealed that 71 percent of Americans support using pound animals, who would otherwise be put to death, for research; 26 percent oppose using such pound animals.

Use of animals is declining due, in part, to the efforts of organizations like PETA. Cosmetics companies now rely much less on the notorious Draize eye irritancy test, in which substances are dropped into the eyes of unanesthetized rabbits to test for sensitivity. In fact, many consumer products companies now brag that their goods were developed without animal research. Scientists' use of primates in drug-abuse research has declined by 60 percent since 1988. Fearing a backlash from local antivivisection organizations, many university and private laboratories now follow animal care guidelines much more carefully. Animal researchers also carry out their work with greater secrecy.

Outlook

The battle over animal experiments is being fought on several fronts. Pro-research organizations like Americans for Medical Progress are lobbying Congress to pass the Animal Enterprise Protection Act, hoping to protect scientists and researchers from physical harm and harassment. Organizations like PETA strive to teach children to protect animals. More and more young teens are choosing to be vegetarians. PETA is also introducing so-called student choice legislation in many states. Student choice mandates that a teacher announce two weeks prior to a classroom dissection that students may choose not to participate. California and Florida have already passed student choice legislation. In Maine, dissection in school is prohibited. By targeting children, PETA hopes to strengthen animal protection in the future. The pro-research lobby argues that America will lose many potential scientists because students never receive the chance to become excited by hands-on biological research.

The American Medical Association and the pharmaceutical industry—two powerful lobbies—strenuously support continued freedom to experiment on animals. It seems unlikely that the antivivisection lobby will succeed in banning experiments anytime soon.

14. Is the Government Spending Enough on AIDS Research?

YES

The federal government spends a vastly disproportionate amount on AIDS. In 1993 the U.S. Public Health Service spent $2 billion on cancer research, $770 million on heart disease research, and $1.3 billion on AIDS research. That year in the United States 500,000 died from cancer, 700,000 from heart disease, and 34,000 from AIDS. On an average basis, the research money spent per death was $3,700 for cancer, $1,000 for heart disease, and a whopping $38,500 for AIDS.

Just because the AIDS lobby gains funds more effectively than other medical lobbies does not mean victims of the more widespread diseases should suffer.

Overspending on AIDS diverts not only funds but also research personnel. The total government research budget remained essentially stagnant over the last few years. Extra dollars going to AIDS means fewer dollars for dozens of other diseases.

AIDS research also funnels top researchers from work on other illnesses. The world only mints a limited number of biochemists and other specialists each year. With the strong government emphasis on AIDS, a disproportionate number of researchers abandon work on other diseases, fearing only AIDS research will get funded.

Overfunding AIDS discriminates against women. Although many women die from AIDS, a much larger number die from breast cancer, yet breast cancer research commands only *one-tenth* the government funding of AIDS research.

AIDS will grow more slowly than predicted. During 1991 and 1992 a consensus of "experts" anticipated 54,000 and 61,000 new U.S. cases, respectively. Because of the success in spreading the safe-sex message, the real numbers of new cases were 46,000 and 47,000 for those years. As even more Americans learn about the risks of AIDS, the number of new cases will level off.

Drug companies will pay for much of the research. The government needlessly funds much research into potential AIDS vaccines and cures that drug companies, motivated by the high potential profit, would gladly sponsor.

N O

Because AIDS strikes the young and healthy, funding is much too low. Tragically, researchers of various diseases must compete for federal dollars. While cancer and heart disease primarily afflict older people, AIDS mainly kills those in their twenties through forties. To fairly compare diseases, statisticians use a measure called "years of potential life lost before age 65," known as YPLL. By this measure, AIDS and cancer each deprived Americans of 1.4 million years of life in 1993. Those dying of heart disease lost 1.2 million years. Since the YPLL for AIDS is expected to surpass that of cancer starting in 1994, AIDS research funding should *exceed* that for cancer and heart disease.

AIDS is deadly, communicable, and out of control. Unlike most other U.S. diseases, AIDS spreads quickly and extensively. YPLL and deaths from cancer, heart disease, diabetes, and stroke are expected to increase by less than 10 percent during the first half of the 1990s. However, YPLL for AIDS will increase from 150 to 350 percent during the same period.

The World Health Organization estimates that by decade's end, 1.5 million Americans will be HIV-positive. Worldwide, the figure could easily exceed 40 million. By other estimates, 100 million could be HIV-positive by the year 2000.

The cost of treating AIDS patients worldwide will top $15 billion for 1995 alone. The more we spend today for finding a vaccine and cure, the more lives and money we can save later.

The virus is particularly dangerous because it evolves so quickly. Not only can HIV hide within human cells, it can also vary its chemical makeup. At any time a new strain could become undetectable and untreatable. Funding must grow to prevent a sudden upswing in AIDS worldwide.

AIDS research enhances our understanding of many other diseases. Insights we gain from studying AIDS have already increased our knowledge about cancer, infectious diseases, immunology, hematology, neurology, and pulmonary medicine.

Background

In a perfect world where the federal government generated a surplus, the sick would not need lobbies to compete for limited medical research dollars. Unfortunately, lobbies must compete. Over the last decade the many groups serving AIDS victims have attracted the most new funding.

In 1981, when AIDS first gained notice, gay men constituted the vast majority of its victims. The gay and lesbian community—well organized, educated, and generally distrustful of the medical establishment—quickly secured funding from Congress despite initial opposition from President Reagan. What started with $200,000 of federal funding for AIDS research, education, and treatment in 1981 expanded to nearly $2.1 billion by 1993. In 1992 private AIDS charities raised an additional $575 million to $850 million, compared to $355 million for the American Cancer Society and $235 million for the American Heart Association.

The AIDS lobby's success extends beyond raising funds for research, education, and treatment. Activists increased patient access to new AIDS drugs during investigational stages and speeded up regulatory approvals of drugs. They even convinced a major pharmaceutical firm, Burroughs Wellcome, to reduce the price of its AZT medication, widely used by AIDS patients.

The massive concentration of research on a single disease resembles the "war" on cancer declared during the Nixon administration. Just as that war in the 1970s made limited inroads against cancer, the vast sums spent on AIDS during the 1980s and 1990s have had mixed results so far. More than a hundred drugs are being tested in clinical trials in the United States. The government has sponsored AIDS research leading to a number of drugs that alleviate some symptoms of the disease. But, as AIDS activists quickly point out, a cure or even a vaccine still seems very far away.

AIDS patients must compete for funds not only with victims of other diseases but also with other AIDS patients. In many localities the largest number of AIDS sufferers are no longer gay white men but rather African-Americans, ethnic minorities, intravenous drug users, and women. Organizations that service heterosexual patients in these communities must compete for funds with groups primarily serving gays. Some gay activists believe funding for AIDS will never rise substantially so long as gays, minorities, the poor, and drug abusers remain the major victims. They predict spending will rise dramatically if AIDS spreads widely within the white heterosexual community.

Owing to the great number of volunteers helping AIDS organizations, the cost of treating a typical AIDS patient from diagnosis to death has actually declined over a recent three-year period, from $102,000 to $70,000. Although the Centers for Disease Control (CDC) predicts the number of U.S. AIDS deaths will level off in the mid-1990s, the costs per patient will probably rise as new medicines become available. That may substantially increase total federal AIDS funding, though not necessarily for research funding.

Outlook

Funding of AIDS research will continue to grow, though not at the meteoric rate of the 1980s. However, if a new strain broke out or the number of victims grew faster than expected, Congress would reevaluate funding levels. President Clinton, thankful for the gay community's support during the 1992 election and ever mindful of future elections, has proposed spending several billion additional dollars. But a Republican-dominated Congress will likely resist such a substantial increase.

Competition for research funds will come more directly from feminists and breast cancer victims who are employing techniques used by the AIDS lobby, including letter-writing campaigns and public demonstrations. Aside from seeking more research funds, the breast cancer lobby, too, wants faster access to new drugs and increased insurance coverage for experimental cures.

The debate over health care reform could inspire the various lobbies to join forces in gaining more research funds for all, and in further streamlining the research and delivery of new drugs. More likely, the competition between lobbies will heat up.

15. Should the Government Run Our Health Care System?

YES

Only the government can cap out-of-control health care costs. In 1994 for the first time, American spending on health care will exceed $1 trillion annually. If present trends continue, total health care costs will grow 13.5 percent annually for the next five years.

Only the government has the regulatory and financial strength to cap or negotiate lower fees with insurance companies, physician groups, and other health providers. Government can also reduce the oversupply of expensive medical specialists while ending the shortage of family and general medicine physicians. Only the government can effectively end today's monstrously expensive administrative and billing systems.

Thirty-seven million Americans live without health insurance. Each month another 100,000 Americans lose their health care benefits. Too often the elderly must choose between food and medicine. Offering decent health care to all Americans is more than an ethical obligation. It will result in a healthier, more productive society from which we all benefit.

The government can best allocate health care fairly. The government does not fund our health care system now, although collectively we already pay for it. Ultimately, whether a major overhaul comes or not, each of us pays for all U.S. health care through our taxes and through higher prices for the products and services of companies that provide health insurance for their workers. Only the government has the ability and incentive to fairly distribute the costs and benefits of health care.

Only the government can stand up to the health care industry. The lobbies opposed to health care reform include physicians, whose income would decline, and the health insurance industry—a bureaucracy that would largely disappear under major reform. Since the health care industry has little incentive to cut costs, only government intervention will work. Otherwise, the health care industry will continue to drain our health care dollars.

N O

No true health care crisis exists. Of the 37 million uninsured half will become insured again within four months. Many of the 10 to 15 million chronically uninsured are under the age of twenty-five and choose not to pay for health insurance since they rarely need it.

Seventy-five percent of presently insured Americans are happy with their health care. Why force sweeping changes on this vast majority? We can help the chronically uninsured by providing health care subsidies rather than by overhauling the entire system.

Our care is costly because we enjoy the best in the world. Americans spend more per person on health care than do people in any other country, but by many measures our care is the finest. For example, the Japanese pay less, but they receive production line treatment from doctors who see nearly fifty patients a day.

Under national health care, bureaucratic administrators will make your medical decisions. Only you and your doctor can decide the treatment that is right for you. A government-controlled system would let bureaucratic gatekeepers limit your access to costly, but effective, therapies and specialists. Do you want government agents deciding which treatments you get, where you get them, and from whom?

Government health care will ultimately force many consumers into HMOs. Some health reform plans, to reduce costs, will push many patients and doctors into health maintenance organizations (HMOs), which generally provide a lower quality of care than traditional fee-for-service plans. HMOs average one physician per 800 members—about half the ratio of the general population. HMOs typically withhold a portion of doctors' annual salaries to ensure they meet stringent HMO targets for limiting patient access to specialists and hospitalization.

Jobs will be lost. Sweeping health care plans that require small businesses to insure all their employees will force mass layoffs. Estimates suggest between 200,000 and 3 million jobs could be lost.

Background

Two factors drive the push to reform our health care system. First are the millions of uninsured who must rely on crowded emergency rooms for all medical care. Second is cost—$1 out of every $7 spent in the United States goes for health care—the highest in the world. Long gone are the days when all insured patients could visit any doctor, who could order any test or treatment, prescribe any medication, and charge whatever he or she wanted, with an insurer automatically picking up the bill.

Several different visions for health reform have given birth to a variety of proposals. All proposals fall along a continuum ranging from total regulation to total competition. The single-payer alternative, given no chance of passing Congress, calls for the most regulation. Modeled after Canada's system, it would allow the federal government to collect all money for health care, set all prices, and pay all the bills. At the other extreme, the most vocal proponents of competition call for little real reform of the present system.

Only a compromise has any chance of passing Congress. Plans advocated by Democrats and liberals generally favor universal coverage for all citizens and rely on some government regulation to achieve true reform. Most Republicans and conservatives—ever reluctant to increase governmental intervention and not anxious to provide universal coverage—concentrate on using market forces to bring down health costs. Most members of Congress agree on one point: the buying and selling of health insurance is terribly inefficient and must submit to some government regulation or other change.

During his campaign President Clinton promised to make health care reform a major goal of his administration. Clinton has expended enormous effort and political capital trying to honor his word. Led by Hillary Clinton, hundreds of policy experts wrote Clinton's 1,342-page bill, the Health Security Act, introduced into Congress in October 1993.

President Clinton's Health Security Act borrowed elements from both the regulation and competition camps. It proposed to rely on market forces by letting different health care companies compete for patients. At the same time Clinton wanted enough federal control to ensure universal coverage. In early 1994 several lobbies began a brutal public relations campaign to defeat the Clinton plan in the various congressional committees considering it.

Most vocal was the Health Insurance Association of America (HIAA), representing over 270 companies who might go bankrupt if the Clinton plan passed. The HIAA produced the highly publicized television commercials of the fictional Harry and Louise debating the future of their health care. Also prominent in opposing the Clinton plan was the National Federation of Independent Business (NFIB), representing many small businesses, who object to Clinton's requirement that all companies, even tiny ones, contribute to their workers' health care costs.

As a result of the antireform publicity campaign, America's support for health care reform dropped dramatically. A March 1994 *Washington Post*/ABC News poll found exactly half of Americans believe a reformed health care system would serve them better than the present system. Only six months earlier an additional 22 percent of Americans had supported reform.

Outlook

The Republican near sweep of the 1994 elections substantially changes the picture. Although many Republican lawmakers favor moderate health-care reforms, other issues will likely dominate their legislative agenda. If a compromise does come in 1995 or 1996, it will not include universal coverage or the comprehensive restructuring championed by President Clinton. Republicans favor small changes designed to lower health-care costs and increase coverage. This might include new rules that would forbid insurance companies from denying benefits to patients with preexisting conditions. Companies might be required to offer, though not pay for, health-care insurance to all their employees. Other reforms sponsored by some Republicans, such as insurance subsidies for the poor, are probably too expensive to survive the cost-cutting agenda of today's Congress.

16. Should the United States Ban Human Cloning Research?

YES

Cloning would be used for immoral purposes. In cloning's near future, infertility clinics could offer scrapbooks of children showing their appearance, intelligence level, and temperament. You could then order a cloned embryo—an exact genetic duplicate of any child—implanted in your uterus or in a surrogate mother.

In time, scientists may even grow extra people for use as spare parts or for human slaves. Unfortunately, human history shows that military and other potentially destructive technologies—once available—get misused. The United States is one of the few countries where you can already buy human sperm and eggs from catalogs detailing the donors' characteristics. How long before we produce standardized human beings on an assembly line? The risks and dangers of cloning technology far outweigh any benefits to society.

Cloning violates respect for the individuality of life. According to nature's and God's design, each person is a unique, exceptional being, with a face, voice, and body all his or her own. Only the occasional identical twins break that rule. Cloned people would be robbed of their value as individuals. We would end up prizing genetically engineered people for their desirable genetic characteristics, not as unique, inherently precious human beings.

Cloning today may result in eugenics tomorrow. We must protect the diversity of the human race or face a homogenized world. Some of today's reproductive technologies, including amniocentesis and abortion, already allow us to destroy lives we deem unworthy.

If we allow cloning research to evolve, we face a very troubling future. Who decides which humans will serve as the model for cloning? Which race, ethnic group, sex, body type, personality, and level of intelligence will dominate? What government agency or corporation can we trust to make such decisions? A society practicing eugenics by creating life is little better than Nazi Germany, which practiced eugenics by destroying life.

N O

Cloning could solve medical problems for millions of people. Today's hopeful parents with infertility problems deserve the right to use cloned embryos so they may bear children. Parents who might produce a child with a dreaded disease, such as sickle-cell anemia or Tay-Sachs, should be allowed to use cloned embryos to test for the disease—a vastly superior method to those currently available.

In the not-so-distant future, parents of a desperately ill child should have the chance to grow that child's identical twin so he or she can donate life-saving tissue or bone marrow. Americans use transplanted eyes, kidneys, and other organs. Why shouldn't patients who can only use tissue from a close genetic relative receive the same chance?

Cloning research itself poses no danger. Even if scientists can someday clone entire humans, clones pose no threat to humanity. Biology itself poses no risk; one could come only from a totalitarian government that controls human reproduction. Just because cloning technology improves does not mean we will suffer from the type of all-powerful government portrayed in Aldous Huxley's *Brave New World*. Popular disapproval and religious customs will prevent the widespread use of cloning.

Clones will not suffer a loss of individuality. In human history, millions of twins and triplets have lived happy, productive lives. The few cloned twins in the future would adjust just as well to not being unique.

In principle, scientific research should not be banned. Unless research leads to obvious and immediate public dangers, such as chemical or biological warfare, governments should never prohibit scientific research. The U.S. government can decline to fund cloning research, or can regulate scientists, but a ban on basic research stifles scientific progress. Even with a ban, Kevorkian-like researchers would still provide desperately needed infertility services to those needing them.

Background

The word "clone" derives from "twig" in ancient Greek, suggesting the technique popular among gardeners of cutting a piece of plant and rooting it to create a duplicate. Many people think of cloning as the use of a nonreproductive cell to create an identical being. Such cloning, popularized by the movie *Jurassic Park,* will remain in the realm of science fiction for a very long time. Nevertheless, some famous people, including Saddam Hussein, have approached scientists to save their tissue for cloning when the technology eventually becomes available. Cryogenics practitioners claim that magazine publisher Malcolm Forbes and clothing designer Halston had tissue samples frozen before their deaths.

In October 1993 researchers Jerry L. Hall and Robert J. Stillman of George Washington University Medical Center, Washington, D.C., announced the first cloning of a human embryo. The story made front-page headlines around the world. The relatively simple, perhaps misnamed, "cloning" by Hall and Stillman is called "twinning" by some scientists. They took seventeen defective microscopic human embryos, destined never to grow beyond the thirty-two-cell stage, and multiplied them into forty-two embryos. Although animal researchers first employed the same techniques years ago, no one dared cross the barrier to use human embryos. Hall and Stillman's main goal was to help infertile couples who can produce only one embryo at a time. A baby results only 10 to 20 percent of the time when scientists use in vitro fertilization to create a single embryo. If scientists could clone embryos the chances of successful pregnancy would increase substantially.

World reaction was swift and mostly unfavorable. The Vatican's official newspaper proclaimed the United States had entered "a tunnel of madness." The Japanese Medical Association called the experiment unthinkable. French President François Mitterrand said he was horrified. These countries and more than twenty others employ commissions to set policies on reproductive technologies. In Germany, for example, cloning a human embryo would result in a five-year prison sentence. No such laws exist in the United States.

The American public finds the cloning of human embryos worrisome. In a November 1993 *Time*/CNN poll, three-quarters of Americans said they disapprove of cloning. Forty-six percent want a law making human cloning illegal; 40 percent believe research should be stopped temporarily.

Cloning research receives its impetus and most of its money from the prospering *in vitro* fertilization industry. In 1985, Congress set up a Biomedical Ethics Advisory Committee to make recommendations on such issues as cloning. Committee members fought continually over abortion ethics, never addressing other issues, until the committee's charter expired in 1989.

Outlook

Many in Congress want to establish a new committee to decide such issues as the cloning of embryos. Senators Edward Kennedy (D-Massachusetts) and Mark Hatfield (R-Oregon) lead this effort. The National Institutes of Health may also form their own panel. Although President Clinton favors creation of a national bioethics panel, he has not yet initiated one. No one knows how a new panel could avoid the battles over abortion that seem to overshadow most reviews of reproductive technology.

Until the United States creates clear biomedical policies, ethical issues will be fought publicly and with rancor in the media and courts. Compromise will prove difficult between those who argue that reproductive and genetic engineering tampers with the laws of God and nature, and those who believe science must remain unfettered and that U.S. business must be allowed to compete on all technological fronts with Japan.

In the twenty-first century scientists may succeed in eliminating certain hereditary diseases, enhancing human physical characteristics, and permanently improving future generations of people. As long as progress in reproductive and genetic engineering serves to alleviate human suffering, few will condemn research. However, a worldwide suspicion that this type of engineering will fundamentally alter the human race seems likely to control such technology for the foreseeable future.

17. Should We Punish Parents Who Rely on Faith Healing for Their Fatally Ill Children?

YES

To save lives, the state must sometimes limit individual autonomy. Protecting the health and safety of children is an established principle of American jurisprudence. It even permits infringements on the constitutional requirement to protect religious freedoms. The ruling of the California Supreme Court in a 1988 case, *Walker* v. *Supreme Court,* is typical of state laws. This court declared that the right of a parent to rely exclusively on prayer must yield when a child's health is seriously jeopardized. The U.S. Supreme Court agrees with such rulings.

Religious exemption laws are unconstitutional. In some states certain religious groups, such as Christian Scientists and Jehovah's Witnesses, have gained special exemptions from blood tests, prophylactic eyedrops for newborns, and health education for schoolchildren. Arizona and Connecticut specifically name Christian Scientists as recipients of special rights.

These religious exemptions are unconstitutional because they violate the antiestablishment clause, which forbids special privileges for specific religions. Christian Science parents unfairly manipulate these laws in cases where faith healing results in a child's death.

Faith healing violates normal health standards. In the largest, most recent study the mortality rate of Christian Scientists, who neither drink nor smoke, was still *significantly higher* than the control group. Only their refusal to use medical treatments can explain this. The Christian Science claim that faith healing works is untrue, and may actually be responsible for lowering their members' life expectancy.

Society must punish these parents to prevent future needless deaths. Upon learning of a child being denied lifesaving medical treatment, the state takes custody and provides care. But often, religious sects hide their mistreatment of children. The only way for the state to save children's lives is to make an example by punishing parents. Just as the state saves lives by criminalizing homicide, so must we punish this form of child abuse.

N O

The state has no right to dictate its views to an established religion. The several hundred thousand adherents of Christian Science believe that illness is rooted in the mind. They think ignorance, fear, and sin cause disease, and that only Christian Science prayer can restore health. Christian Science beliefs about treating illness comprise the core of their religion, and conventional medical healing totally conflicts with their faith. The state has no right to force any established religious group to conform to the majority's beliefs.

The Constitution protects freedom of religion. The First Amendment prohibits the federal government from interfering with a religion. State constitutions also guarantee religious freedoms.

Medicine is far from perfect. Daily, we read about the tragic failings of hospital treatments and doctors' inability to cure numerous ailments. Many patients and their families choose alternatives to conventional medicine. Faith healing is a legitimate alternative.

The government and medical insurers recognize the legitimacy of faith healing. Christian Science practitioners and nurses send invoices to their patients. Just as with medical expenses, the U.S. Internal Revenue Service permits Christian Scientists to deduct faith healing expenses from their income tax returns. Health insurers also accept the validity of Christian Science. Medicare, Medicaid, Blue Cross/Blue Shield, and hundreds of health insurance companies reimburse Christian Scientists for their faith healing charges. If such major American institutions accept faith healing, why do the courts harass Christian Scientists and other religious groups?

Haven't these parents suffered enough? Losing your child is one of life's worst tragedies. Surely, we need not force the parents to suffer even further by bringing them to trial. We do not cast suspicion upon the bereaved parents of children who die in hospitals. Those who choose faith healing should receive the same compassion.

Background

Before the advancement of modern medicine, parents were not criminally liable for choosing faith healing over medical care for their sick children. English common law and pre-twentieth-century American laws exonerated parents who, in good faith, chose the healing method they felt worked best. But by the middle of this century, most courts would accuse parents of criminal negligence for withholding medical treatments proven to work in a certain percentage of cases. In the eyes of the courts, medical science has improved so much that impartial standards for care now require parents to use conventional medicine. Today, in most states faith healing is certainly permissible, though most authorities do not consider it a substitute for medicine.

Christian Scientists—by far the largest U.S. sect practicing faith healing—do allow members to visit dentists and optometrists. Church members often use physicians for relatively simple, noninvasive procedures like setting a broken bone or delivering a baby. But only Christian Science ministers using faith healing are supposed to treat other ailments.

State courts and the U.S. Supreme Court have consistently ruled in favor of compulsory medical care for children, even when contrary to religious beliefs. Courts must balance three competing interests: the parents' First Amendment right to free exercise of religion, the child's right to lifesaving medical care, and the state's responsibility to protect life. In the last few decades courts have ordered vaccinations, blood transfusions, and other life-sustaining treatments for children. The Supreme Court agreed with a Pennsylvania court, which held that although adults may choose to become martyrs themselves, they may not make martyrs of children too young to decide on their own. The doctrine behind such rulings—called *parens patriae*—allows the state legally to assume the role of parent for some children. With older children who can speak for themselves or when the situation is not life-threatening, courts have sometimes bowed to religious freedom.

Nevertheless, most states still have some kind of religious exemption laws giving religious groups certain privileges. Colorado, Louisiana, and Texas recently passed new exemptions. In Louisiana, for example, parents are not negligent who use faith healing with a reasonably proven record of success instead of conventional medicine. Such legislation virtually grants Christian Science, which cites its own statistics of successful healing, equal standing under state law.

Massachusetts, the birthplace of Christian Science, has been central in tackling the parental negligence issue. Until recently, Massachusetts law held a child was not neglected because a parent relied on spiritual healing. It said, "Parents who fail to provide medical services to children on the basis of religious belief are expressly precluded from imposition of criminal liability." Before that law was repealed in 1993, the much publicized case of David and Ginger Twitchell came to trial. This Boston couple used spiritual healing on their two-and-a-half-year-old son as he slowly died in agony from a bowel obstruction. A simple operation would have saved the boy's life. In July 1990, after finding them guilty, the court sentenced the couple to ten years' probation and required that their remaining three children receive regular medical checkups. But a higher state court overturned the manslaughter conviction because the original jury never learned that Massachusetts law allowed parents to rely on faith healing. In another highly publicized case concerning Christian Scientists, a Florida couple was convicted in 1992 for relying on spiritual healing while their ten-year-old diabetic daughter died from a lack of insulin injections. This conviction, too, was overturned on appeal. However, during the last decade more than twenty parents in other states have been convicted for failing to provide medical care to fatally ill children.

Outlook

Most of the recent cases are still in the process of appeal. Despite religious exemption laws many states are likely to continue prosecuting parents who fail to treat their children's life-threatening illnesses. But most judges and juries, rather than imprison parents, will give them suspended sentences and order conventional medical treatment for their other children. This may satisfy neither side. Christian Scientists will claim infringement on their religious freedom while others will see the punishment as a deterrent insufficient to protect future sick children.

18. Should the Government Control Pharmaceutical Prices?

YES

Prices have risen at outrageous rates. According to a government study, wholesale drug prices rose by an incredible 128 percent between 1980 and 1992, nearly *six times* the overall rate of inflation. In 1993 alone, the prices that prescription drugmakers charge wholesalers increased no less than 15.5 times the producer inflation rate. Childhood vaccination prices rose 1,000 percent in the 1980s.

Older Americans suffer from unfair price hikes. Most older people lack insurance that covers medications. According to the American Association of Retired Persons, approximately 8 million people over age forty-five must cut back on food, heating fuel, and other necessities to pay for drugs.

How many times must a patient pay? When Johnson & Johnson gained permission to use its sheep-deworming drug, levamisole, to treat colon cancer in people, they raised the price one hundredfold from $15 to $1,500 per year, even though they had used $11 million of National Cancer Institute money for researching its use in humans. A large number of other drugs are developed in government laboratories or with the help of taxpayer money. Why, then, should patients pay a second time in the form of inflated prices?

Special tax breaks to pharmaceutical firms manufacturing in Puerto Rico cost us even more: $3 billion yearly in lost revenues to the Treasury. The pharmaceutical industry is one of the most profitable in America. While per share earnings for all companies on the Standard & Poor's Index rose only 7 percent between 1988 and 1992, earnings of the ten largest U.S. drug firms increased 18 percent. Why should the American people subsidize these profits?

Price controls will not reduce research. Drug firms claim lower prices will reduce research on lifesaving drugs. Today only 16 percent of their sales go to research, while 25 percent go to bloated administration and promotion budgets. Since drug development forms the heart of their business, firms will never sacrifice it.

N O

Developing new drugs is enormously expensive. On average a new drug takes twelve years and costs over $200 million to bring to market. A few profitable drugs must cover the cost of testing thousands of chemical compounds.

Price controls will reduce research. Since drug research is extremely risky, companies need a financial incentive. Several companies, fearing future price controls, have already declined to develop new taxpayer-sponsored drugs for cancer and AIDS. Small biotechnology companies must raise capital to fund new drug research. Yet the fear of price controls has already reduced investment in small firms.

Drug prices are stabilizing. In 1993 wholesale drug prices rose their smallest amount in twenty years, accounting for inflation. Pharmaceutical firms are already controlling prices.

Controls will make little difference in health expenditures. Prescription drugs account for only 7 to 10 percent of the total consumers pay annually on health care. Even with substantially reduced drug costs, the nation would save only a small fraction of total health care expenditures.

Some drugs actually save money. Certain ulcer drugs save billions of dollars by helping patients avoid surgery. Another drug, Neupogen, prevents infection in cancer patients and saves seven times its cost in hospital expenses. Drugs are cost effective.

U.S. firms must recoup their losses at home. Many foreign countries strictly regulate drug prices and profits. Our drug firms must recover their research-and-development costs back home.

U.S. firms must make their profits quickly. Patents on new drugs last only seventeen years. Since it takes twelve years to bring new drugs to market, companies must recoup their investment in only five years, before generic drugmakers produce their own cheap versions.

Why harm an industry with a trade surplus? The last thing we need is to make American companies less competitive. Our drug firms create a trade surplus of over $1 billion each year. Why threaten this?

Background

Prescription drugs are particularly conspicuous in the debate over health care reform. The key issues concerning health care—who pays for it, what it costs, who has access, who profits, and the quality of care—seem particularly focused in the debate over pharmaceuticals. One side evokes desperately ill patients who can not afford lifesaving drugs. The other describes an industry producing miracle drugs at pennies per dose to save millions of lives every year. Each side brings to the table an impressive array of statistics.

The most outspoken criticism of drug prices has come from Senator David Pryor (D-Arkansas) and his friends President Bill and Hillary Clinton. In response, major drug firms, aiming to thwart congressional action, are curbing price increases. Some of the largest firms have announced they will cut their staff by up to 10 percent, mainly in marketing and administrative posts.

Between them, the pharmaceutical firms employ 30,000 "detail men" who visit physicians, shower them with free samples, gifts, and dinners, all to promote their high-priced brand of drugs. Since doctors do not pay for the drugs, they do not mind prescribing them. Most insured patients, responsible only for a $5 co-payment charge, also do not object.

But the market is changing. As federal and state health agencies, hospital groups, and health maintenance organizations (HMOs) buy a greater percentage of drugs, fewer of these well-paid "detail men" will be needed. HMOs and governments also drive down drug prices through volume discounts and by demanding the most cost-effective drugs. The flood of so-called me-too drugs will also drive down drug costs. These cheaper drugs differ chemically from the patented versions but frequently treat the same ailment just as effectively. Will all these market forces lower prices enough to satisfy President Clinton?

That is hard to predict. In mid-1993 seventeen drug firms promised to keep the prices of existing drugs in line with the rate of inflation. In exchange and to avoid antitrust problems, they requested permission from the Department of Justice to discuss prices among themselves. Some drug executives admit pharmaceutical firms could survive cuts in their revenues. They will protect research-and-development budgets because the future well-being of the companies depends on yet undeveloped drugs.

Foreign countries do not provide a clear example of what we should expect from price controls. France and Austria, where price and profit regulations are very strict, perform relatively little new drug research.

But in Canada, with price controls imposed in 1987, spending on drug research has more than doubled.

The American public is certainly open to government intervention. A February 1994 ABC News/*Washington Post* poll found that 70 percent of Americans support federal price controls on hospital and doctor fees, pharmaceuticals, and other medical expenses.

Outlook

Proponents of price controls look to Canada as a possible model for the United States. Canada's Patented Medicine Prices Review Board has succeeded in slowing the rise of drug prices there. At the minimum, an American review board would reprimand companies whose prices it determined were excessive. American drug firms fear government access to their confidential data and fear price controls would follow.

Another solution is to allow high prices for new, breakthrough drugs, but control prices on other drugs. Senator Pryor and his allies believe this will spur innovation while providing more Americans with affordable drugs. Some members of Congress would like to charge companies for research paid for by taxpayers. Another proposal would limit profits to a certain percentage above the firm's actual R & D and production costs. Yet another proposal calls for the government to become a drug wholesaler, gaining leverage from the huge quantities it would buy. The pharmaceutical companies are lobbying hard to avoid all these challenges to their independence. The Republican-controlled Congress will probably defeat the more sweeping of these proposals.

19. Should Random Drug Testing Be Allowed in the Workplace?

YES

Testing saves lives. Alcohol and many drugs reduce the user's perceptual facilities and motor coordination. The news abounds with stories of industrial and transportation accidents in which an impaired machinery or passenger train operator caused major loss of life. If drug testing prevents just one major accident, like the next *Exxon Valdez* oil-tanker tragedy in Alaska, it is worth the expense.

Federal and state statutes require employers to furnish a safe environment for all employees and customers. That sometimes means weeding out workers who present serious dangers to themselves and others.

Testing saves money. According to the Research Triangle Institute, employee drug abuse costs the United States $60 billion annually. Companies with employee drug-screening programs can save a fortune in insurance premiums, lower employee turnover, provide better quality products and services, reduce employee theft, and increase productivity. Drug abusers use expensive health care services at a rate eight times higher than drug-free people. The absenteeism rate is four times higher and workers' compensation filings are five times greater among drug users.

Not only so-called hard drugs cause problems. When a computer operator for the reservation system of a major airline got high on marijuana, he neglected to load a key computer tape. That resulted in eight hours of downtime and lost reservations costing the company $19 million.

Testing helps society at large reduce the drug scourge. Drugs contribute to crime, urban blight, and many related family and social problems. Employers bear a civic responsibility to screen out drug addicts. Since most people work, the workplace serves as a perfectly logical place to identify addicts. If drug users realize they cannot find adequate work, it may motivate them to stop taking drugs. While America is losing the war on drugs, employers wield the most powerful weapon: the paycheck.

N O

Employers should not be in the business of law enforcement. Giving an employer the power to test employees for casual drug use that occurs off the job represents a frightening expansion of employer power—at the expense of everyone's personal privacy. Let the police and courts enforce drug laws rather than give free rein to corporate witch-hunters.

False positives on tests can unfairly point the finger. Laboratory error, passive exposure to marijuana smoke, and even common over-the-counter drugs such as Sudafed, Contac, aspirin, and even poppy seeds and herbal teas can falsely indicate the presence of a controlled substance.

False positives put everyone in danger of unfairly losing his job. Some employees even stop taking the prescription or over-the-counter medications they need to avoid failing a drug test.

Testing harms employee morale. By testing, the employer sends the message that workers cannot be trusted. Studies show it is disruptive, demoralizing, and reduces employee loyalty. Many workers who do not take drugs still suffer needlessly by worrying they may test positive.

Tests are ambiguous. Tests cannot distinguish between drug use that day, which might impair the person, and earlier use. They also fail to discriminate between heavy, chronic users most likely to cause accidents and occasional users. Tests infringe on a person's autonomy to spend leisure hours in activities of her own choosing.

Studies fail to show that drug use causes job performance problems. Drug users differ from nonusers in many respects. Factors other than drug use may account for the work problems of these employees.

Testing can easily lead to abuse by employers. The urine tests that commonly check for drugs can also reveal pregnancy or diseases. Employers can easily misuse drug testing to obtain this privileged information about a current or prospective employee.

Background

Is drug testing the witch-hunt of the 1990s or a cost-effective, life-saving measure? According to the American Management Association, 85 percent of large American corporations now require drug screening for potential employees, current employees, or both. Given the high average cost of nearly $50 per test, more large firms test for drug use than small ones. A survey of *Fortune* 500 firms revealed that 21 percent periodically test all employees working in sensitive positions, 8 percent randomly test all such employees, and another 8 percent periodically test all current employees.

A large majority of Americans have been found to favor testing. In June 1992 a Gallup/CNN/*USA Today* poll asked if Americans would favor new laws encouraging mandatory drug testing in the workplace. Seventy-one percent said yes, 26 percent said no, and 3 percent had no opinion.

Bodily samples such as urine, blood, hair, and breath can all serve to test for drug or alcohol use. Urine tests are the most commonly used because of their accuracy, but they are also the most intrusive. Employers test on a periodic basis (a predetermined timetable), for probable cause (an accident or unusual behavior), for reasonable suspicion (repeated absenteeism), or on a voluntary basis. Random testing, in which employees only learn of the screening the day it happens, generates the most controversy. Approximately one-half percent to one percent of all employees test positive. Ninety percent of these test positive for marijuana. Some employers dismiss those who test positive; others give employees the option of drug rehabilitation or treatment.

Some employers choose alternatives to drug tests. These include behavioral or mechanical aptitude tests, often using computer software, that directly measure a person's ability to perform his job safely and efficiently. Other employers train supervisors to spot problem workers before accidents occur. Many companies provide educational programs to prevent drug abuse.

The Department of Defense first used urinalysis to screen for drugs in the late 1960s and early 1970s when American soldiers returned from Vietnam. As tests grew more accurate and in response to a drug-related accident on an aircraft carrier, the military substantially expanded its testing in the early 1980s. In 1986, Ronald Reagan ordered compulsory testing of all job applicants and employees in executive branch agencies of the federal government. Congress then passed the 1988 Drug-free Workplace Act, requiring any company obtaining a contract with a federal agency worth $25,000 or more to provide a drug-free workplace. Additional government regulations now require random alcohol and drug testing for more than 7 million workers in the transportation and chemical industries.

When the Greyhound Corporation announced it would screen all its drivers in the mid-1980s, many companies followed suit. In 1989 the Supreme Court ruled in two cases that although drug tests constitute a search, they are reasonable if the "compelling interest" of public safety exceeds the individual's right to privacy. In both cases the Court found for the employer.

Some states have enacted strict laws regulating when and how employers may test their workers. Certain states allow only pre-employment screenings or tests of suspected abusers. Many states allow random tests but only for employees in safety-sensitive positions. California, often the harbinger of change, passed a law granting the right of privacy to private sector employees who wish to avoid testing.

In 1992 the National Labor Relations Board declared that drug testing will now be part of mandatory bargaining. As a result, labor unions will become much more active in protecting workers' rights in testing disputes.

Outlook

Random drug testing is one of several workplace issues—along with employers spying on workers on and off the job—likely to evolve over the next few years. As unions become more involved and as additional states regulate testing, the number of permissible situations for random testing may decline. But the overall number of Americans tested will certainly rise.

Money Matters

20. Would Dramatic Tax Cuts Improve the Economy?

YES

Past cuts led to sustained economic recoveries. The two major recent cuts in the federal income tax occurred in 1975 and from 1982 to 1983. After the 1975 cut, the United States experienced an immediate economic rebound that lasted fifty-eight months. The 1982–83 cut resulted in a ninety-two-month recovery—the longest period of economic health since the end of World War II. The so-called Reagan miracle of the 1980s was in large part due to his tax cuts.

Tax cuts give consumers more to spend. Consumer spending usually generates economic recoveries. Across-the-board tax cuts put more cash in consumers' pockets, which leads to more spending, followed by greater industrial output, business investments, and rising employment.

With lower taxes, workers feel a greater incentive to work harder, since they pocket more for their efforts. As a result, productivity improves, which ultimately makes America more competitive. Tax cuts improve the U.S. economy in both the short and long run.

Tax cuts give small businesses more capital to invest. Several hundred thousand small businesses in the United States with incomes over $200,000 annually file their taxes as individuals (subchapter S corporations). These firms are the engines of job growth in this country. When punishing taxes on these companies are eliminated, they will hire more workers and become more productive.

It makes no sense to raise unemployment taxes to pay for unemployed workers. The economy is much better served by lower taxes on the businesses that can actually hire new workers.

Savings and investments will grow under tax reductions. With more disposable income as a result of lower taxes, and higher after-tax returns on investments, consumers will save more. That increases the capital available for borrowers. If the wealthy can retain more profit from high-risk investments, they will put more capital into ventures that stimulate the economy.

N O

Tax cuts mainly benefit the rich. When President Reagan reduced federal income taxes in the early 1980s, the wealthiest taxpayers gained the most. They bought luxury products and put their money into unproductive investments like junk bonds. Many also invested abroad. The rich generally ignored investments that would have created jobs or otherwise stimulated the U.S. economy.

The Reagan cuts did not produce an economic miracle. The economic recovery in the mid-1980s was an expected cyclical recovery, not a result of tax cuts. In fact, the recovery arrived during and after the tax *increases* of 1982 through 1984.

The flashy tax-cut promises of politicians do not serve the economy. The politicians who typically suggest tax cuts may attract voters, but they do not improve our economy. The problems of the U.S. economy—the massive deficit, the decaying infrastructure, massive layoffs, high consumer debt, evolution from a manufacturing to a service-based economy—require long-term solutions. Politicians should focus on retraining workers, investing more in research and development for high-growth industries, creating incentives for consumer savings, and devising other solutions to specific problems. Short-term measures like tax cuts can hurt our economy.

Tax cuts increase the deficit. Reagan's major economic legacy to us was the dramatic growth of our deficit. He cut taxes but not spending. President Bush also failed to cut spending. As a result, our national debt now exceeds $4 trillion.

Many economists believe reducing the deficit is an economic priority. Over the last decade our huge deficit has resulted in a dwindling pool of capital for investment, poor U.S. productivity, the terrible burden of paying interest on the debt, and other economic ills. The worst medicine for our economy is a further reduction of government revenues and increased government borrowing to meet spending needs.

Background

Before World War II only a small number of wealthy Americans paid an individual income tax. During World War II taxes rose dramatically and were applied to a much larger percentage of the population. Although taxes fell slightly during peacetime, they increased again to finance the Korean War during the early 1950s. After that, combined federal, state, and local taxes grew steadily, from 22.5 percent of gross national product (GNP) in 1954 to a high of 28.2 percent of GNP in 1969. Total tax rates remained near that level during the next two decades.

A backlash against the historically most unpopular taxes—the property tax and the income tax—grew in the late 1970s and early 1980s. Voters in several states followed the lead of California by revolting against rising property taxes. Nationally, voters elected Ronald Reagan, who promised to cut the federal income tax and reduce the high inflation plaguing the American economy.

In 1981 the Republicans succeeded in passing the Economic Recovery Tax Act (ERTA). In retrospect, despite appearing to dramatically cut the federal income tax, ERTA actually did little more than compensate for the tax-increasing effects of economic growth, inflation, and "bracket creep" (occurring when a person's inflation-driven salary pushes her into a higher tax bracket even though her real earning power remains stagnant or even falls). Nevertheless, ERTA resulted in the federal government collecting hundreds of billions of dollars less than it would have otherwise collected.

The Reagan administration's tax-cutting philosophy is often called supply-side economics. Supply-siders argued that the dominant federal fiscal policy until 1980 was "demand management," a policy first advocated by the economist John Maynard Keynes which attempted to increase employment and economic growth through increased government spending and high taxes on the wealthy. Reaganites maintained that not only did high taxes discourage the wealthy from investing productively and increasing the pool of available capital, but the tax structure before Reagan also transferred money to the poor and middle class who spent, rather than invested it. In the late 1970s the United States spent only 19 percent annually of its GNP on private investment, while the booming economies of Japan spent in the mid-30s and of Germany in the mid-20s. The Reaganites believed that supply-side policies—intended to encourage investment and reduce government spending—would improve the U.S. economy.

During the 1980s the U.S. government rewrote the federal tax laws more often and with greater changes than ever in our history. During each of the three years following Reagan's huge 1981 tax cut, Congress voted for tax increases in an attempt to offset the mounting federal deficit and the financial problems of the Social Security program. The government's debate on taxes ended with the most sweeping restructuring in our tax laws ever—the Tax Reform Act of 1986.

Liberals and Democrats argue that Reagan's major tax cut of 1981 mainly benefited the rich, devastated the poor by the resulting cuts in social programs, and drove the federal deficit so high it forced tax *increases* the following years. Conservatives and Republicans believe the tax cuts were never given a chance to work because profligate spending by Congress actually forced the subsequent tax increases.

Outlook

Cutting taxes is a key part of the Contract with America, the Republican proposals for legislative action signed by more that 300 Republican politicians in 1994. Republicans hope to continue the strategy begun by former President Reagan of cutting taxes for upper- and middle-income Americans, and still balance the federal budget in a few years. Some of the proposed cuts include tax credits for families with children or elderly dependents, repeal of the marriage tax penalty, tax breaks or business investments, increases in the size of the gifts and estates exempt from taxation, and greater tax benefits for individual retirement accounts.

The tax cuts proposed in the Contract with America would total some $220 billion over five years, paid for by cuts in federal spending. According to some estimates, balancing the federal budget by 2002 would cost an additional $700 billion. Since Republicans are loath to cut social security and defense spending, cuts would come from welfare, education, housing, and social programs. President Clinton is likely to exercise his presidential veto power to prevent the more extreme tax cuts proposed by the Republicans.

21. Does Welfare Perpetuate Poverty?

YES

Welfare fosters dependency. By removing the need to work, welfare, which generally refers to the program called Aid to Families with Dependent Children (AFDC), creates generations of people with no incentive to become productive or self-reliant. Paying people to be dependent encourages more of them to live that way.

Welfare destroys the work ethic. The values that help people support themselves include pride, self-respect, hope, industriousness, and mutual assistance. Self-supporting people usually believe that work is rewarding and desirable. But welfare undermines these values. Why bother working hard for the minimum wage when the government will simply hand you money?

Accumulated welfare benefits often pay better than work, providing incentives for most single welfare mothers to decline paying jobs. A few years ago when New York City sent letters to 100,000 AFDC recipients encouraging them to join job or training programs, only one percent signed up.

Only work can break the cycle of poverty. Millions of undocumented aliens, who do not receive welfare, hold menial, low-skill jobs. Yet, because they are working, they stand a real chance of rising from poverty.

Welfare encourages illegitimate births and discourages marriage. Welfare rewards single welfare mothers with more money if they bear additional children out of wedlock. When poor women marry, their chances of escaping poverty improve dramatically. Stable, two-parent homes have a much better likelihood of standing on their own. But by rewarding illegitimate births, the welfare system perpetuates broken homes and poverty.

Life for the poor has deteriorated under welfare. In the last two decades billions have been spent on welfare, yet life for the poor has become worse. More people receive assistance today than twenty years ago, yet more people live in poverty. The number of AFDC recipients increased by nearly a quarter from 1990 to 1993.

N O

Don't blame the victim. Calling welfare recipients unwilling to work is cruel. The poor suffer terrible deprivations. They receive insufficient educational and employment opportunities, and live in crime-infested neighborhoods. The meager government benefits they receive are hardly an incentive to remain impoverished.

A weak economy and industrial decline—not welfare— perpetuate poverty. Fewer people today can support a family because of structural changes in the U.S. economy. The manufacturing and low-skill jobs that employed many underclass dwellers of northern cities moved overseas or to rural and suburban areas. As cities became centers where professionals and managers could find work, African-Americans with the proper education and work skills prospered, while those without these advantages lost their jobs. The argument that welfare causes poverty arose from a historical coincidence. Our economy has been weaker in the last twenty years than from 1945 to 1973. Since 1973 we have experienced two deep recessions, small productivity increases, and high unemployment, all of which caused poverty. In the 1970s poverty rates stopped falling just as Medicaid, food stamps, and other new welfare programs expanded. These programs did not cause poverty, but moderated its impact.

Single-parent families are often driven into poverty. Single mothers often have no choice but welfare. Either they must work continually—thus neglecting their children—or end up on welfare. The failure of fathers to fulfill their parental obligations, no-fault divorce, and the reduced payment of court-ordered child support all contribute to poverty. Only 15 percent of children in two-parent households will experience poverty in any given year, compared to 50 percent of single-parent children. Welfare does not create single-parent families, poverty does.

Few recipients spend their lives on welfare. Only 2 percent stay on welfare for more than a decade. Half of all recipients get off within two years.

Background

The argument that welfare perpetuates poverty grew popular among conservatives during the Reagan presidency. It originated largely from the book *Losing Ground* (1984), by sociologist Charles Murray, who argues that the only way to stop the cycle of poverty and dependency is to end welfare payments.

Does welfare perpetuate poverty? Probably both sides are partially right. Welfare presents us with a terrible dilemma: its benefits and its harmful effects intertwine. By curbing aid, we lower the already harsh living standards of millions of people. Yet we must avoid creating a dependency on such aid.

The recession of the early 1990s and persistent unemployment rates added many people to the public-assistance rolls. Today 14 million individuals receive cash from the Aid to Families with Dependent Children program, an increase of nearly 25 percent from 1990 to 1993. AFDC costs $16 billion per year—excluding health care and housing costs.

Liberals point out that some of the stereotypes about welfare are wrong. On average, AFDC families are not much larger than nonwelfare families. The perception that most welfare recipients are inner-city blacks is also incorrect. Only 40 percent of AFDC recipients are black. However, half of all AFDC children are born out of wedlock, compared to 10 percent within the general population, which conservatives believe contributes enormously to poverty and welfare dependency, especially in the inner cities.

AFDC constitutes one percent of the federal budget and a little over 3 percent of the average state budget. Payments to the poor are dropping. Over the last twenty years AFDC payments fell by 42 percent when adjusted for inflation. The average monthly payment today for a single mother with two children is $580.

In 1988, Congress passed the Family Support Act, which is intended to help AFDC recipients receive job training. However, with the act seriously underfunded and its goals so limited—only 10 percent of all AFDC recipients participate—few improvements are expected.

Presently, most states are freezing or reducing welfare payments because of tight budgets and attempts at welfare reform. Those attempts include denying extra payments to single mothers who bear additional children, maintaining their benefits if they marry, paying for job training, and docking the pay of teenage parents who quit high school. So far, forcing recipients to work or learn—often called workfare or learnfare—shows limited success. Unfortunately, with the unemployment rate hovering near 6 percent, many newly trained workers cannot find jobs.

Outlook

Starting in 1995 Wisconsin may lead the nation with its tough "Work Not Welfare" program, which requires all welfare recipients to work, or start training for work, within one month of receiving benefits. Other states may try to follow the Wisconsin program. New Jersey's "family cap" experiment, which refuses to increase welfare benefits to recipients who bear additional children, may also be imitated by other states.

During the 1992 presidential campaign Bill Clinton promised to "end welfare as we know it" by changing not only the payment system but also the culture of dependency among welfare recipients. In June 1994, President Clinton proposed his goals for welfare reform, including a two-year limit on AFDC benefits to virtually all recipients. To help recipients survive, Clinton also called for job training and child care for welfare mothers, cracking down on fathers who evade paying child support, and the enactment of universal health care coverage. Liberals regard Clinton's plan as callous to the poor, particularly children. Conservatives find it too ineffectual and costly.

A Republican-controlled Congress will likely support much more stringent forms of welfare reform that include fewer benefits and less training for recipients. One group within the Republican party would like to put 1.5 million welfare families into work programs by the end of the century. Another proposal, intended to discourage unwed mothers from bearing children, would allow states to stop distributing payments to all children born to mothers under twenty-one. States could use welfare money instead to set up group homes or orphanages for those children whose mothers could not support them. The most conservative Republicans propose to permanently cut benefits for all young mothers on welfare, whether they are willing to work or not. Another stringent proposal would deny benefits to all children of unmarried mothers under age twenty-six, cutting 3.5 million children from the welfare rolls.

Although some form of national welfare reform will clearly arrive during 1995, President Clinton will almost certainly veto the harsher proposals.

22. Should Social Security Payments Be Tied to Need?

YES

Cuts are necessary to reduce the deficit. In 1993 entitlement programs consumed nearly half the federal budget, a staggering $738 billion. Of that total, Social Security commands the largest portion, $319 billion. Unless we curb government spending, those now entering the workforce will face a runaway federal deficit and skyrocketing payroll taxes.

Limiting Social Security benefits can save federal dollars. Shaving just a portion of those benefits received by the very rich could generate nearly $30 billion.

More federal dollars go to America's elderly than to its youth. Thirty years ago children benefited most from federal social spending. Today's seniors, however, who constitute only 12 percent of the population, reap nearly one-third of *all* government spending.

Retirees receive more than they contributed. Owing to substantial increases in benefits in recent years, an average American retiring today at age sixty-five can expect to recover his full contribution to the Social Security fund, *with interest,* by age seventy-one. After that, he receives pure profit courtesy of the American taxpayer.

Affluent seniors claim a disproportionate share of federal benefits. Overall, Americans living below the poverty line receive only one-sixth of federal entitlement money; families with taxable incomes above $50,000 receive nearly 20 percent of the money. The most affluent American families collect close to 10 percent of all federal subsidies for retirement.

Young, lower-paid workers subsidize the elderly rich. The young pay rising Social Security taxes, knowing full well they may never recover their contributions to the fund. Social Security recipients, supplemented by personal savings and private pensions, boast higher average incomes than those young workers.

The demand for diminishing resource dollars will only increase. In 1950, 120 workers paid into Social Security for each retiree receiving benefits. By the year 2030, however, when the baby boom generation retires, the proportion of contributors to recipients will drop to two to one, not enough to sustain a viable pension system.

N O

Social Security is *not* an entitlement program. Social Security is a contributory insurance program that warrants separate consideration from other government spending programs. Monies earned by hardworking Americans are held in trust for them until retirement. To deny promised benefits would mean breaking the government's contract with its citizens.

Benefits have already declined. Retirees could once hope to reap twice as much in benefits as they contributed to the fund. Not so since Social Security's 1983 reform, which drastically increased payroll taxes. Those retiring now will *not* recover their full contribution. To limit their benefits would only cheat them further.

The federal government forces us to pay Social Security. The investments in stocks or bonds we might choose instead would pay much better. To then deny us the paltry return on our Social Security investment is appalling.

Slashing benefits will only increase poverty among the elderly. Nearly two-thirds of those over sixty-five claim annual household incomes below $20,000. As pension plans become less generous and interest rates remain low, even well-off retirees will increasingly depend upon Social Security as a primary income source.

Payroll taxes do not overly burden indigent families. Since 1983 low-wage workers have received tax rebates through the Earned Income Tax Credit. Moreover, the lowest income retirees receive nearly three-quarters of their preretirement wages, while the wealthiest receive only a quarter of their own preretirement maximum wages. Consequently, Social Security succeeds in its goal to reduce hardship and poverty among the elderly.

Limiting benefits will not achieve substantial savings. President Clinton himself admits that reducing the Social Security benefits of the wealthy would produce only modest revenues. In a program whose expenditures run into the hundreds of billions of dollars each year, such low returns do not justify depriving beneficiaries of their just compensation.

Background

In 1935, President Franklin Roosevelt signed the Social Security Act into law, creating an all-inclusive entitlements program designed to protect citizens from destitution in their old age. According to the plan, workers would contribute to a "trust fund," via payroll taxes, which the government would then invest. In return, the government would provide financial security to all contributors in their senior years, regardless of their personal financial situation. Not surprisingly, such a program received widespread political support from all sectors of society.

Congress, however, soon abandoned the "trust fund" model. Beginning in the early 1940s, Social Security began using current contributions to pay pensions. With worker-taxpayers outnumbering pensioners by more than 120 to 1, Congress had little difficulty maintaining low taxes and generous pensions. As the system continued to generate surpluses, the tax base rose significantly, and with it payroll taxes. Simultaneously, the average pension rose from 28 percent of preretirement pay to 35 percent.

During the 1960s and 1970s, as increasing numbers of taxpayers reached retirement age and fewer new ones entered the workforce, concern for Social Security's viability mounted. Nonetheless, Congress continued to approve higher retirement payouts. To keep the system solvent, payroll taxes were likewise raised.

In 1983, with Social Security facing imminent default, Congress adopted a new method of funding to meet growing demands on the nation's retirement system. This reform sought to protect future pensions by resurrecting the original idea of a national trust fund. The plan called for the accumulation of reserves, beginning in the 1980s, that would swell to several trillion dollars in subsequent decades. These reserves would help cushion the predicted drain between 2010 and 2030, when the massive, aging baby boom generation will begin collecting benefits.

Despite this reform problems with Social Security persist. The 1983 plan mandated the establishment of reserves to be invested in Treasury bonds. While these securities do pay interest to the pension account, Congress uses Social Security's reserve funds both to finance current government spending and to make the federal deficit appear smaller. Compromised by these bookkeeping manipulations, the pension account is not growing fast enough to meet the financial needs of beneficiaries in the coming century.

With the federal deficit growing, Social Security surpluses offer a potential source of money for a financially strapped administration. During 1993 the Clinton administration began discussing means testing (the computation of benefits based on income) as a way to save money. According to a January 1992 Gallup/*Newsweek* poll, 67 percent of Americans would support increased taxes on Social Security benefits for the wealthy. In 1993 the Democratic-controlled Congress voted to raise from 50 percent to 85 percent the federal tax ceiling on Social Security benefits received by wealthy recipients. These new taxes on approximately 5 million Americans were expected to raise $32 billion in revenue over five years.

But such changes to Social Security are politically dangerous. Until now, Social Security has remained exempt from budgetary restraints connected with deficit reduction. Lawmakers worry about the political clout wielded by Social Security beneficiaries, who constitute one of the largest voting blocs in the nation.

Outlook

Many Republicans promising to safeguard Social Security benefits were swept into office during the 1994 election. The Republican Contract with America includes the proposed Senior Citizens Fairness Act, which would repeal the 1993 tax increase on the Social Security benefits of wealthy citizens. Nevertheless, despite the political strength of America's seniors and the resolve of Republicans, changes to the Social Security system may come in a few years if America hopes to balance the budget.

Some politicians propose to lower payouts or delay the retirement age. Senator Daniel Patrick Moynihan (D-New York), fearing that large surpluses provide too great a temptation to inflate benefits, suggests returning to the old system of using current contributions to pay benefits. Other politicians would preserve the surpluses but privatize them, letting individual workers determine how to invest their contributions.

23. Are High Salaries Ruining Professional Sports?

YES

High salaries destroyed the 1994 baseball season. During the summer of 1994 greedy players, already favored by a salary arbitration system that often awards players the entire amount they request, refused to negotiate a sensible team salary cap with the owners. That led to the worst strike in baseball history.

High salaries alienate fans. Baseball players like Bobby Bonds make more than $7 million per year. That translates into $45,000 per game, more than the average fan earns in a year. Some fairly mediocre players collect the average baseball salary of over $1 million per year. Fans resent these salaries and are starting to rebel against paying high ticket prices to support them.

High salaries may put baseball and other team sports in serious financial trouble. In 1989 major-league baseball teams collectively earned $200 million, their best year ever. In 1991, however, earnings dropped to $100 million. According to a study by the baseball club owners, they collectively broke even in 1992, but eighteen of twenty-six teams lost money. Having added two expansion teams, nineteen of twenty-eight teams lose money now.

Over three years the salaries of the Seattle Mariners baseball team tripled, from $8 million to $24 million annually. According to the owner, the team now loses $10 million a year.

Football, basketball, and hockey teams already sell more than 90 percent of their tickets. The combination of soaring salaries and stagnant revenues may force teams into bankruptcy.

Teams in smaller cities cannot stay competitive. Because they can not afford exorbitant salaries, teams in small cities must settle for lesser players. As a result, the richest teams will win consistently, ending fair competition.

The focus on money erodes the spirit of sports. What happened to playing for its own sake? Or to the love of the game? Insanely high salaries change the great games of America from true sports into mere businesses.

N O

Superstars make money for their team. Most high-priced players captivate the fans and expand interest in their sport. Owners pay a lot for star players because stars increase attendance at the stadium. One or two thousand more fans per game earns many extra millions for owners in sales of tickets, parking, food, and souvenirs. Increased television ratings also earn more money.

In a free market economy, stars deserve the highest rewards. Why shouldn't they earn whatever the market will bear? No one forces owners to pay high salaries or fans to buy tickets. Superstars offer extremely rare skills. Since the demand for star players exceeds the supply, they deserve every penny they make. The 1994 baseball strike was caused by greedy team owners trying to reduce the players' fair compensation.

Sports careers last a short time. Very few athletes can compete more than twelve to fifteen years professionally, even if they avoid injuries. Athletes have every right to capitalize on their limited careers.

Lack of profitability does not indicate economic weakness. Baseball and other teams serve as superb investments for their owners. The Seattle Mariners baseball team was sold for $125 million in 1992—a huge increase over their 1981 price of $13 million.

Since teams are privately held, owners can use "creative" accounting to show a profit or loss for any particular year.

Richer teams do not dominate any sport. In baseball, basketball, and other sports, win-loss records and league championships have been distributed with little regard for the size of the local market. New franchise teams and young teams do take time to establish themselves, but no proof exists that wealthy big-city teams dominate their sport.

From 1982 to 1992 only five of the twenty-six major-league baseball teams failed to reach postseason play. Furthermore, no single team captured consecutive World Series titles from 1978 to 1992.

Background

The first highly paid superstar of baseball was Babe Ruth. In 1923 he became the first player paid $50,000 a year, a huge sum in those days. When told his salary exceeded that of the U.S. President, Ruth replied, "Well, I had a better year than he did." No player topped Ruth's salary for several decades. At his peak Ruth earned $81,000, about eighty times the average American salary in his day. Today a very good (but not truly great) ballplayer earns perhaps $4 million a year, more than 170 times the average American wage.

In 1941, the year Joe DiMaggio hit in fifty-six consecutive games, he made $37,500, about ten times the average player's salary that year. Not until 1976 did baseball salaries begin to escalate substantially. Two factors drove them up. First, larger television audiences increased revenues. Second, the free agency system permitted baseball players to negotiate with any team after six years and submit their salary requests to arbitration after only three years. Prior to 1976 players had to remain with one club unless traded or released. If a player did not like his contract, the team could fire him. Since the start of free agency, average salaries of baseball players jumped from $46,000 in 1975 to more than $1 million.

Today, more than 100 baseball players earn over $3 million a season. Battles about money, particularly about team salary caps, have come to overshadow professional sports. The 750 members of baseball's Major League Players Association began their season-ending strike to prevent owners from imposing caps.

A March 1993 poll by E.D.K. Associates found that 66 percent of Americans feel that there should be a limit on how much major-league baseball players can earn. In August 1994 a CBS News poll about the baseball strike reported that 39 percent believe the owners are more in the right, 22 percent favor players, 15 percent blame both sides equally, and 24 percent do not know or care.

After much study and under threat of a court decision, the National Football League (NFL) decided to introduce free agency in 1993. Players with five or more years' experience can sign with any team when their contract is up. Football salaries rose dramatically, but not nearly as much as baseball and basketball salaries. Star quarterbacks still earn less than half the money paid to star baseball players. In 1994 the NFL instituted caps on how much each team could spend on player salaries. The $34 million per team payroll allowed in 1994 controlled runaway salary inflation.

The NFL's new agreement copies elements of the deal basketball players worked out in 1983. In the early 1980s several National Basketball Association (NBA) teams were close to folding. The union agreed to a revenue-sharing contract that limits salaries to 53 percent of NBA sales from admissions and broadcasting. As a result, the NBA is healthy financially. Basketball players, however, now feel this arrangement restricts their full earnings potential.

The average NBA salary, at $1.2 million per year, exceeds baseball's average. Can professional basketball teams afford such salaries? NBA revenues grew from $200 million in 1984 to approximately $1 billion in 1993. So far, it appears the rapidly escalating salaries do not exceed the financial growth of the league. But the wealthiest NBA teams, eager to sign the best players, constantly search for salary cap loopholes. That may significantly escalate salaries further. Basketball's superstars already earn the highest salaries in sports. The Charlotte Hornet's Larry Johnson signed a twelve-year, $84 million contract in 1993. An unknown rookie, the Orlando Magic's Anfernee Hardaway, signed for thirteen years at $65 million before ever playing a game in the NBA.

National Hockey League (NHL) salaries, at $500,000 per year on average, are the lowest among the major team sports. Arguments between players and owners over revenue-sharing plans, salary arbitration, free agency, and formulas for rookie salaries have severely interfered with the 1994–1995 professional hockey season.

Outlook

If the baseball owners succeed in negotiating salary caps or a change in the salary arbitration system, baseball salaries would likely decline. The strike has focused the anger of many baseball fans who feel that players are overpaid crybabies *and* owners are greedy business people. Fan backlash may ultimately reduce baseball revenues and salaries. But fan enthusiasm, revenues, and salaries seem headed ever upward for basketball, football, and hockey players.

Schools and Rules

24. Should the Government Continue Funding Bilingual Education?

YES

Immigrants deserve a good education. Adults who take immersion language courses know the difficulties they will face. But young children, especially those recently arrived from abroad, can feel totally lost. When their school forbids them to use the only language they know, youngsters feel discriminated against, isolated, and punished. Schools *should* teach English to foreign students, but in a humane, compassionate way. When bilingual education is taught properly, children *do* gain self-esteem and, according to some studies, go on to higher academic achievement.

Bilingual education was never given a chance to succeed. During the Reagan and Bush years federal funding for bilingual education fell dramatically. Today state and local bilingual programs are notoriously underfunded and oversubscribed.

Studies show it takes an average of five to seven years of academic instruction to learn English beyond a superficial level. However, most federally funded bilingual education programs limit students to three years.

Language policy has historically been used to exclude certain minorities. At different times our government has attempted to prevent American Indians, African-Americans, and Mexican Americans from becoming literate in English and from becoming citizens. Until the Voting Rights Act of 1965, so-called literacy tests were used to prevent nonwhites from voting. Today efforts to dismantle bilingual education recall our long exclusionary history.

English has never been the glue of U.S. society. There never was a golden age when we all spoke the same language.

English is not threatened in America. Most immigrants realize that learning English is crucial to their economic advancement. And a majority of Spanish-speaking immigrants *do* learn English. We are not headed toward two separate cultures and languages.

A multicultural, multilingual population makes America competitive. The increasingly global economy favors nations whose businesspeople speak the language of more than one country. Bilingual education helps America produce such people.

N O

English holds America together. We are a country of great cultural and social diversity. Nonetheless we bind the melting pot together with one common language: English. Otherwise, we risk becoming dangerously divided along political, social, and linguistic lines, like Canada, Sri Lanka, and various African countries, where two main languages conflict. If our fast-growing Spanish-speaking population fails to assimilate successfully, America will suffer. In our pluralistic society, the government must advance similarities to unite the nation, not subsidize differences among us.

Bilingual education has failed. Until the 1960s, when the government began funding bilingual education, immigrants learned English because they had no choice. Immigrants recognized then as they do today that proficiency in English is a key to economic success. The goal of bilingual education, as stated by Congress, has been to teach students English. But many bilingual programs teach primarily in Spanish or another foreign language. As a result, the dropout and school failure rates are very high among Hispanic students who gain only limited English proficiency. Owing in part to poor English skills, only 50 percent of all Hispanic high school students graduate.

We have spent over $2 billion since Congress passed the Bilingual Education Act of 1968. But instead of helping immigrant children, we have perpetuated their life in linguistic and economic ghettos. To create a separate Spanish-language "track" for Hispanic students hurts their ability to become part of our nation.

Only language immersion works. Bilingual education ignores the "time on task" tenet accepted by most educators: the more time students spend learning a subject, the faster they learn it. No wonder some Hispanic youngsters fail to learn English. Some spend only forty minutes a day receiving English-language instruction in their bilingual programs. If students were forced to immerse themselves in English, they would succeed far more quickly.

Background

In the United States, approximately 6.3 million children age five to seventeen speak a language other than English at home. Of these, 14 percent speak English poorly or not at all. Spanish is the home language for the vast majority of these youngsters. During the 1980s the number of school-age children who speak another language grew by 41 percent, while the total number of schoolchildren nationwide decreased by 4 percent.

The federal government began funding bilingual education in 1968 through Title VII of the Elementary and Secondary Education Act (ESEA). Funding grew until the Reagan and Bush administrations opposed it. Between 1982 and 1992 federal funding was cut in half, adjusted for inflation, to $170 million annually.

Bilingual education usually means using a student's native language at least part of the time until she becomes proficient in English. Several types of bilingual education are used today. The English as a Second Language (ESL) method gradually teaches students English through extra classes beyond their regular instruction. The Structured Immersion method teaches all subjects in English at the student's level of understanding. Teachers comprehend the native language but usually respond to questions only in English.

Using a third method, Transitional Bilingual Education (TBE), students learn math, science, and other nonlanguage subjects in their native tongue until they are ready for regular classes. A fourth method, Two-way Bilingual Education, is expected to grow in future years. Classes using this method mix interested native English-speaking students with native speakers of another language. Students learn both languages. Other subjects are also taught in both languages.

The vast majority of new immigrants in America do learn and use English. Seventy-five percent of Hispanic immigrants who live in the United States speak English daily. Immigrants to the United States lose their native language more quickly than immigrants almost anywhere else in the world. Typically, the first generation learns just enough English to survive financially. The second generation speaks English at school and work, while retaining their native tongue at home. But by the third generation, English dominates.

Does bilingual education help or hurt non-English-speaking students? Lobbies on both sides of the issue present studies proving their point of view. On one side is the National Association for Bilingual Education (NABE), whose mission is to increase spending on bilingual education and to rally educators around a single nationwide method of bilingual teaching. NABE's opponents argue that its real goal is to keep the Hispanic political elite in power by maintaining a separate Hispanic culture and language.

The other side of the controversy is represented by organizations such as English First, U.S. English, and Learning English Advocates Drive (LEAD). Their agendas focus on making English the official language of the United States. Nineteen states have passed "English Only" legislation, outlawing official use of other languages, primarily Spanish. But these laws have not yet affected bilingual education or been tested in the courts. Despite lobbying efforts these groups have failed to pass a constitutional amendment to declare English the official language. Their opponents argue these groups are thinly disguised anti-immigration lobbies motivated by xenophobia and racism.

Outlook

The Clinton administration supports bilingual education. In February 1993, Education Secretary Richard Riley set the tone by describing bilingualism and multiculturalism as an American strength. A few months later, after a Stanford University policy group recommended additional government spending for bilingual education, a Hispanic member of the group was appointed director of the U.S. Office of Bilingual Education.

Although Democrats and Republicans traditionally cooperate on many education issues, Republicans have not championed bilingual education. The drive of the Republican-led Congress to reduce spending may result in cuts to bilingual eduction programs.

The young, fast-growing Hispanic population in America will continue to make bilingual education an important issue. So, too, will the burgeoning job market for bilingual speakers, especially in Florida, California, and Texas.

25. Should Condoms Be Distributed in Schools?

YES

Teens will have sex no matter how much we try to "educate" them against it. The median age for first intercourse among today's high school students is 16.1 years for boys and 16.9 for girls.

Most teens assimilate a moral code not from home, but from the media and their friends. The average viewer of prime-time television sees about 9,000 instances or suggestions of sexual intercourse per year. Few teens will listen to a parent who says "don't have sex," when classmates and most media icons say "do."

The rate of teenage pregnancy is out of control. According to the Centers for Disease Control (CDC) in Atlanta, more than one million teenage girls in the United States become pregnant each year. The rate of teenage pregnancy has more than tripled since 1964.

Only condoms can prevent the spread of AIDS. Each year 2.5 million teens contract sexually related diseases, including AIDS. The rate of AIDS cases among teens has risen 62 percent in a recent two-year period. Since abstinence is an unrealistic goal, only condoms—a barrier contraceptive—can stop this tragedy.

Too many teens have no access to contraceptives. According to the CDC, about 25 percent of sexually active teens do not use contraceptives. Many are too embarrassed, scared, or poor to buy them. Others lack a sense of responsibility. School is the only place where the necessary sex education and distribution of contraceptives can succeed.

School-based contraceptive programs have proven to work. Some of the oldest contraceptive programs, in clinics serving St. Paul, Minnesota, schools, show dramatic drops in local student pregnancies. Other countries offering easy access to contraceptives also reveal much lower rates of teenage pregnancy.

Contraception for teens is an economic necessity. Not only do teenage mothers often ruin their own lives, but taxpayers must also support them through welfare and social services. Contraception can help stop this cycle of poverty.

N O

Contraceptives encourage promiscuity. Many teens feel unprepared for sex, but if their teachers and school principals encourage the use of condoms teens feel pressured to have sex prematurely. Distributing condoms in schools sends teens the wrong message.

Teens can not handle contraceptives responsibly. Studies reveal that after one year, 10 percent of all teens using contraceptives become pregnant. After two years, 24 percent become pregnant. Contraceptives give teens a false sense of security, encouraging more to have sex and increasing the number of unwanted children and abortions.

"Old-fashioned" rules work. We must return to the traditional controls over teens that used to prevent pregnancy. We must teach premarital abstinence and attach great shame to young parents of illegitimate children. That moral code worked for generations; it can work again.

The only sure way to avoid pregnancy and AIDS is through abstinence. Teens need something worthwhile to strive for and believe in. But if we assume they have no self-control and willpower, if we constantly shove contraceptives at them, of course they will never accept abstinence.

Emphasize better ways to reduce teenage pregnancy. Studies show teens who can hope for educational and career advancement are much less likely to get pregnant. Let's combat the root causes of teenage pregnancy: ignorance, poverty, poor self-esteem, broken homes. Give teens emotional and financial incentives to graduate from high school and *not* get pregnant.

Distributing contraceptives in schools undermines parental authority. Parents, not schoolteachers, are the primary teachers of ethical behavior to children. Parents should make the decision about whether their children can receive birth control. If parents teach abstinence at home, how can we let schools sabotage their moral authority?

Schools should be for learning. Schools are not social service centers or medical dispensaries. They should focus on teaching the three R's and other traditional subjects.

Background

The sexual revolution of the 1960s and 1970s led to a loosening of societal restraints against premarital sex. Today, by age nineteen, 50 percent of unmarried women and 60 percent of unmarried men are sexually active. As a result, U.S. teens have one of the highest pregnancy rates in the Western world—twice that of England and seven times that of the Netherlands. U.S. teens' use of condoms rose from 23 to 47 percent in the 1980s. Does this indicate that the use of contraceptives has increased or decreased teenage pregnancy? Both sides offer impressive statistics to argue their case. A majority of experts believe that if enough money were spent to educate teens about sex and provide them with contraceptives, the rate of pregnancy and sexually transmitted diseases (STDs) would drop. But a vocal minority—mainly fundamentalist Christians—argue that only teaching abstinence will substantially lower unwanted births and STDs.

In 1973 a St. Paul, Minnesota, family planning health clinic became the first to distribute contraceptives in or near a school. This clinic reduced unwanted teenage pregnancies and served as a model for other clinics around the country. These clinics provide a wide range of services, including sex education and counseling, pregnancy tests, and condom distribution. A moderately strong parental and religious resistance has always opposed these clinics. At first, most clinics only provided such services with parental permission. In recent years condoms have been distributed without parental permission, counseling requirements, or fees to the students in some school districts, particularly in major cities.

In 1991, New York City became the first city with such a program, probably because the city's rate of reported AIDS cases among thirteen- to twenty-one-year-olds is seven times the national average for that age group. A fierce battle erupted, pitting school authorities, public health officials, and gays against the Catholic Church and parents. Condoms are now freely available to New York City's 270,000 public high school students. However, local school boards in many other parts of the country have refused to allow condom distribution, or have permitted it only with parental permission or as part of a counseling program, which frequently dissuades students from participating. A 1991 Roper poll reported that 67 percent of Americans believe condoms should be available in high schools; 47 percent believe junior high schools should also make them available.

A second battle about school-distributed contraceptives is being fought over Norplant. This new drug—contained in silicone rubber capsules implanted in a woman's arm during a ten-minute operation—provides 99 percent effective birth control for at least five years. Most of the pro and con arguments regarding condoms also apply to Norplant. In addition, opponents of Norplant argue it gives girls a false sense of security because they may be reluctant to insist their boyfriends use a condom, exposing themselves to AIDS. Some African-American opponents call Norplant a tool of slow genocide, since schools offer it mainly to cut the birthrate of black girls.

So far, only the Baltimore public schools—known for some of the highest teenage pregnancy rates in the nation—offer Norplant to their students. The Laurence Paquin School, run exclusively for pregnant girls or young mothers, is serving as the nation's first testing ground for Norplant. Most girls are happy with the drug, though a few have requested the simple surgery to remove the capsules.

Outlook

The future of contraceptives in schools will be determined by hundreds of local school boards nationwide. But it could also be strongly influenced by Surgeon General Dr. Joycelyn Elders. When she was confirmed as U.S. surgeon general, the Clinton administration signaled its intention to bring Dr. Elders's activist, pro-contraceptive approach to a national level. As head of the Health Department in her native Arkansas, Dr. Elders had promoted sex education, condom distribution, and Norplant for crack-addicted prostitutes. While she was in Arkansas the teenage pregnancy rate rose, but at a slower rate than the national average.

However, Dr. Elders has initiated little effort to reduce teenage pregnancy on a national basis since taking office. Now that voters have swept many conservative Republicans into Congress, the Clinton administration is unlikely to take the lead in promoting widespread contraceptives programs.

26. Should Prayer Be Banned in Public Schools?

YES

The Constitution guarantees separation of church and state. Every American is free to practice any religion he or she chooses or to practice no religion at all. Public schools are an agency of the state. Forcing students to attend prayers, even if they remain silent, violates the First Amendment.

School prayer discriminates against the minority. A primary goal of the Constitution is to protect religious and other minorities. Freedom of worship is a fundamental right that cannot be subject to public vote or to the whims of either elected or appointed officials. If a government shows preference toward one religion—or toward religion in general—it automatically discriminates against others.

There is already ample opportunity for prayer in our lives. You are free to pray at church, at home, and even silently to yourself at school. The Constitution does not deny a belief in God or forbid Bible study in private life. But the state cannot sponsor any public expression of religion.

School prayer harms nonbelieving children. At prayer time the child of a religious minority would face three unpleasant choices. First, he can leave the classroom, branding him as "different" or "weird." Second, he can stay and refuse to participate—considered immoral or even satanic by some in the majority. Third, he can join prayers he might find offensive. These choices—between going against his beliefs or facing the hostility and ridicule of teachers and classmates—are unacceptable.

The separation of church and state protects us from strife. Many of the world's bloodiest conflicts today are fought between different religions. The fighting in Bosnia and Ireland, recent wars within Lebanon and between Iran and Iraq, were all fought between different religions. By not imposing religion on our own minorities, we help prevent internal strife.

N O

The Constitution is meant to protect freedom of religion, not freedom *from* religion. While the First Amendment was meant to prevent the government from giving preferential treatment to one religion, it did not ban prayer in school. Its authors never intended to banish religion from American public life and treat it as some sort of social infection. The Supreme Court has gone much too far in erecting a wall between church and state.

Religion is already accepted in our public lives. American currency is inscribed with the motto "In God We Trust." The Pledge of Allegiance and the national anthem—recited and sung at public school ceremonies nationwide—also mention God.

Our forebears intended religion to be part of our public life. The same founders who wrote the Constitution also voted to give land to a private religious society that spread the gospel. The Continental Congress also paid for chaplains to say prayers.

The rights of the majority also need protection. American civilization places a very high value on the role of a Supreme Being who created us and fills us with his spirit. Religious minorities may practice any religion or remain nonreligious, but they have no right to make believers ignore the Judeo-Christian values of American civilization. Schools are the proper place to teach children these values.

School prayer is not coercive. Students often opt not to participate in all kinds of school activities. Just because an activity is available—such as joining a sports team—does not mean it is coercive.

We must improve America's moral climate. It is no coincidence that the moral and social decline of this nation and the breakdown of our family unit have coincided with the banning of God from our classrooms. The failure of American public education has directly followed the banning of school prayer by the Supreme Court in the late 1960s.

Background

The First Amendment states the following: "Congress shall make no law respecting an establishment of religion, or prohibiting the free exercise thereof." In the 1940s the Supreme Court made the first of many rulings designed to eliminate religious practice and prayer from public schools. By forbidding the "establishment of religion," the Court argued that neither the states nor the federal government could set up a church, aid any religion, or even aid all religions. Justice Hugo Black wrote for the majority in a 1947 case that "the clause against establishment of religion by law was intended to erect a wall of separation between church and state. . . . [t]hat wall must be kept high and impregnable." Proponents of school prayer claim the Court has misinterpreted this so-called establishment clause, and that it only prevents governments from establishing a state religion.

Since the 1940s the Supreme Court has used its interpretation of the First Amendment to prohibit from public schools the reading of prayers, distribution of Bibles, religious instruction, teaching of creationism, moments of silence, and posting of the Ten Commandments. Many school districts, particularly in southern and rural communities, have continued school prayers for decades despite Supreme Court rulings. Reciting the Pledge of Allegiance and singing the national anthem, both of which mention God, have remained legal. According to a 1993 Gallup poll, 58 percent of Americans disapprove of the Supreme Court ban on school prayer, down from 70 percent in 1963.

Most recently, in the 1992 case *Lee* v. *Weisman,* the Court found that officially inviting guests to say prayers at high school graduation ceremonies was unconstitutional. Many schools now use students to say graduation prayers, but at least two lower courts have ruled this also unconstitutional. The Supreme Court has not yet heard a case regarding students leading prayers during graduation. A Phi Delta Kappa survey found that two-thirds of responding schools continued graduation prayers in one form or another in 1993.

The Reagan and Bush administrations, despite putting several conservative members on the Court, were unable to change its basic stance on this issue. Members of Congress, led generally by southern representatives and senators such as Jesse Helms, have tried to return prayer to schools by proposing legislation, resolutions, and more than six hundred constitutional amendments. None of these efforts have succeeded in wresting control of the school prayer issue from the Supreme Court. In 1984, however, Congress enacted the Equal Access Act, which requires secondary schools that receive federal funds to allow student religious groups to use school facilities. Religious groups may *not* use these facilities as part of standard educational activities, if the school has organized them, or if a teacher is present. The Supreme Court declared the act constitutional in 1990.

Most of those fighting prayer in schools are religious minorities, nonbelievers, and civil libertarian organizations like the American Civil Liberties Union (ACLU). At the other end of the political spectrum, some small, fringe religious groups object to school prayer for an entirely different reason. They believe the watered-down, nondenominational general prayers agreed upon for public use by committees are not really prayers at all.

Outlook

The Supreme Court, grassroots activists, and Congress will all share a hand in deciding the future of school prayer. The Court is expected to maintain the "high and impregnable" wall between church and state, keeping school prayer illegal, though permitting minimal use of school buildings after hours for religious clubs. Religious conservatives are expected to accelerate a trend of recent years of electing fundamentalist Christians to school boards. As a result, those communities whose majorities strongly desire school prayer will continue to practice it, unless organizations like the ACLU sue the local boards.

The Republican-controlled Congress may eventually enact a congressional amendment that guarantees the right to voluntary school prayer. A congressional amendment must first gain two-thirds majorities in the House and Senate, and then be ratified by three-quarters of the state legislatures.

27. Should All Students Study a Multicultural Curriculum?

YES

Multiculturalism teaches tolerance. Multicultural education celebrates the racial, cultural, and ethnic diversity of American citizens. It demonstrates that each distinct group has its own value and warrants respect. Through multicultural teachings, students learn to relate more effectively to individuals, whatever their racial or ethnic origin.

The metaphor of America as a melting pot is inaccurate. Although we may share certain traits, America is not a nation of people sharing a common identity. Rather, it is a nation of groups whose race and ethnicity define their lives. America already *is* a multicultural nation.

Eurocentric education excludes the experience of minority children. The predominance of Western European teachings in the schools damages the self-image of minority students. These children feel neglected by a curriculum that mainly extols the works of Dead White European Males. Deprived of a past in which they can take pride, their academic performance suffers.

In New York City alone, one-quarter of those under age ten are children of non-English-speaking immigrants. Another large segment is African-American. Why should these children be required to learn a history based almost exclusively on European traditions and ideas, a history that has little meaning in their own lives or experiences?

Multiculturalism raises minority self-esteem. A good multicultural curriculum deals equitably with four non-European cultures: Native American, Latino, Asian American, and African-American. Consequently, minority children acquire newfound self-esteem and self-respect that displaces feelings of racial and ethnic inferiority. Moreover, this curriculum instills pride in past ethnic accomplishments and furnishes necessary role models to encourage future academic success.

Multiculturalism does not threaten American unity. As school curricula expand to incorporate broader multicultural elements, some conflict and divisiveness may arise. Ultimately, however, multicultural education will help forge a society based upon inclusion and equality, recognizing the rich diversity of all its people.

N O

Multiculturalism is divisive. Through successive waves of immigration, public schools have served to assimilate and unify diverse peoples so that they thought of themselves as American citizens. Multicultural education separates people according to their ethnicity, race, religion, or sexual orientation. It turns ethnicity into a person's defining characteristic. Such arbitrary classification often exaggerates existing differences, exacerbates long-held animosities, and deepens divisions between races and nationalities.

We must not diminish America's Western tradition. For over two hundred years the traditions of Western Europe have served as the cornerstone of American education. Those democratic ideals that today define America first took root in ancient Greece and Rome and later developed in Great Britain and elsewhere in Europe. Multicultural education diminishes the importance of American democracy, its origins, and its institutions.

The commonality of education is lost. Rather than employ one common standard and teach universally accepted ideals and traditions, multiculturalists promote a separate history and a separate set of values. This results in segregated children who may lack the knowledge necessary to function as productive citizens.

America does acknowledge its cultural diversity. Minorities may have been unrecognized in the past for their contributions to American society. Today's schools, however, do introduce students to the accomplishments of diverse races and cultures, but within the context of their impact upon a unified America defined by Western ideals. Martin Luther King's birthday and Black History Month are widely celebrated.

Historical accuracy suffers under multiculturalism. Under the guise of promoting self-esteem and ethnic identity, some multiculturalists deliberately distort history. Certain Afrocentric curricula, for example, teach children that black men discovered America long before Christopher Columbus; that Cleopatra was black; and that Egypt, not ancient Greece, was the birthplace of "Western" science and philosophy. Does teaching myth and false history truly benefit the children of America?

Background

For much of this century the image of the United States as a cultural melting pot prevailed. But since the 1960s the civil rights movement and waves of Hispanic and Asian immigrants led all minorities to discover newfound pride in their distinctive heritages.

During the 1960s and 1970s college campuses played host to the first debates on multicultural education. Minority students and faculty, who claimed to find little to identify with in Western traditions, demanded and won curriculum reform.

Multiculturalism soon spread beyond college campuses. In 1987, California adopted an inclusive social studies curriculum for its public schools that became a model for multicultural education nationwide. It significantly increased the time devoted to the study of non-European cultures. In addition, it acknowledged the multiracial aspect of American society, past and present.

California's large ethnic and racial groups continue fighting to increase the time spent on their cultures and history. Numerous school board meetings turn into shouting matches as activists battle over which textbooks to buy and how to supplement them.

Like California, New York City revamped its social studies program for public schools starting in 1987. The new curriculum significantly minimized Western traditions. A full-year course on Western European history was reduced to one-quarter of a year. Despite these sweeping changes, in 1989 a more radical New York task force on minorities determined that American institutions and culture had intellectually and educationally oppressed African-Americans, Asian Americans, Latinos, and Native Americans for centuries. The task force insisted upon further reform.

In 1991 a new commission recommended that the social studies curriculum be revised further to accentuate the role of nonwhite cultures. At the forefront of reform in the New York school system and elsewhere have been radical Afrocentrists such as Professor Leonard Jeffries of the City University of New York, who espouses the belief that blacks are inherently superior to whites because of their skin pigment.

Equally controversial have been a series of African-American Baseline Essays, first introduced in 1989 as a curriculum resource for teachers in the Portland, Oregon, school system. These essays present a radical Afrocentric perspective to history that contradicts traditional teachings about the origins of Western civilization. According to this Afrocentrism, ancient Egypt, as a black African culture, gave birth to the science, medicine, philosophy, and arts so long attributed to ancient Greece. Teachers in Portland have the option of teaching this point of view.

Outlook

Despite arguments by white historians that Afrocentrism is not serious scholarship, its influence in elementary and secondary school curricula continues to spread. Guilt over past wrongs inflicted upon black Americans has made some nonminority members hesitant to challenge Afrocentric programs. But a majority of white historians, often led by the two-time Nobel Prize winner Arthur Schlesinger, are attempting to fight the more radical Afrocentrists.

Multicultural education also continues to grow at the university level. According to the National Endowment for the Humanities, 78 percent of American colleges and universities *do not* require any courses in the history of Western civilization. However, numerous institutions, including Dartmouth, the University of Wisconsin, and Mount Holyoke, *do* require courses in Third World or ethnic studies. Increasingly, students at universities insist that the professors who teach ethnic studies courses be members of the same ethnic group. At the primary and secondary school level, too, minority teachers increasingly are sought to teach about their own culture and history.

In late 1994 a federal education panel with members from thirty-five national organizations, including the American Historical Association, released new standards for teaching American history, world history, and social studies. These standards and curricula, designed for kindergarten through twelfth grade, deemphasize Western civilization and thought, but do not accomodate the more extreme beliefs of some multiculturalists. If these voluntary standards are approved by a U.S. Department of Education bipartisan council, they may be adopted by many public school systems and serve as a compromise among the various factions fighting over multicultural education.

28. Should the Government Subsidize Private Schools Through Vouchers?

YES

Private schools achieve superior academic results. According to the federal government's National Educational Longitudinal Survey, math and reading proficiency is much higher among students attending private schools than among their public school counterparts. With the nation's public schools failing miserably to educate our students, private schools are often a parent's only recourse.

School vouchers help parents afford the best education possible for their children. Vouchers help defray tuition costs and would permit all children, especially those from low-income families, the same opportunity for a quality private school education as those whose families can easily afford it.

Parental choice saves taxpayer dollars. As an example, each public school student costs the state of California approximately $5,200 a year to educate. Because they are run much more efficiently, many private schools cost only $2,600 per year. Under a proposed voucher system, each student would receive a $2,600 credit to enroll in a private school, ultimately saving taxpayers $2,600. Such a program would save billions of dollars annually as increasing numbers of children transfer to private schools.

Vouchers secure the survival of private schools. As the discretionary income for working- and middle-class families continues to decline, so too does enrollment in private schools, particularly in the parochial schools that serve inner cities. A voucher system would increase funding to these vital institutions.

Overcrowding in public schools will ease. In California alone, public school enrollment is projected to grow by 200,000 students annually through the year 2000, straining an already congested system. An increasing number of private and parochial schools have room for the additional students that voucher programs will attract, thereby reducing public school congestion.

Private school vouchers induce public schools to improve. Under a free market system, public schools will face the loss of their brightest students to private schools. To thwart that exodus, public schools will be forced to overhaul their outmoded, bloated bureaucracy and adopt innovative teaching methods.

N O

Voucher programs rob public schools of critical funds. To finance vouchers, monies would be skimmed from already strapped public schools. This decrease in funding could prompt deep spending cuts in school transportation, security, classroom supplies, and staff, leaving inner-city schools in far worse condition than at present.

Vouchers subsidize discrimination. Traditionally, private schools have always set their own admission standards, often based on gender, English proficiency, intelligence, financial status, or religion. Why should taxpayers finance private institutions that promote segregated student populations?

Public schools become the dumping ground for the unwanted. Under a voucher system, private schools pick and choose students according to their own criteria. Public schools, however, must continue to accept anyone seeking an education, including those with learning disabilities, physical handicaps, behavioral disorders, or language deficiencies. These special students require additional services too costly for private institutions to willingly provide.

Poorly run or fringe private schools could take advantage of voucher programs. Concerned taxpayers fear that bizarre religious or political groups, cults, even profiteers will be allowed to operate schools subsidized with public money, yet be immune from government oversight.

There is no private school advantage. Tests administered by the National Assessment of Educational Progress, a congressionally backed study group, indicate that public schools are on equal academic footing with reputable private schools. Students from private and public institutions performing the same coursework demonstrate no major differences in achievement. If public schools provide quality education, why promote private education through vouchers at all?

Private school vouchers are too expensive. The program defeated in the 1993 California elections would have cost the state nearly $1 billion a year for the 550,000 students already attending private schools. Initiating such an extravagant entitlement program for kids who can already afford private schools is a luxury most states cannot afford.

Background

A recent wave of dissatisfaction with America's public schools has prompted the search for new methods to improve education, one of which is school vouchers. The basic plan would allow those parents who wish to remove their children from the public school system to apply government-issued vouchers toward tuition costs at private educational facilities.

The school voucher concept is not new. Forty years ago Nobel Prize–winning economist Milton Friedman suggested such a plan, but received little support. In the 1980s, Great Britain studied the feasibility of a voucher system. After much debate, however, the legislature chose to retain its control over government-operated schools, permitting parents a limited choice among *only* those schools. "Choice" in Great Britain did not extend to private schools (called public schools there).

In the early 1990s the voucher concept resurfaced in California, where the public school system was in dire financial straits. Statewide, per capita spending for schools continued a downward spiral. Standardized test scores and the overall quality of education were also declining.

To confront California's education crisis, members of the Libertarian and Republican parties, together with prominent businessmen, came together in 1993 and drafted Proposition 174, the Parental Choice in Education Act. Under this proposal, the state would issue a $2,600 educational voucher for each child, to be redeemable at any private school accepting the child.

Initially, Californians appeared receptive to the proposal. However, on the eve of the 1993 elections, opponents to the measure, backed by well-funded school unions, waged a $10 million media blitz that ultimately turned public opinion against the proposal. Californians, fearing excessive tax increases and further degradation of their school system, rejected Proposition 174 by a two-to-one margin.

The election defeat has not derailed the voucher movement in California. Surveys indicate that 95 percent of those voting against the measure did so because they believed that specific plan was flawed. Many still support the basic concept of parental choice and would support new proposals.

Numerous communities outside California are also seriously considering school vouchers. Although no statewide programs yet exist, such cities as Indianapolis, Minneapolis, Detroit, and Milwaukee have adopted pilot programs similar to Proposition 174, though on a much smaller scale. Milwaukee's program, for example, accepts only low-income families. Students receive $2,970 vouchers from the state that parents pay to the private school of choice. No additional tuition charges are permitted. So far, the program has received high marks from parents, though student scores on standardized tests reveal no apparent academic improvement.

Elsewhere, the voucher concept is meeting with some resistance. In Oregon and Colorado, proposals patterned after Proposition 174 failed by two-to-one margins. In May 1993 the Pennsylvania legislature narrowly defeated (by a mere thirteen votes) a school choice measure that would have granted vouchers equal to $700 for elementary and $1,000 for high school tuition at private institutions. But the measure is far from dead. Analysts predict that school choice will play a pivotal role in Pennsylvania's 1996 gubernatorial race.

Outlook

In the mid-1990s legislative initiatives are under consideration in thirty-four states to promote school vouchers. Nationally, education reformers see the school voucher plan as one of many proposals, including charter schools and open enrollment within public school districts, that have the potential to revitalize America's educational system.

Meanwhile, in California proponents vow to push for a revised referendum, most likely for the 1996 ballot. This new voucher plan will offer more financial advantages to low-income families while limiting support to the wealthy. In addition, it will recommend a gradual phase-in statewide, as well as some government supervision of private schools to ensure accountability. As California's educational troubles continue to mount, this tempered version of Proposition 174 has a far greater chance of appeasing voters. Should the California proposition pass, other states will likely follow.

29. Should Affluent School Districts Be Forced to Aid Poorer Ones?

YES

The current funding system is inherently unfair and unconstitutional. Property taxes constitute about 40 percent of all funds raised for elementary and secondary education in the United States. Typically, an affluent school district might spend *three times* more per student than a poor one only a few miles away.

Many state constitutions provide for educational equity, quality, uniformity, and access for all students. The current system in most states violates these provisions.

Conditions at poor schools make good education virtually impossible. America's underfunded grade schools typically have no librarians, and no art, music, or physical education teachers. They frequently hold classes in coatrooms and furnace rooms. Class sizes sometimes approach forty students.

Increased spending directly improves education. A recent study by a Fordham University professor shows that each additional $100 spent per year on classroom instruction in high schools results in eighteen additional points on a student's SAT scores.

Some critics claim that infusions of cash for inner-city schools have failed to produce results. But much of this money goes toward nonacademic needs such as school security and maintenance. When increased spending can be used for up-to-date textbooks, equipment, and good teachers, education does improve in poor districts.

Redistributing property tax revenues is the best way to achieve equality. As an example, the impoverished North Chicago school district has one of Illinois's highest property tax rates—$7.33 per $100 of assessed value. It raised only $1,638 per student in 1992 because of low property values. Nearby Lake Forest raised $14,143 per student on the much lower tax rate of $1.32 per $100 because of high property values.

Only by taking some funds from wealthy districts—sometimes called Robin Hood plans—will we properly educate all our children. Otherwise poor children will remain forever locked in the cycle of poverty, as parents will never be able to afford a better neighborhood with better schools for their own children.

N O

Spending large sums does not improve education. Many people intuitively feel that increased spending will automatically help students get better educations. In the last thirty years the United States has increased spending for education by 205 percent, adjusted for inflation. Yet most educators agree that American education has deteriorated during this period. Average spending per student rose from $2,500 in 1966 to almost $5,200 per year in 1989 (in constant dollars). Yet the average combined math and verbal SAT test score declined from 960 to a little over 900 during the same period.

A state like New Jersey, which adopted extensive funding equity laws in 1990, has yet to show a change. For example, Jersey City's schools doubled spending to $9,200 per student, yet still only a third of its high school students graduate, compared to nearly 72 percent nationally.

No studies conclusively show that increased teacher salaries or higher school spending helps students learn better. We have spent decades pouring billions into the black hole of education. To waste more money makes no sense—we need to focus on curriculum and standards.

Local people need to determine their own level of taxation. The failure of inner-city schools to provide a proper education may be caused by a host of problems, including a poor family life and drug abuse. It is unfair to take money from the middle class, who struggle hard enough to pay their bills.

Let states and the federal government increase their share of funding for public education. Taking money from localities violates their freedom to decide how local tax dollars get spent.

Education can improve with the resources at hand. Some school systems in states like Maine and Kentucky have improved high school grades and SAT scores through new rigorous curricula. By increasing the time spent on academic subjects and reducing the number of nonacademic subjects and after-school activities, public schools can provide good education without additional spending.

Background

To date, the educational funding practices in forty-one states have been challenged in court at least once. Currently, about half the states are being sued over issues of school funding equity or the closely connected issue of school adequacy. Usually the parents in poor school districts, or the districts themselves, bring suit. Of the $200 billion spent each year on elementary and secondary education, states pay 48 percent, localities pay 46 percent, and the federal government covers 6 percent. During the boom early and mid-1980s, money was relatively plentiful for education. But since then, scarce resources have put funding equity back into the limelight.

In many states, the state supreme court has battled the legislature over this issue. Typically, parents from poor districts sue, the court orders the governor and legislature to come up with an equitable funding scheme, the plan proves inadequate, parents sue again, and the legislature redrafts its funding formula. To achieve equity, states often combine three methods, which include increasing their payments to poor districts, controlling the educational spending of wealthy districts, and using a Robin Hood plan to take local property tax dollars from wealthy districts and distribute them to poor ones.

The first lawsuits seeking to change school funding practices were filed in 1968, against Texas and California. In 1973 the U.S. Supreme Court ruled that the Constitution did not grant equal access to education as a fundamental right. The Court preferred to let states and localities decide this issue, as they had for so long. In the mid-1970s equity advocates won a series of battles when the supreme courts of Texas, New Jersey, and other states agreed that education was a fundamental right protected by state constitutions. Through the mid-1980s a majority of state courts upheld the existing situation. But since the late 1980s a majority of state supreme courts have mandated changes that require equitable financing.

Some states try to raise additional money for education by increasing personal, sales, or corporate taxes. But they run into immediate trouble with the taxpayer reform movement. In a direct blow to educational funding, taxpayer revolts in California and Colorado have capped property taxes. When Democratic legislators and former Democratic Governor Jim Florio in New Jersey raised taxes and redirected funds from wealthy suburban school districts to poor urban ones, Florio's popularity dropped dramatically. The governor and some legislators were replaced by Republicans in the 1993 election. Until improved state economies reduce the pressure on state budgets, the school funding issue will continue to pit the poor against wealthy and middle-class taxpayers.

Outlook

A few states are taking radical action not just to create financing equity but to improve education statewide. In 1993, Michigan became the first state to pass a law prohibiting the use of property taxes to finance public education. In March 1994, Michigan voters overwhelmingly accepted a statewide increase in the sales tax from 4 to 6 percent to replace those lost educational revenues. The state also set minimum spending levels for poor education districts and ceilings for wealthy ones.

In Kentucky, an activist chief judge on that state's supreme court was asked to rule on the funding equity issue. Instead, he declared Kentucky's entire public education system in violation of the state's constitution for its inadequacy. That forced the Kentucky Assembly to redesign the entire elementary and secondary school system. The numerous reforms include increased local control of educational policy and financial rewards for schools whose students excel. The reforms, started in 1990, have already narrowed the spending gap between rich and poor school districts by a third, and improved educational standards statewide.

Some other states will likely follow the examples set by Michigan and Kentucky. A focus on educational *adequacy* may someday replace the issue of funding equity. If Oklahoma, the first state sued over adequacy, is forced to radically improve its educational system for all students, suits in other states will surely follow.

Combat Fatigue

30. Should We Exclude Women Soldiers from Ground Combat?

YES

Women are physically weaker than men. Front-line fighting requires great strength and endurance. The average woman's upper-body strength is only 42 percent of the average man's. Infantry soldiers must carry up to 110 pounds of weapons and supplies, and be prepared to carry a wounded comrade over very rough terrain. They must physically overpower an enemy in hand-to-hand combat. A slow or weak member jeopardizes the whole unit.

Today U.S. basic training gives easier physical tests to women because they are weaker. But in real combat, women need the same strength as men.

Women could harm unit bonding. A small combat unit must be a cohesive, self-reliant force. The men might take unnecessary risks for the women or go easy on them, which could result in low morale, poor fighting effectiveness, and even unnecessary deaths. In Israel's 1948 War of Independence it tried using women in combat. This disastrous experiment ended after only a few weeks. The female casualties so demoralized the male soldiers that the unity of their forces was ruined.

Undeniable tensions between men and women in the U.S. Armed Forces already cause problems. Women must worry about sexual harassment. Such barriers to camaraderie and unit bonding are dangerous in battle. Soldiers must eat, sleep, bathe, and live together for days or weeks at a time. Mixing the sexes in infantry units simply will not work.

Most women are not killers. Fighting a human being to the death requires a level of brutality and violence impossible for most women. Numerous studies show that people with high testosterone levels are capable of substantially greater aggression. Most women produce much less testosterone than men.

Winning wars with minimal casualties comes first. Combat units should never serve as a testing ground for social change. We cannot afford to sacrifice our military's effectiveness in the interests of social equity.

N O

Exclusion discriminates against women. Combat experience is an important criterion for career advancement within the military. Training in elite units such as the Rangers almost guarantees future promotions. Female soldiers do not receive these opportunities and soon run up against the "brass ceiling." Without the experience of leading soldiers into battle, few women will ever rise to the rank of general, or even colonel.

Women can improve military effectiveness. The military would manage its resources more efficiently if all qualified personnel could contribute. For example, in the 1989 U.S. action in Panama the 82nd Airborne Division had to leave home one of their best intelligence analysts who specialized in Panama—because she was a woman. Can we afford to waste qualified soldiers?

Modern warfare puts all combatants at equal risk. In the past those fighting on the front lines were clearly at much higher risk, but the weapons of today put most combatants (and many noncombatants) at risk. Rules designed to protect women soldiers do not work. If women can work as medics and combat pilots, why not allow them in the infantry?

Similar arguments against women were once used against African-Americans. Before President Harry Truman integrated the armed forces, racists claimed that blacks could not follow orders, would lower morale, and were psychologically unprepared to lead whites. All these claims were proven untrue. Women deserve the same chance to prove themselves.

Many women are strong enough. According to some tests, 20 percent of women are strong enough to compete with the weakest 20 percent of men in infantry training. These top 20 percent of women want to fight and deserve the chance.

Men and women can fight together. In Vietnam, the main concern was if blacks and whites could bond. When the bullets started flying, the problems disappeared. The same will be true of men and women.

Background

Although women have served in the U.S. Armed Forces since World War II, only since the Persian Gulf war has their role triggered a major controversy. Several milestones led to the expanded role of women soldiers.

In 1948, Congress passed the Women's Armed Forces Services Integration Act, which sanctioned military careers for women but also included restrictions on their range of service. These restrictions, known as the combat exclusion laws, prohibited the air force, navy, and marines from assigning women to aircraft, ships, and other forces "engaged in combat missions." Although these laws do not explicitly mention the army, it established policies that exclude women from jobs, missions, and locations likely to involve direct combat.

In 1967 ceilings on the number and grades of military women were eliminated. The end of the male draft and inauguration of the All Volunteer Force in 1973 dramatically increased opportunities for women. Three years later women were admitted to military academies.

Women first participated in combat during the 1989 fighting in Panama. Although supposedly restricted to flying transports, two female helicopter pilots ferrying troops were fired on during a battle against the Panamanian Defense Forces. In another incident, a female captain leading a U.S. military police unit engaged in a firefight.

During the 1991 Persian Gulf war the line between combat and non-combat missions grew more clouded as women flew helicopters, and worked as medics, truck drivers, and in a variety of other support jobs throughout the region. The U.S. media was flooded with stories about war-bound mothers saying goodbye to weeping toddlers, two U.S. women held prisoners of war, and the eleven female U.S. soldiers who died. Our first experience seeing women come home in body bags, however, did not cause a public outcry.

In April 1993 then-Secretary of Defense Les Aspin lifted the prohibition against women flying many combat aircraft and serving on naval surface ships. The army has continued restrictions on its air cavalry and special operations aircraft, arguing these are part of ground combat units.

In January 1994 the Pentagon announced a new policy allowing women to serve in some combat support jobs. The policy still forbids women to serve in ground combat, but no longer excludes women from dangerous military assignments. Women will be allowed to fly helicopters that fly cover for tanks and be assigned to air defense artillery groups. But as of late 1994, one-quarter of army jobs, including infantry and armor units, will remain closed to women.

This issue stirs great debate among feminists. Some argue that the only way for women to achieve equality and power is to serve equally in the most important institutions of our society, including the military. Others believe women will humanize the military and change the brutal male culture that dominates it. Antimilitary feminists argue that women should not fight because fighting itself is wrong, and the military simply serves the interests of American elites.

Outlook

A key undecided issue is not only *whether* women will be permitted to fight in combat, but if they will be *required* to. Members of Congress have suggested an army trial program to observe women in combat under test conditions. If the program shows some women are indeed physically and psychologically able to fight, and that women do not lower the effectiveness of fighting units, what then? According to informal polls, very few army women want to join the infantry. Should every woman face the same combat risks as every man? Can women expect true equality if they do not accept the same dangers? An army trial program may only substitute one controversy for another.

Today some 230,000 women constitute 11 percent of our armed forces. It remains unlikely that any will soon join infantry units. Resistance in the military and among key members of Congress is strong, and military downsizing decreases the need for women candidates to compete for ground combat units. Unlike homosexuals, whose vocal lobbyists work to gain them equal access to military jobs, women have no organized lobbying effort around this particular issue.

31. Should the U.S. Armed Forces Save Countries Under Siege?

YES

The United States has a moral obligation to save innocent lives. As the world's remaining superpower, only America possesses the military might to effectively intervene in many situations abroad. Like it or not, this gives us a special obligation to help others in need.

During World War II we failed to bomb the Nazi concentration camps, which ultimately might have saved millions of lives. In this decade we could have easily prevented mass killings in places like Bosnia, Rwanda, and Haiti.

U.S isolationism creates serious dangers. President Clinton's focus on domestic affairs signals a new self-absorbed America. Not since the 1930s have we exhibited such isolationism, but our passivity will only result in future bloodshed.

The world watches carefully when the United States fails to stop the genocide in places like Bosnia. This sends a comforting message to extremists and nationalists in Russia, the Ukraine, and various other former Soviet states. Our inaction inspires North Korea and Iran to develop nuclear weapons and Saddam Hussein to continue his aggression against the Kurds. Our passivity shows the world that we now tolerate military expansionism.

If we fail to curb aggression in Asia, Europe, and the Caribbean, and do not stop nuclear proliferation, hostile countries and new Hitlers will surely take advantage of the situation. As the saying goes, power abhors a vacuum.

U.S. isolationism causes lost opportunities. Through two world wars and forty years of the cold war, we stood fast against our enemies. Now that we have won, instead of exerting our leadership worldwide, helping democratic regimes flourish, and allowing a truly effective global economy to develop, we have turned our backs.

Our defeat of communism created chaos in many countries. We must maintain our position as the world's military and political leader. We should not lose the opportunity to create a climate of peace and prosperity.

N O

Places like Bosnia, Rwanda, and Haiti are not central to our vital interests. At any given time dozens of low-grade wars or insurgencies persist around the globe. There will always be more conflicts and civil wars than we can deal with. Most have little to do with the United States. Many wars, like the ones in Bosnia and Rwanda, are based on age-old hostilities between tribes, religions, or ethnic groups. Beyond offering humanitarian aid to refugees, the United States has no responsibility for or interest in getting involved.

The only time we should risk the lives of our soldiers is in situations where U.S. security or economic interests are directly endangered. Conflicts like those between Muslims and Christians in Bosnia are tragedies, but that does not obligate us to sacrifice American lives.

The United States can no longer police the world. The massive U.S. debt is proof enough that we cannot afford to pay for the security of others. Most of our recent military involvements required help from our allies. Even the 1991 Gulf war and the Somali relief effort were multilateral—conducted and paid for by a group of countries. Involvement in too many military situations will quickly exhaust our financial and diplomatic capital.

The last thing we need is to become mired in another Vietnam or some other costly obligation halfway around the world. The British involvement in Northern Ireland started as a peacekeeping action in 1969 to keep the Protestants and Catholics apart. It has now cost thousands of lives.

Militaristic superpowers make enemies. If we act like a bully or an unwanted guest in foreign conflicts, other nations will band together to counterbalance our influence. That does not mean secondary nations will go to war against us, but it does mean they will act against our interests.

Background

From its earliest days the United States has wavered between isolationism and interventionism. With the exception of World War II, each of the wars we fought during this century was followed almost immediately by a period of inwardness. After these quiet periods, the natural American instinct to right some wrong regains control. Even during the cold war our sense of obligation to protect democracy and liberty always battled with our natural reluctance to shed American blood.

The United States has enjoyed the unusual luxury of avoiding most threats from foreign powers. The world's military crises in this century played out far from home. Although we like to imagine ourselves as magnanimous defenders of liberty, our involvements in both world wars were triggered by foreign attacks. German submarines sank eight U.S. ships before Woodrow Wilson brought America into World War I. Only after the Japanese attacked Pearl Harbor did we enter World War II.

From the beginning of the cold war in the late 1940s to its end in the early 1990s, U.S. foreign policy remained straightforward. Most American administrations during that period focused on containing what they saw as a hostile, expansionary Soviet Union. Most U.S. foreign policy and certainly most U.S. military involvements were deeply influenced by our battle with communism.

The Vietnam War substantially reduced America's willingness to fight overseas. American conservatives believed U.S. involvement in Vietnam would stop the "domino effect" of spreading communism. Liberals viewed the conflict in Vietnam as a civil war far outside America's sphere of influence. Neither side expected the United States to actually lose the war or to suffer from the deficits and inflation it caused at home.

Since Vietnam, American administrations have limited themselves to low-risk conflicts where the United States has a vital interest, the goals are clear-cut, and an exit for U.S. troops is readily available. In many post-Vietnam conflicts the United States simply supplied arms and training to one side so our own troops did not fight. A combined aversion to losing another war and tight budgets keep us from major military involvements.

With the breakup of the Soviet Union and the Warsaw Pact, our foreign policy lost its strong anticommunist anchor. Not only is the United States safe from immediate dangers, but our NATO allies and major trading partners, whom we would feel compelled to protect, are also safe. While George Bush's focus on foreign policy helped him win the 1988 presidential election, he lost the 1992 election because of it.

Americans clearly want to fix problems at home first.

In the early 1990s the conflict in Bosnia dominated foreign policy news. But despite almost nightly television pictures of horror and brazen aggression against civilians, and despite President Clinton's campaign promises to become involved, the United States chose to rely on diplomacy and a few low-risk air strikes.

When American troops led a U.N. multinational force into Somalia toward the end of the Bush administration, they saved hundreds of thousands from starvation and the anarchy that reigned. Unfortunately, there were hundreds of American casualties. Operation Restore Hope, intended as a purely humanitarian mission, soon extended U.S. military involvement far beyond what the American public would tolerate. The Somali intervention—once discussed as a possible model for post–cold war military intervention—revealed the declining American taste for foreign adventures, even those to protect lives and liberty.

Outlook

What would inspire the United States to take up arms in the future? Any real threat to our national interests, such as a reconstituted Soviet Union, Chinese military expansion, a North Korean invasion of South Korea, or an attack on our NATO allies, would certainly change the picture. But the days of risking substantial military involvement to save a small country not vital to our national interest seem long gone for the moment. Small-scale military actions, however, assisting the people of nearby nations to remove tyrannical rulers—such as in Panama or Haiti—remain a potential American policy.

32. Should the United States Dramatically Reduce Defense Spending?

YES

Today economic, not military power is crucial. The real battle today pits the United States against the world's economic powers such as Germany and Japan. We desperately need to become competitive in world markets. This means spending part of the nearly $300 billion annual military budget on education, nonmilitary research, and rebuilding our infrastructure.

Let our wealthy allies pay for their own defense. Germany and the other European nations can afford to pay much more for NATO's upkeep. Japan, too, can pay much more for its own defense.

We face little direct military threat. For the last seventy-five years we have assumed that a foreign power, or combination of powers, could threaten our national security. But today, with the collapse of the Soviet Union and the Warsaw Pact, no country could possibly challenge the United States.

Many weapons we plan to build are not needed. Some of the high-ticket weapons under development were designed to fight World War III against the Soviet Union. Why build the navy's Arleigh Burke destroyers, with their AEGIS combat system geared to fight hordes of incoming Soviet missiles and aircraft? The F-22 and B-2 aircraft do not function as promised, cost a fortune, and no longer serve a purpose.

We can mothball many existing weapons. Despite the vastly diminished nuclear threat, we still maintain nearly 10,000 strategic nuclear warheads. We still own 16,000 tanks. A country like Iran, a potential enemy, keeps only 500 tanks. Why do we still operate fourteen aircraft carrier groups at nearly $10 billion each? According to *The Bulletin of the Atomic Scientists,* five would be enough.

The military should not serve as a jobs program. Maintaining high spending levels just to save defense jobs makes no sense. A major study shows that the money needed to create one defense job could create two jobs in other industries.

N O

The nuclear club is growing. North Korea may well possess nuclear weapons. Pakistan, which certainly has the bomb, could be taken over by anti-American militants. China maintains a large nuclear arsenal. Libya and Iran are trying desperately to acquire nuclear weapons. Can we really afford to let down our guard?

Several conflicts can erupt at once. North Korea, the Middle East, and half a dozen other hot spots could require U.S. intervention at any time. If our weakened military can meet only one or two challenges simultaneously, other nations might start opportunistic local wars.

Why would we suddenly abdicate our role as the only superpower and our clout in international affairs? We still need a substantial troop presence in Europe and Asia and a large navy showing the flag worldwide.

The former Soviet Union could still threaten us. The Russians and Ukrainians still possess nearly 30,000 nuclear weapons and a vast array of conventional weapons. A hostile authoritarian government could endanger us again. What if an ultranationalist like Vladimir Zhirinovsky comes to power?

Don't let the "hollow military" return. After World War II we scaled down the military so quickly that our poorly equipped and trained soldiers were easily routed by the North Koreans in 1950. After the Vietnam War our slashed defense budget created the famous "hollow military" of poorly trained, undisciplined troops. Must we repeat history?

We must maintain a viable defense industry. What happens if we do go to war and cannot build a new generation of weapons quickly? If we let our defense suppliers disappear, our capacity to meet future needs could prove disastrous.

Our defense budget costs only 4.5 percent of the gross national product today. According to the *Congressional Quarterly,* the cost will drop to only 3.4 percent of GNP by 1997, the lowest level since 1948. Surely, we can afford that low level of spending.

Background

In response to the end of the cold war, the Bush administration announced substantial cuts in the U.S. military, including a 25 percent cut in manpower, to be reached by 1996. In the so-called Base Force, a prudent minimum proposed by the Bush administration, the army will shrink from eighteen to twelve active divisions, the navy from fourteen to twelve carriers, the air force from twenty-four to fifteen active fighter wings, and the Marine Corps from three to 2 ⅔ active divisions. Many studies suggest deeper reductions could still maintain America's presence in Europe and South Korea. The Brookings Institution believes seven active army divisions and nine aircraft carriers would suffice. Brookings calls for a total defense budget of $170 billion annually, about 60 percent of the 1993 level.

Other groups suggest even deeper reductions. For example, *The Bulletin of the Atomic Scientists* proposes reducing our strategic nuclear warheads from about 9,750 to 780, our tank force from 16,000 to 2,000 of our most advanced models, our army ground forces from 1.8 million to 180,000, our navy from 420 vessels to 120, and the Marine Corps from 200,000 active soldiers to about 50,000. Its experts believe such a scaled-down military could adequately defend U.S. interests at a cost of only $115 billion per year. The chances of such an extreme reduction are virtually nonexistent.

Others prefer to decrease the defense budget by revamping many existing weapons instead of building new ones. Planes, tanks, and ships can be dramatically improved by adding new electronics, engines, and weapons systems. For example, the marines decided to upgrade their Cobra helicopter with new avionics, engine, night-vision equipment, and missiles rather than buy a new attack helicopter.

Some budget cutters hope to reduce interservice rivalries and redundant forces. For example, the navy's air force covers many parts of the world from carriers, while land-based air force planes could do the job much more cheaply. The army's various rapid deployment forces duplicate those of the marines.

A key factor influencing congressional spending decisions is the loss of jobs in the defense industry. According to the Office of Technology Assessment, up to 1.4 million defense jobs may disappear by 1995. Half a million of these are uniformed soldiers and other Defense Department employees, and about 900,000 others are in defense plants. The number of defense contracting firms has already shrunk from 120,000 during the height of Reagan's military buildup in the 1980s to less than

30,000 today. Many defense factories cannot successfully convert themselves into plants making civilian products.

Congressional representatives resist closing larger firms, particularly those within their districts. Several presidents have failed to shrink the Grumman Corporation plant in Bethpage, New York, which produces some aircraft the military does not really want, because of the influence of the New York congressional delegation.

Congress also fights reducing the National Guard, which provides jobs and money in home congressional districts. Although the army wants to cut the guard from ten to six divisions, opposition is growing.

Outlook

When President Clinton took office, he proposed military cuts over five years of $60 billion beyond those proposed by the Bush administration. With Republicans in control of Congress, Clinton will certainly not achieve these reductions. Many Republicans call for increases in military spending. Some champion a return of the Star Wars antimissile defense program sought by President Reagan. Others push for building more B-2 bombers, increasing troop salaries, and improving combat readiness. But since Republicans are loath to cut spending for Social Security and other entitlements, finding funds to pay for an increased military budget will prove difficult. As a result, the Pentagon budget will probably remain fairly constant for the next several years.

Nevertheless, the U.S. military will have changed dramatically during the 1990s. By the year 2000 more than a hundred military installations will have closed. The military portion of the U.S. gross domestic product will drop from the late 1980s high of 6 percent to 3 percent by the new century. The U.S. Armed Forces, once designed to fight simultaneously on two major fronts against the Soviet Union, will become a more specialized force designed to fight regional conflicts and terrorism, yet still be able to win a single large-scale war.

33. Should Out-of-the-Closet Gays Be Banned from the Military?

YES

Trust, confidence, and unit cohesion would suffer with gay soldiers. Soldiers must live in very close quarters for long stretches of time. They share dormitories, tiny rooms, showers, and toilets during training, on cramped ships, and in the field. Modesty becomes impossible. Just as we do not want members of the opposite sex infringing on our privacy, so too soldiers have a right not to live in close quarters with homosexuals who may look upon them in a sexual manner.

Combat requires soldiers to place compete trust in one another. It requires knowing that each member of the unit will lay down his life for you. For a small combat unit to stay alive it must share common values and grow into a tight, disciplined team. The gay lifestyle deviates from military values and threatens fighting effectiveness within a unit.

Gays harm morale and discipline. Many straight soldiers simply will not take orders from an openly gay officer. The fundamentally male, macho hierarchy of the military makes mixing straights and gays impossible.

Gays harm America's image abroad. U.S. soldiers serve in many countries where, for religious or cultural reasons, homosexuality is considered an abomination. Gay soldiers would offend these countries and harm America's prestige.

Gays would be more prone to disciplinary problems. On average, gays have higher rates of alcoholism, promiscuity, and suicide than the population as a whole. The military needs to reduce—not increase—these problems.

Gays would be imperiled. Fragging, in which officers are murdered by their own soldiers, is an unfortunate fact of military life during wartime and peacetime alike. Gay officers and soldiers would be endangered by their own men who find their lifestyle detestable. The highly publicized murders of gay soldiers in the last few years highlight this danger.

N O

Gays have already served with distinction. All evidence indicates that gays and lesbians serve with the same distinction as heterosexual soldiers. Gays can be found at all ranks and in all branches of the military. The Pentagon's own studies indicate that homosexual recruits perform as well as heterosexual ones.

Gays do not harm morale. Although gay military men and women may not publicly acknowledge their sexual lifestyle while on duty, many feel comfortable being gay while off duty. It is no secret who is gay and who is straight in today's military. Besides, the military tends to attract conservative-leaning people who share most values of their fellow soldiers.

No harm has come from gays serving in other countries. Countries such as Canada, Israel, and Australia all permit homosexuals to serve in their military. No ill effects of any kind have been reported.

Questions about unit cohesion and morale were also raised at one time by fire and police departments in the United States. But gays now serve with equal ability as police officers and firefighters throughout America.

Our military adapts well to change. When African-Americans were first integrated into the service in the 1950s, the military establishment predicted numerous calamities, including loss of morale and discipline. Whites, they argued, simply would not serve with blacks. Today the military is America's most successfully integrated institution.

The ban on gays is very expensive. In the 1980s our military spent an astonishing $500 million ferreting out gay soldiers and training more than 10,000 replacements. Can't we spend this money more effectively?

Combat effectiveness will not suffer because of gay soldiers. On the battlefield soldiers care only about staying alive and winning. Better training and weapons and superior forces win battles. Who is straight or who is gay makes no difference.

Background

As far back as the Revolutionary War, General George Washington court-martialed and dismissed one of his soldiers for sodomy. Nonetheless, laws against sodomy did not exclude homosexuals from the military until World War I. In 1981 the army adopted a regulation requiring all gays to be dismissed, regardless of their service record. The next year in a policy directive on the topic, the Department of Defense announced: "Homosexuality is incompatible with military service. The presence in the military environment of persons who engage in homosexual conduct or who, by their statements, demonstrate a propensity to engage in homosexual conduct, seriously impairs the accomplishment of the military mission."

Until the Clinton presidency, about 1,400 soldiers were dismissed from the four services each year for their alleged homosexuality. Openly gay soldiers had no recourse. The military has always been allowed to manage its internal affairs with little outside interference from Congress. Traditionally, when soldiers sued the military for violating their constitutional rights, the Supreme Court sided with the armed forces, arguing that the military, as a specialized society, knows what is best for itself.

Bill Clinton first proposed ending the military's ban on homosexuals during the presidential campaign of 1992. So limited was criticism of his proposal at the time that he and gay activists assumed the nation was ready for a change. However, as a newly inaugurated president he faced massive resistance from inside and outside the military. When he contemplated issuing an executive order ending the ban against gays, the large number of angry protests prevented him.

Much to his surprise and anguish, this issue dominated the first few months of Clinton's presidency. He directed then-Secretary of Defense Les Aspin to find a compromise satisfactory to gays and the military establishment. The battle moved into the courts and into hearings by the Senate Armed Service Committee, under the leadership of Senator Sam Nunn. This conservative Democrat, who has a reputation as a defender of the military's status quo, proposed a compromise policy known as "don't ask, don't tell, don't pursue." Under the policy, gays need not admit to their homosexuality upon enlistment. The policy states that "homosexual conduct is grounds for separation," but "sexual orientation is considered a personal and private matter . . . unless [it] is manifested by homosexual conduct." The policy was designed to end witch-hunts aimed at suspected gays; a gay soldier openly practicing homosexuality still faces discharge.

So the battle is not over. But the courts no longer automatically side with the armed forces on issues of military personnel. In January 1993 the U.S. District Court in Los Angeles ruled the navy unjustified in dismissing Petty Officer Keith Meinhold after he admitted his homosexuality during a television interview. The court also prevented the Defense Department from "discharging or denying enlistment to any person based on sexual orientation in the absence of sexual conduct which interferes with the military mission of the United States." In October 1993 the Supreme Court overturned the U.S. District Court ruling, which paved the way for the "don't ask, don't tell" policy. The case is being considered by a lower appeals court.

Outlook

America's gay community, generally an educated and affluent group, envisions for itself a great civil rights struggle similar to the one for black equality in the 1960s. America's conservative and religious right see fighting gay rights as another battle for traditional American values. Since President Clinton met such resistance on this issue, he is unlikely to expend much more political capital supporting gays in the military. Without a champion in the White House, gays must wait for the courts to advance their cause.

The Supreme Court may someday be asked to decide whether *any* limitations on gay conduct in the military are constitutional. At the moment gay rights activists believe the Supreme Court would continue to allow the military to set its own policy on personnel matters.

Culture Wars

34. Should the Government Fund Sexually Explicit or Blasphemous Art?

YES

The withdrawal of funding for controversial art amounts to censorship. Like all other citizens, artists enjoy the right to say whatever they choose and to create any type of art they wish. Any attempt by Congress to prejudge art, to control it through a political agenda, or to interfere with the democratic processes of the National Endowment for the Arts (NEA) is unconstitutional censorship.

The government has traditionally funded different types of free speech. Washington spends taxpayer dollars to keep the airwaves open to differing opinions, to prevent monopolies among communications companies, and to provide money to political candidates. The government also allows all nonprofit organizations and churches to remain tax-exempt, giving them a financial chance to advance their beliefs and agendas. If the government supports all these forms of free speech, why should artists be treated differently?

The funding of art must remain nonpolitical. The peer review system, in which a panel of artists determines which candidates receive NEA grants, is the only fair system. Artists can best judge one another's work. Otherwise, every political fringe group will try to twist government-funded art to serve their own purpose.

Many of the worst totalitarian regimes in history, such as the Nazis, banned what they considered "degenerate" art. If our government defines state-sanctioned art, doesn't that in turn create our own category of degenerate art? Art needs to be challenging, provocative, and sometimes controversial to maintain our free society. Otherwise, art risks becoming the political tool of the established powers.

The NEA budget is already tiny. The NEA spends under $200 million per year for arts subsidies. The German government spends $4.5 *billion* for their arts programs. Our arts budget is hardly an extravagance. The number of art works that some find offensive is also minuscule.

N O

Congress must spend public money wisely. Robert Mapplethorpe's photographs of graphic sadomasochism and homoeroticism, and of naked, sexually provocative children, have a right to exist, but taxpayers should not be forced to *subsidize* them. Andres Serrano's photograph of a plastic crucifix submerged in his own urine, called *Piss Christ,* has the right to exist, but the NEA should not have paid $15,000 to help create it. This is not a free speech issue but rather a question of misuse of public money.

We elect members of Congress to use their best judgment to make laws and spend taxpayer funds. At a time when children go hungry in America, we should not spend one dime on this so-called art. Strained finances aside, certain standards of morality and public decency and value must apply.

The public has a right to regulate how tax money is spent. Our elected officials appoint watchdog agencies to control and regulate spending in virtually all government offices. Even the Pentagon, which has the authorization to spend some money secretly, is regulated by Congress. Why shouldn't cultural expenditures be subject to the same controls?

Making choices is not censorship. The government does not owe all things to all people. Not every artist who walks up to the public trough can be supported. Just because we refuse to subsidize something does not mean we censor it.

Art should compete in the free market. Most other creations, products, or services of American workers must survive based on their own merits. Why should offensive art be subsidized? Let these photographs sell on their own strengths.

The government should not denigrate religion. The Constitution, to protect religious minorities, prohibits government from establishing or promoting religion. Surely, it also prohibits government from sponsoring sacrilege against a religion.

Background

The current controversy over government funding of the arts began in 1985. Conservatives, members of the religious right, and certain members of Congress criticized the work produced by artists receiving grants from the National Endowment for the Arts, state arts councils, and other groups dispensing public funds. Representative Richard Armey (R-Texas) first tried to eliminate the NEA for funding gay literary magazines. Others objected to art they described as pornographic, obscene, blasphemous of Christian symbols, and degrading of the American flag and other national symbols.

The arts community fought back in Congress and the media, arguing that these works deal with major issues such as racism, war, poverty, sexuality, AIDS, and the environment, and that the personal lifestyle of an artist does not determine the quality or value of art. The NEA argued that most grants are matched at the local level and given to arts councils, which select peer review panels, which in turn choose who receives money. In creating the NEA in 1965, the Senate called for full artistic freedom. Peer review panels are intended to prevent Congress or government bureaucrats from interfering with decisions about aesthetics or artistic merit.

A key moment came in June 1989 when the Corcoran Gallery of Art, in Washington, D.C., dropped their planned exhibition of photographs called *Robert Mapplethorpe: The Perfect Moment.* A small number of the photographs did contain graphic representations of homosexual sex, including a picture of one man urinating into the mouth of another and a self-portrait of Mapplethorpe with a bullwhip protruding from his anus. The Corcoran Gallery did not want to become embroiled in debate about the photographer's work and did not want to endanger its NEA funding.

Senator Jesse Helms (R-North Carolina) has been one of the most outspoken critics of the NEA. In 1989 he tried to attach an amendment to an NEA appropriations bill that would have prohibited funding of obscene works depicting sadomasochism, sexual intercourse, homosexual acts, and sexuality involving children. It would also have prohibited art that defamed a person's religion, national origin, sex, age, race, or physical handicap. This so-called Helms amendment was contested even by Republicans, who argued Shakespeare's work, *Tom Sawyer,* and other classics would fail the Helms test. A watered-down version, called Public Law 101-121, based on the Supreme Court's legal definition of obscenity, did pass, but the wording of this legislation is so vague that both sides complain about the results. Although the NEA tried to obey this law by requiring a written promise from artists not to use government grants to create obscene art, many artists refused NEA money under these conditions. The NEA lost a court challenge and has stopped asking artists for a signed statement.

Debate about NEA funding is part of a much larger debate in our society concerning different concepts of morality and the competing social and cultural agendas of the left and the right. This battle has raged over the content of television, movies, books, magazines, and educational curricula. It involves various branches of government, special interest groups, and the courts. NEA funding became such a flash point because taxpayer money is involved. According to a March 1992 *Reader's Digest* poll, 73 percent of Americans believe strongly or at least somewhat that the government should not use tax dollars to support artists whose works are obscene, pornographic, or blasphemous.

Outlook

Today conservatives continue to press for stricter controls on government spending for the arts. Artists maintain that the Helms initiative has chilled the freedom of artistic expression in America. The NEA and state arts councils take great care now not to let the most offensive—or daring and challenging—art receive taxpayer funds.

The controversial battles of the late 1980s and the 1990s have transformed the NEA. Its current chairperson, actress Jane Alexander, has attempted to mollify Congress by consulting many of them, especially Senator Helms, about NEA's funding directions.

35. Do the Media Have a Liberal Bias?

YES

Polls find most journalists are liberal. A 1985 *Los Angeles Times* poll of large newspapers found that for every reporter identifying him- or herself as conservative, three identified themselves as liberal. On issues such as abortion, school prayer, and gun control, the majority of newspeople consistently support the liberal viewpoint. Fewer than 25 percent said they voted for Ronald Reagan in 1984. According to the often-cited 1981 Lichter-Rothman poll, at least 80 percent of reporters voted for Democratic candidates in presidential elections from 1964 to 1976.

Personal convictions influence professional objectivity. According to the Media Research Center, during the 1988 presidential campaign reporters questioned Republican candidates about liberal issues two and a half times more than they questioned Democratic candidates about conservative issues. Networks as a whole also reveal their bias. Over the years the Public Broadcasting Service (PBS) has steadily selected documentaries and programming that brazenly promote liberal tenets.

Conservatives consistently receive bad press. During election campaigns analysts use an objective system to count which candidates receive the most favorable and unfavorable news stories. According to media experts Maura Clancey and Michael Robinson, Reagan's bad press outnumbered his good press ten to one in the 1984 election. Meanwhile, more than 50 percent of the stories about the Mondale-Ferraro ticket were favorable—most unusual during a campaign.

Few members of any given news organization understand, never mind champion, conservative thinking. Working in such a biased environment, journalists cannot help reflecting their personal, liberal-leaning viewpoints in their story selection, editing, and presentation.

Conservatives' achievements are often overlooked. Conservative good deeds receive no more praise from the news media than conservatives themselves. In 1983, with Reaganomics in full swing, changes in the U.S. economic figures were overwhelmingly positive. Yet most stories aired by the big three networks on their evening news broadcasts presented a decidedly negative, gloomy image of the economy.

N O

Conservatives dominate radio and TV talk shows. Each night moderates and conservatives monopolize the Public Broadcasting Service's *MacNeil/Lehrer NewsHour*. According to Fairness and Accuracy in Reporting (FAIR), fewer than 10 percent of the guests hail from labor or public interest groups or minority organizations.

In many other television programs, right-wing conservatives—John McLaughlin, Pat Buchanan, William Buckley, and Rush Limbaugh—own the airwaves. Rebuttal from the left is conspicuously absent. Even the one designated liberal on *Crossfire,* Michael Kinsley, confesses he is not a true left-winger.

The conservative press is growing stronger. In only two years the circulation of the staunchly conservative magazine *Spectator* has jumped by 700 percent to 251,000. The circulation of *National Review* is also up dramatically.

The competitive spirit overrides political loyalties. Journalists by nature are skeptics, turning a doubting eye in *all* directions, not just to the right or to the left. The goal of most journalists is to find the truth and further their own careers.

Reporters work hard for impartiality. There is no hard evidence that reporters' personal views actually influence their stories. In fact, some journalists go to extremes to maintain their neutrality. Leonard Downie Jr., executive editor of *The Washington Post,* abstains from voting and encourages his staff to do likewise.

The media have proven to be no friend of Bill Clinton. If the news media have a liberal bias, what accounts for their less than gracious handling of Clinton during the 1992 presidential campaign? Some of the most scathing stories about Clinton originated at the supposedly liberal *New York Times* and *Los Angeles Times.* Clinton's Democratic affiliation provided him little protection from media charges ranging from adultery to political cronyism.

Since his election the media have steadily attacked Clinton on a host of issues. The media's obsession with the Whitewater inquiry removes any doubt that Clinton receives special treatment.

Background

Most Americans feel there is no place in the news for personal viewpoints and that journalists, whatever their convictions, should strive for total objectivity and fairness in reporting. Earlier generations grew up on a different kind of news. During the golden age of radio in the 1930s and 1940s, "news and comment" programs flourished. Journalists such as Lowell Thomas, Paul Harvey, and Ed Murrow recapped the news of the day, and then, based on their own personal views, provided informed analysis of those events.

With the Vietnam War and Watergate came a new breed of investigative journalist in pursuit of stories that would effect change. They brought with them an unrelenting desire for complete disclosure, provoking accusations of bias from all camps, but particularly from the right.

One of the loudest protests came in the late 1960s and early 1970s when then–Vice President Spiro Agnew publicly attacked the news media, the first senior government official to do so. Not surprisingly, he directed his attacks against the media he considered liberal. Agnew denounced television networks and newspapers with their multiple media holdings, contending that they held too much sway over public opinion. Republican politicians have led the attack against a supposedly liberal media bias ever since.

Today the federally subsidized PBS has emerged as the latest lightning rod for media criticism. A recent study conducted by the Center for Media and Public Affairs concluded that public television's programming does favor the liberal view. Another advocacy group, Fairness and Accuracy in Reporting, quickly countered with evidence of a conservative bias at PBS. While admitting that some documentaries do advance liberal themes, FAIR argued that a significant number of conservative commentators and pro-business personalities appear regularly on PBS programs, sometimes on a daily basis, to promote their views.

Unlike PBS, most major news agencies do not receive federal subsidies but are profit-driven businesses. Ten large business and financial corporations control the three major television and radio networks, as well as several dozen subsidiary TV stations, national magazines, newspapers, book publishers, and motion picture companies. As with any well-run business, the news media's first obligation is to turn a profit for their owners.

With corporate America controlling the purse strings of the news industry, some feel the American media have become too tame, too homogeneous. Differences between the three major networks' broadcasts are insubstantial. Each network straddles the same political fence, hesitant to shift too far in either direction for fear of alienating viewers or sponsors. Those complaining about the media's homogeneity argue that only a handful of programs, such as *Nightline,* provide an opportunity for real discussion or dissent.

What do journalists themselves say about bias? Many acknowledge that the very nature of their work can create an appearance of liberalism. It is their job to challenge the status quo, specifically those in power. From 1980 to 1992 that power rested with conservatives. By investigating possible wrongdoings within the Reagan and Bush administrations, the media inevitably elicited charges of biased reporting by those receiving the closest scrutiny. But many journalists dismiss the charge of liberal bias, admitting instead to an antiestablishment bias.

According to a January 1988 *Time*/Yankelovich poll, 46 percent of Americans believe the media tend to be fair in their reporting, 20 percent detect a liberal bias, 10 percent a conservative bias, and the remainder are not sure or cannot determine the type of bias.

Outlook

Despite the vigor with which the media have investigated President Bill and Hillary Clinton over Whitewater and other possible improprieties in Arkansas, conservatives argue that the media treat Clinton with kid gloves. Liberals claim that Whitewater proves the essential nonbias of reporters. Both sides will continue to present convincing statistics "proving" their point of view. This issue will never be resolved, nor is it likely to disappear.

36. Should the Government Regulate Violence on Television?

YES

Children watch far too much violence on television. According to an American Psychological Association study, the average American child watches twenty-seven hours of television each week. Before graduating from elementary school, an average American child sees 100,000 acts of violence and 8,000 murders on television.

Most of this violence does not occur on late-night television. According to the National Coalition on Television Violence, the average children's show contains thirty-two acts of violence per hour, compared with six per hour during prime time. With wide access to cable, pay-per-view, VCRs, and full-length movies, parents have difficulty controlling their children's access.

Exposure to violence leads to aggressive, antisocial behavior. In more than 3,000 studies conducted over the last three decades, social scientists proved that both children and adults imitate the violence they see on television. Young children in particular cannot distinguish between fantasy and reality. After watching the Ninja Turtles hit on television, children hit their friends. Some children feel like victims of violence. Others become so callous they lose all empathy for victims. Television teaches children that violence is the right way to resolve problems. Owing in part to television, youth violence has become a serious public health problem.

Studies of adults show the more violence a person watches, the more violence he or she exhibits. Suicide rates climb after dramas about suicide. Homicide rates rise after nationally televised boxing matches.

The television and entertainment industry has little incentive to regulate itself. Violence draws the largest audiences. The real business of these companies is not providing programs to audiences but rather providing audiences to advertisers. A reduction of violent programming directly hurts profits.

Despite thirty years of promising to voluntarily reduce violence on television, the industry has continually dragged its feet and obstructed efforts. Only binding regulations on the quantity and nature of violence will work.

N O

Studies of television violence contain serious flaws. Violence is a subjective judgment. Is a slapstick routine in which someone slips on a banana peel violent? Is a magic trick sawing a person in two? Pro-regulation activists count such incidents in their studies. How do you explain studies that reveal some children who watch "wholesome" shows like *Sesame Street* act aggressively afterwards?

Censorship of television programs violates the First Amendment. Our Constitution expressly provides for freedom of the press. With the exception of blatant obscenity, the government may not tell television networks what to broadcast or the public what to watch.

If we start by censoring violence on television, what comes next? The media must remain free or we will begin losing our democratic freedoms.

Where and how do you draw the line? How do you define unacceptable violence? Killing? Punches? A shove? A verbal insult? A raised voice? Should we censor a highly praised television documentary about the Civil War that contains all these forms of "violence"? Will we ban football games since they contain tackling? Should we edit out a car crash in a documentary about the dangers of drunk driving? Should we ban the TV show *America's Most Wanted,* which has helped capture several hundred fugitive criminals? The government should not be in the business of making such decisions.

Television simply provides what the public demands. Television, like most businesses, is market-driven. TV executives did not *create* an appetite for graphic or realistic depictions on television. The public wants these programs and has the right to watch them.

Television does not cause violence. Poverty, ignorance, poor education, easy access to guns, and alcohol and drug abuse lead to violence. The only way to create a more peaceful society is to attack these root causes.

Background

Congress held its first hearings on the impact of television violence on children in 1952, practically the dawn of television. Many more have followed. The National PTA, the American Medical Association, the American Academy of Pediatrics, the American Psychological Association, and other major groups have warned of the link between TV violence and aggressive behavior. Numerous organizations have formed to fight violence on TV. Yet the quantity and severity of violence have continued to escalate. Since the 1950s the television industry has argued that it can police itself.

In 1990, Senator Paul Simon (D-Illinois), one of the most outspoken critics of television, succeeded in his efforts to have Congress pass the Simon-Glickman Television Violence Act. It allows an antitrust exemption for the major networks to draft a common policy on violence. In December 1992, only a few days before House hearings on violence, the networks released a policy statement agreeing to control gratuitous violence and scenes glamorizing violence. They also promised to curtail realistic violence in children's programs, scenes where children are victims, and scenes combining sex and violence. The networks also agreed to show the *consequences* of violence.

In October 1993, Attorney General Janet Reno appeared at a Senate Commerce Committee hearing to threaten the television industry with government regulations if it failed to control violence itself. She argued that the regulation of violence is constitutionally permissible. The Supreme Court has never directly addressed the constitutionality of government restrictions on television content. However, in March 1994, Reno backed down by saying the television industry was making progress toward limiting violence.

Reno was responding to an announcement a month earlier in which most of the major TV and cable networks promised to fund an outside monitor to track and annually report on the violent content of programming. Senator Simon agreed this concession was a major turning point. Other critics of television feel different.

Advocates working to limit violence and sex on television range from the feminist left to the religious right. Some propose to expand the legal definition of obscenity to include things ranging from violent depictions of rape on television to the lyrics of satanic cults on rock videos. The current definition of obscenity, clarified in the 1973 Supreme Court decision *Miller* v. *California,* applies only to sex, not violence.

Many other proposals to limit violence have been debated. One would initiate a rating system, much like that used for movies, with a warning to flash on the screen before each show. The cable industry has endorsed a ratings system. Some critics propose tax breaks for TV companies that fund research on violence. Others suggest that the Federal Communications Commission (FCC) should levy fines on and withhold licenses from stations showing excessive violence, the method already used to control indecency.

One of the most dramatic ways to control violence involves using the so-called V-chip, a technology that would allow parents to block any program with certain violence ratings. The cable industry is amenable to this new technology, though the television networks resist it.

Despite all these proposals and an interested Congress, regulation is difficult to push through. The FCC may not police violence under current laws, which prohibit censorship. Few members of Congress want to risk infringing on First Amendment rights. Most still believe the best way to achieve a balance between retaining free speech and responsibility toward children is through industry self-regulation.

Outlook

With both Attorney General Reno and Senator Simon relaxing their pressure on the industry, government regulation seems unlikely anytime soon. Nevertheless, several senators and representatives continue to promote antiviolence legislation, particularly plans to use V-chip technology.

Entertainment trends will soon make regulation even more difficult. Before long, the three major networks will compete in most homes with hundreds of cable channels, home satellite services, and interactive multimedia, all of which contain violent programming. Many children will continue to watch whatever they wish.

37. Does Pornography Incite Violence Against Women?

YES

Pornography propels some men toward sex crimes. While no one can definitively determine what causes human behavior, studies have revealed that pornography can incite violence. From 1980 to 1985 Professor William Marshall of Queen's University, Ontario, Canada, studied 120 men who had raped women or molested children: for about 25 percent of these men, viewing pornography was a major catalyst propelling them toward deviant behavior. For men with certain personalities or those predisposed to commit sexual offenses, pornography can easily act as the trigger.

Some of the men Professor Marshall studied said they intended to use pornography for masturbation; after becoming aroused they decided to find a woman or child to rape. Others told Marshall they intended to rape before viewing pornography and deliberately used it to prepare themselves for a sexual assault.

The 1986 Attorney General's Commission on Pornography (the Meese Commission), led by then–Attorney General Edwin Meese, concluded that, when tested in a laboratory setting, exposure to violent pornography increased punitive behavior toward women.

Pornography sends many harmful messages. Pornography portrays women—and sometimes children—as easily accessible and willing objects of sexual abuse and exploitation. It breaks down all societal taboos against molestation and violence. It invites viewers to use and then discard women.

According to the 1986 Meese Commission, even pornographic magazines and films devoid of explicit violence usually portray women in humiliating or degrading poses. The commission concluded that extensive viewing of even these relatively tame materials leads the viewer to believe that rape or other forms of sexual violence are less harmful than they might otherwise believe.

Pornography itself is an act of violence against women. Feminist scholars like Catharine MacKinnon are right in saying pornography acts as an inducement and spur to rapists, much like ordering a trained attack dog to "Kill!" Pornography literally acts as a form of assault.

N O

Most researchers agree pornography has not been proven to cause violence. The United States first considered this issue seriously in 1970 when a commission appointed by President Lyndon Johnson found no credible data linking exposure to pornography with delinquent or criminal sexual conduct.

For political reasons, the 1986 Meese Commission tried very hard to find such a link. It asked for an independent review of existing evidence showing a relationship between sexually explicit materials and violent sex crimes. The review, by Professor Edna Einsiedel of the University of Calgary, found no such link. The commission then asked Surgeon General Dr. C. Everett Koop to find evidence. Aside from one irrelevant study conducted under laboratory conditions, Dr. Koop found that crimes are not inspired by viewing *nonviolent* pornography. Commissions in Denmark, Canada, and England also found no link between pornography and violence.

Pornography may actually reduce sexual crimes. According to a recent Danish study, the incidence of rape and other sexual offenses has declined in countries with freer access to pornography than the United States. The study reviewed rape reports from 1964 through 1984 in Denmark, West Germany, Sweden, and the United States. Only the United States—where local obscenity laws are often strict—reported an increase in rapes.

Pornography acts as a masturbatory safety valve that prevents rape. Feminists who call pornography a form of violence against women ignore its major benefit: pornography provides a harmless release for men.

Viewing violence, not pornography, inspires violence. According to Professor Edward Donnerstein, a University of Wisconsin psychologist and key witness at the Meese Commission hearings, exposure to violence can lead to violent behavior. Movies like *Rambo* cause increased violent tendencies, as do explicitly violent pornographic movies. But if you remove the violent scenes from either type of movie, violent tendencies in the viewers disappear. If you remove the sexual content but leave the violence in, violent tendencies remain.

Background

The possible link between pornography and violence is at the center of several issues, most importantly censorship. Pornography is defined as any writings, photographs, movies, or drawings that show sexual activities. Using this definition, an August 1993 poll by the National Opinion Research Center found that 57 percent of Americans believe pornography leads people to commit rape, 34 percent do not believe so, and 9 percent do not know. Pornographic films actually depict less explicit violence than commonly thought. Two recent studies of such films found that sexual violence occupies approximately 4 percent and nonsexual violence another 4 percent of their running times. The explicit violence in pornographic films has declined since 1970, while such films have become more sexually explicit.

Materials showing sexual acts involving anyone under eighteen are illegal. Other pornographic materials receive protection under the First Amendment right to free speech. However, individual communities may censor pornography as they see fit. In 1973 the Supreme Court decreed that sexually explicit materials could be judged obscene if an average local person finds them "patently offensive," if the materials are sexually "morbid or shameful" by local community standards, and if the materials lack political, artistic, scientific, or literary value. Not only can a community bar pornography, but the producers and distributors of such materials may also be subject to criminal prosecution. However, few people have been indicted on obscenity charges. Local courts tend to protect First Amendment rights despite the eagerness of some prosecutors to jail pornographers in response to outraged juries.

Efforts to censor pornography have frequently pitted conservatives, the pro-family lobby, and the religious right against the press, the American Civil Liberties Union (ACLU), and liberals. In recent years some prominent feminists, particularly Professor Catharine MacKinnon of the University of Michigan Law School and essayist Andrea Dworkin, have taken up the battle against pornography. Their radical argument that all heterosexual sex is a power struggle in which men assert their dominance over women led to a novel attempt to ban pornography. They maintain that because pornography harms women, it violates their civil rights. In the early 1980s they succeeded in having the Minnesota legislature pass an ordinance defining pornography as discrimination against women. Any woman who felt harmed by a pornographic image could seek redress from the local Civil Rights Commission. The ordinance was declared unconstitutional in 1985. MacKinnon has also helped write antipornography laws in Canada.

Conservatives hope to fight pornography by gaining financial compensation for its alleged victims. In 1992, Senator Mitch McConnell (R-Kentucky) sponsored the Pornography Victims' Compensation Act, which would permit victims of sex crimes and other violence allegedly inspired by obscene materials to sue the producers and distributors responsible for those materials. The act was often referred to as the Bundy bill because serial killer Ted Bundy blamed pornography as the cause of his crimes. Despite support from the religious right and the feminist left, the act has so far failed to pass Congress.

Early versions of the act that sought to allow lawsuits against all kinds of sexually explicit materials were clearly unconstitutional. The 1992 version targeted only child pornography and obscene materials, neither of which receive protection from the First Amendment. But many liberals worry that the act's vague language would seriously impinge on the First Amendment. It could define many relatively tame movies and pop songs as child pornography. Even worse, the act could scare the media out of printing or broadcasting any crime stories that might inspire "copycat" crimes—a substantial infringement on free speech.

Outlook

Does pornography really incite violence against women? The antipornography lobby would receive a tremendous boost from strong evidence linking the two. While little evidence shows that pornography directly causes violence, pornography is probably one influence among many for men with a proclivity for sexual violence. Without strong evidence in either direction, the courts will probably continue to grant considerable First Amendment protection to pornographers, and federal antipornography legislation will continue to fail.

38. Should Same-Sex Marriages Be Legal?

YES

Marriage laws discriminate against gays socially. Marriage is much more than a mere private contract. Marriage endorses a couple's integrity and their acceptance by civil society. Through marriage, the state, our community, and our families publicly recognize the emotional and economic commitment of two people who wish to spend their lives together. Denying the 25 million gay Americans so basic a right is oppressive.

Gays contribute to society in countless ways. Like all of us, they work, vote, and pay taxes. Why shouldn't they be allowed the simple dignity of marriage just like everyone else?

Marriage laws also discriminate economically. In most places, gays cannot acquire the many tangible benefits conferred by marriage, including coverage under their spouse's health and pension plan, and the right to inherit property free of taxation. Although fringe benefits can make up to 40 percent of a worker's compensation, gay spouses rarely receive them.

Gays can be shut out if their partner dies. Gays often lose the right to visit their lover in the hospital and the authority to make medical decisions and funeral arrangements. The surviving partner even loses the right to continue living in a rent-controlled apartment if his or her name is not on the lease.

Encouraging monogamy helps curb the AIDS tragedy. Laws recognizing gay marriage will help to legitimate monogamy and curb promiscuity. Among other benefits will be a reduction in the spread of AIDS.

Gays should no longer need to hide their sexuality. Despite the increased opening of society, many gays still feel compelled to conceal their lifestyle. Gays who come out of the closet may lose their jobs or be rejected by their parents. By accepting the legality of gay marriage, however, society can help to bring greater mainstream acceptance to gays, diminishing the emotional hardships and discrimination they suffer.

N O

Procreation is a main purpose of marriage. Beyond partnership, the main function of marriage is to provide an economic and psychological foundation in which to successfully rear children. With the exception of a tiny minority of gays and lesbians who bear or adopt children, most homosexuals do not become parents.

All governments establish laws to promote continuation of human life on the planet. Society must favor certain practices and discourage others. We can best serve the future by encouraging heterosexual marriages and the families they usually produce.

Gays can easily gain many legal and economic protections. Any two people, including gay couples, can use joint-tenancy agreements, power-of-attorney agreements, proxies, wills, insurance policies, and other documents to obtain many of the benefits shared by married couples. No material need exists for our nation to recast its most sacred institution.

The gay lifestyle sends a wrong message to the young. Despite more than a decade of safe-sex public education, homosexual sex remains a major cause of spreading AIDS. In the midst of the AIDS epidemic, legalizing homosexual marriage sends the message to young people that gay sex is an acceptable choice.

We must not discard our Judeo-Christian traditions. All our religious, moral, and legal codes support heterosexual marriage and the traditional family unit. Alternative lifestyles should be tolerated, but we cannot simply throw away thousands of years of our established marriage customs just to please a vocal minority.

Our nation is in the midst of a social and moral breakdown. Many of our problems stem from the decline of our ethical codes and the dramatic reduction of traditional two-parent families. We need to reaffirm—not dilute—our social and moral traditions by fostering heterosexual marriages. To legalize gay marriage announces our government's acceptance of our moral decline.

Background

The movement to accord gay marriage the same legal and economic standing as heterosexual marriage has taken several small steps forward in recent years. In 1989, when a New York court declared a gay couple a "family," it permitted surviving partners in unmarried straight or gay couples to assume possession over rent-controlled apartments. In 1990, San Francisco voters approved "domestic partners" legislation that permits any two people living together to register themselves, agreeing to share joint expenses. These two cities and a few others allow sick and bereavement leave to the domestic partners of city employees. Only a few cities, all in California, provide health or dental benefits to domestic partners. Dozens of well-known corporations, including Warner Brothers and Apple Computer, recently began providing domestic partnership benefits to gays.

Despite these small changes no city or state permits same-sex marriages, but gays in several states are challenging existing laws. A gay couple has filed a discrimination suit against Washington, D.C., for refusing them a marriage license. The suit charges the city violated the basic human rights of these men because D.C. law forbids discrimination on the basis of sexual orientation. The case is slowly working its way through the courts.

In the strongest challenge to existing marriage laws, three lesbian and gay couples sued Hawaii for the right to same-sex marriages. Hawaii is famous for its multicultural population, liberalism, and tolerance of diversity. A lawyer for the couples identified more than four hundred sections in Hawaii's state laws that grant benefits to married couples, ranging from insurance and employment benefits to lower prices for wildlife licenses.

In May 1993 the Hawaiian Supreme Court ruled that depriving these couples of legal and financial benefits violated the due process clause of the Hawaiian Constitution, which prohibits discrimination based on gender. The Hawaiian Supreme Court sent the case back to the circuit court to decide if the state has a compelling interest in maintaining the ban on gay marriages.

In May 1994 the Hawaiian state legislature, pressured by fundamentalist Christians, passed a law limiting marriage to male-female couples. They hope to bolster the state's position in court that its compelling interest must deny same-sex marriages. A state constitutional amendment to exclude gay marriages failed to pass the legislature despite prevailing public opinion. A January 1994 Honolulu *Star-Bulletin* poll found 58 percent of Hawaiians oppose same-sex marriages, 32 percent favor them, while 10 percent remain undecided.

Many American gays believe that several years from now society will accept the equality of gay marriages, much as interracial marriages required time to become sanctioned. When the Supreme Court declared bans on interracial marriage unconstitutional in 1967, fifteen states still prohibited them.

Some gays feel that while equality in the military serves to measure gays' acceptance as citizens, only gay marriages will signal society's acceptance of gays as full members. Some radical gays, however, disapprove of the push for gay marriage. They argue that gay lifestyles— unique, liberating expressions of change and nontradition—should not attempt to fit into traditional heterosexual institutions. These radicals believe gays should not try to emulate a society that has rejected them.

Only two countries, Sweden and Denmark, recognize same-sex marriages. Denmark's 1989 Registered Partnership Act allows any same-sex couple to register themselves and receive the same rights as married heterosexuals in such areas as inheritance, alimony, and taxation. However, gays may not adopt children and lesbians may not legally obtain sperm from a sperm bank in either country. Lesbians may inseminate themselves if a private donor makes himself available.

Outlook

If the Hawaiian circuit court rules in favor of gay marriages, that will probably set the stage for suits against discriminatory laws in many other states. Other states would then also need to decide if they should accept all Hawaiian marriages. Meanwhile, in localities where no one has yet challenged marriage laws in court, activists will continue to agitate for domestic partners benefits.

Insurance companies, fearing the costs of treating AIDS patients, have so far refused to underwrite health insurance policies for domestic partners. Unless the insurance industry changes its position, or the courts rule insurance practices discriminatory, only self-insured cities or companies making special arrangements will offer health benefits to domestic partners.

39. Should African-Americans Receive Preferential Treatment in Hiring and College Admissions?

YES

We must remedy the past sufferings of African-Americans and other minorities. Blacks have suffered institutionalized discrimination ever since their ancestors were forcibly brought to this country. Just as America feels a moral obligation to give special preferences to our war veterans for their past sufferings, so too have blacks earned a certain preferential treatment. Just as victims of industrial accidents and Holocaust survivors have been compensated for terrible wrongs, so too should blacks be compensated.

So-called race-neutral hiring policies actually discriminate against minorities. More than 85 percent of all available jobs are never advertised. You can learn about many jobs only through word of mouth. But most blacks cannot tie into the "old boy network" through which they might hear about these jobs or be recommended for them. The playing field is not even. Unless we make special efforts to compensate minorities for their lack of access, they will continue to suffer discrimination.

America's workplace is still segregated by race. More than 50 percent of America's garbage collectors and maids are black, while only 4 percent of our managers and 3 percent of our lawyers and doctors are black. Since the days of slavery blacks have been denied good jobs. Only affirmative action can break this legacy.

Affirmative action strengthens the black middle class. Since the Civil Rights Act of 1964, affirmative action by employers has helped enlarge the black middle class. These affirmative action procedures and programs give some minority citizens an equal chance. Blacks now work alongside whites in middle-level, blue-collar, and government jobs they were previously denied. Affirmative action must be maintained and expanded to allow employed minorities to rise above the "glass ceiling" and attain top management positions. At the other end of the spectrum, poor minorities must also get preferential treatment in order to rise from poverty and unemployment.

N O

Affirmative action fosters a victim mentality among African-Americans. Preference programs enforce the black identity as victims of past and present racism. African-Americans desperately need to move beyond this mindset. Many minorities come to question their *own* qualifications. This self-doubt hurts African-Americans deeply. Individuals must ultimately succeed or fail on an equal basis, in open competition. Otherwise, their achievements will always be tainted.

Preference programs create racial tensions. White students and workers expect to receive an equal chance to attend good colleges and advance at work. Righting the wrongs of the past sounds noble. But why should today's whites have to suffer from society's past mistakes? Affirmative action programs give rise to resentment and racial tensions.

Whites are sometimes the victims of reverse discrimination. Although banned by the Civil Rights Act of 1964, a quota system for hiring exists in many organizations. Until recently, some employment test scores were adjusted to create results that fit racial quotas ("race-norming"). Many colleges today admit low-scoring minorities instead of whites with substantially higher test scores. It is unfair to discriminate against whites so other groups can excel.

Affirmative action makes people question the credentials of minorities. Any individual who benefits from a preference program is assumed to be less qualified for the job or school than other candidates. Since the reasons for hiring decisions and college admissions are usually secret, no one knows who benefits from these programs. As a result, the majority feel that *all* minority workers and students are less qualified than their majority counterparts.

Affirmative action has failed to create a more equal society. Most of the beneficiaries of these programs—middle-class blacks—were already positioned to take advantage of them. Ghetto dwellers and the rural poor have gained nothing, although these are the very people affirmative action was supposed to help.

Background

Affirmative action means different things to different people. To Democrats and liberals, it refers to programs, policies, and hiring procedures that remedy and prevent discrimination against minorities, women, and others. To Republicans and conservatives, it refers to an unfair quota system.

The term was first popularized by President John Kennedy in 1961 in an executive order. Federal contractors, he decreed, must use "affirmative action to ensure that applicants are employed . . . without regard to their race, creed, color, or national origin." Subsequent executive orders, judicial decisions, and the Civil Rights Acts of 1964 and of 1991 amplified the use of affirmative action by employers. The Equal Employment Act of 1972 requires all educational institutions receiving federal funds to admit students without discrimination.

Surprisingly, it was the Nixon administration in 1968 that first mandated specific goals for hiring African-Americans. After that many employers and universities moved quietly from goals to quotas.

The first serious challenge to affirmative action came in the 1970s when Allan Bakke, a white medical student denied admission to a California medical school because of its quota system, claimed he was a victim of reverse discrimination. The Supreme Court held (5–4) in *Regents of the University of California* v. *Bakke* that rigid quotas for minority applicants to medical school are not permitted if white students may not compete on an equal basis. However, the Court also stated that race could be a factor in admissions policy. Bakke was eventually admitted.

In later decisions the Court has allowed employers to voluntarily use affirmative action for removing obvious racial imbalances in their workforce. Race or gender, the Court ruled, may be used as *a* factor, *but not the major factor,* in hiring.

Affirmative action is one of today's most paradoxical issues. Many local, state, and federal laws require employers to avoid discrimination on up to nine criteria: race, color, sex, national origin, religion, age, handicap, veteran's status, and sexual preference. At the same time, affirmative action laws require certain employers to give preference to racial minorities, women, and others. For example, companies doing work for the federal government must follow complex procedures that include determining which minorities are underrepresented, creating plans to achieve racial or gender balance, and ensuring that employees meet minimum qualifications. Failure to properly implement plans can result in legal action from minorities claiming racism or from whites claiming reverse discrimination.

Many African-American leaders resent affirmative action for non-blacks. Women and certain ethnic groups now receiving preferential treatment have not suffered oppression or discrimination anything like the legacy of slavery and segregation imposed on blacks. As a result, blacks compete with women and other minorities for limited affirmative action benefits.

In recent years many advocates of preferential hiring policies have adopted the term "diversity" to replace affirmative action. President Clinton is the first president to make diversity a policy at the highest levels. He stated during his presidential campaign that his administration and cabinet would "look like America."

Outlook

The key questions regarding affirmative action are: How much is enough? When will it end? Critics of affirmative action point to the large advances made by the black middle class. We can no longer justify affirmative action policies that discriminate against whites and perpetuate a victim status among blacks, say its critics.

Advocates of affirmative action point out that black unemployment, already twice as high as white unemployment, is expected to grow. The average black still earns only $56 for each $100 earned by the average white. Blacks are still absent from the vast majority of senior level positions in companies and academia. According to the Equal Employment Opportunity Commission, black workers were the only group to suffer a net loss of jobs during the 1990–91 recession. Many blacks and liberals argue that the time has not yet come to end affirmative action.

What will change? Neither new legislation nor court cases will likely transform the affirmative action landscape for a long time. Democratic administrations will seek to increase minority employment through affirmative action, while Republican administrations will fight anything resembling quotas.

40. Do Children in Day Care Suffer Problems Because of Their Parents' Absence?

YES

Nothing can replace a parent's love. While some day care workers may be loving and committed, many are overworked and undertrained. The child care industry employs some of the lowest-paid workers with the highest turnover rates in the country. Their relationship with children is temporary and commercial. Even if day care workers want to give special attention to the children, they cannot always find time. The high ratio of children to workers in some centers means much of the time gets spent changing diapers and providing for other basic needs, rather than in nurturing.

On the other hand, most parents truly love their children and feel eternally bound to them. Especially in the first year of life, children need a level of personal attention and nurturing that only a stay-at-home parent can provide.

Day care children get sick more often. According to a 1980 Centers for Disease Control and Prevention study, children in large, licensed day care centers are more likely to suffer from severe diarrhea, hepatitis, and other diseases. The more hours children spend there and the larger the facility, the more these diseases spread. The superior sanitary conditions at home cannot possibly be re-created in a large institution where workers touch one child after another.

Children in day care suffer psychologically. Studies show that babies in nonmaternal child care more than twenty hours per week during their first year are at increased risk for psychological and behavioral problems later. Day care babies tend not to reattach themselves quickly when reunited with their mother. Day care toddlers tend to kick, hit, argue, and threaten more than children at home. Day care children are less verbal or attentive and less persistent in solving difficult problems. At eight to ten years old these children are still more aggressive and disobedient.

N O

Day care can benefit children. A study found that children growing up in day care while their low-income, unmarried mothers worked scored higher on second-grade math tests than similar children who stayed at home with a mother who did not work.

As a result of their increased stimulation, day care children often jump ahead academically six to nine months, although children raised at home do catch up later. Day care children tend to be less fearful or timid in new situations. They make new friends more easily and learn to cooperate with others. Being at home all day with a parent may not provide enough excitement or variety of experience.

Studies demonstrating psychological problems resulting from day care are flawed. How can you tell what a one year-old is really thinking or what her reactions to her mother really mean in a laboratory setting? In laboratory tests, the day care children's slightly higher tendency to ignore their mother upon reunion may simply mean they show precocious independence, which other children will learn later.

The study of infant development is young and riddled with guess-work. Many studies ignore key factors like the quality of day care. According to Deborah Phillips, professor of psychology at the University of Virginia, no unusual psychological problems arise in well-regarded day care centers where children receive consistent care from the same people.

Children in day care often come from families experiencing financial stress or families in which parents focus more on their careers than on domestic life. These factors, rather than the day care itself, may well cause the psychological problems observed in these studies.

You cannot shelter children from certain diseases. Those kept at home may temporarily avoid exposure to measles, mumps, chicken pox, and colds. Unfortunately, most will contract the usual childhood illnesses once they attend kindergarten or first grade.

Background

Child-rearing methods, like clothing fashions, change overtime. As recently as 1928, John B. Watson, a famed psychologist of his day, advised parents in a child-rearing book that children should never be hugged or kissed or held in our laps. Instead, he advised, we should shake hands with our children to greet them in the morning. During the 1950s day care was unpopular. By the late 1970s, with vast numbers of women entering the workplace, day care became necessary and fashionable, only to fall somewhat from favor today. However, social and economic forces have made day care an integral part of American life. Real earnings of American workers declined by 13 percent from 1973 to 1990, necessitating two paychecks for many families.

Today approximately 80,000 day care centers look after more than 4 million American children. Family day care—where parents in their own home look after other people's children—accounts for another 3.1 million. Owing to the large number of two-income parents and a divorce rate that has resulted in so many single-parent homes, parents spend an average of only seventeen waking hours per week with their children.

In 1986, Jay Belsky, a child development expert at Penn State University, published an article proclaiming that children who spend more than twenty hours per week in day care during their first thirteen months of life suffered higher rates of developmental and behavioral problems later. Belsky relied on the Strange Situation Test, in which a young child is left alone with his mother, with a stranger, or both for varying lengths of time. Depending on how easily the mother can calm the stressed child, psychologists determine how securely attached the child is to his mother. Some researchers believe that insecurely attached young children—whether raised at home or in day care—suffer more psychological problems later. The research of Belsky and others found day care children to be less securely attached.

Belsky's findings were disputed by psychologists for a variety of scientific reasons, and by nonpsychologists for political reasons. Belsky, like other male child psychologists who found evidence of problems among day care children, was discredited by feminists and liberal academics for implying that women should leave the workplace and return to the home. Social thinkers at some Republican think tanks and at conservative and religious colleges believe that women's entry into the workplace has harmed a great number of American children. These conservatives openly call for women to stop working until their children go to school. Feminists argue that nothing should prevent women from enjoying their hard-won gains. Since women are expected to fill 60 percent of new jobs by the year 2000, the U.S. economy would suffer without their contributions. Feminists say that if day care causes problems, the government and employers need to subsidize better day care facilities.

Outlook

Despite disturbing evidence that early day care may cause problems in some children, when parents feel comfortable leaving their children in a high-quality center the children generally thrive. Even if parents feel guilty about leaving their children, the economic realities will not change.

It seems unlikely that further study by child psychologists will uncover dramatic, conclusive evidence that children suffer serious problems from day care. No one contests that unsanitary, poorly run, understaffed facilities are less desirable than upscale day care centers. No one contests that children in large groups who receive little personal attention thrive less than those in smaller groups. But proving that children in decent centers suffer will be difficult.

Most countries assist more than the United States does with caring for young children. Many European governments help pay for or at least regulate large networks of day care centers. Although U.S. lawmakers have considered a variety of measures to ease the burden on parents, nothing beyond tax credits for low-income families exists today. Although President Clinton has talked about helping parents with day care, he is more concerned with advancing two other child-related programs—Head Start and immunization.

41. Should Immigration to the United States Be Drastically Reduced?

YES

The United States is already overpopulated. At the turn of the century we needed thousands of new workers to settle the frontiers and increase our industrial base. But today we suffer from high unemployment, serious air and water pollution, depletion of forests and other natural resources, massive landfills, traffic jams, and a host of other problems caused by overpopulation. Why are we allowing immigration when our population, already 255 million, is expected to grow by 50 percent to 383 million in 2050?

We cannot afford any more immigrants. The largest number of immigrants—over 6.5 million—have settled in California. These immigrants cost California alone an estimated $3 billion annually in extra health care, schooling, and other public services, even *after* you deduct tax revenues contributed by these newcomers.

Immigration harms poor blacks and other disadvantaged groups economically. One-third of new immigrants are high school dropouts. These uneducated newcomers compete directly with poor urban blacks for jobs, educational opportunities, low-income housing, and human services. Across the nation 40 percent of black youths cannot find work, compared with a general unemployment rate of about 6 percent. America must first solve the problems of our own poor. Why do we allow the foreign poor to jeopardize the chances of our own people?

Immigrants endanger American culture. Many foreigners today settle in enclaves of their own people, clinging to their language and cultures. We need to remain a melting pot, not become a salad bowl in which the fractious elements clash.

We should train our own workers, not import skilled foreigners. We may face serious social conflicts in the future unless we prepare our own workers for high-wage jobs and stop relying on skilled immigrant labor. America could become a two-tiered society with a third of our population earning high wages while two-thirds remain stuck in low-wage jobs competing unsuccessfully with the Third World.

N O

Immigrants invigorate America. People who immigrate to the United States are typically younger, healthier, more enterprising and determined, and less afraid of risk than the general population. These traits will help the United States compete in the world economy. Immigrants bring the old-fashioned virtues of hard work, discipline, and family responsibility. Early immigrants built our nation. Newer immigrants can now revitalize it.

Immigrants increase employment. A recent study by the Urban Institute found that each hundred new adult immigrants results in forty-six new jobs. Each hundred people born in the United States results in only twenty-five new jobs.

Immigrants contribute substantially to the U.S. economy. They earn $240 billion and pay over $90 billion in taxes annually. In contrast, recent immigrants receive only an estimated $5 billion in welfare payments a year.

Illegal immigrants support our service industries. We need dishwashers, fruit pickers, nannies, clothing makers, and sweatshop workers to help run our economy. Most Americans will not take these low-wage jobs. In fact, poor immigrants usually take only low-paying jobs that most ghetto dwellers do not want.

Educated immigrants fill jobs no one else can. For the foreseeable future we face a shortage of American-born engineers, chemists, mathematicians, physicists, nurses, and certain business executives. To remain competitive we must fill these high-tech jobs *now*. Without employing highly educated and competent immigrants we would already have fallen behind in developing new medical, computer, electronic, and pharmaceutical technologies. If the United States fails to attract these people, they will immigrate to nations with which we compete economically.

By investing in immigrants, we invest in our own future. The most important natural resource today is human capital. Immigrants bring ideas, the work ethic, and sometimes even capital to our shores. They start businesses, create jobs, and pay taxes. Immigrants help build our future.

Background

Do immigrants harm or help the U.S. economy? The Hudson Institute of America polled thirty-eight top economists, including seven Nobel Prize winners. More than 80 percent of them believe the economic effect of immigration in this century has been very positive. The others said it was slightly positive. For the future, two-thirds believe higher immigration levels will lead to higher standards of living in the United States.

In the 1980s the United States received 8.7 million new immigrants, a number equaled only in the first decade of this century. Today a million new immigrants arrive each year, including at least 200,000 illegals. The United States takes in more immigrants than the rest of the world *combined.* Until the mid-1960s most of these immigrants came from Europe. Today's immigrants come mainly from Asia and Latin America.

Throughout history we have blamed new immigrants for our troubles, particularly during periods of economic stagnation and unemployment. Today, with so many immigrants knocking on the door of the United States and Europe, the mood against them appears particularly ugly. In Germany, foreigners fear for their lives. France now admits no new immigrants.

Of the million immigrants arriving in the United States each year, half are close relatives, spouses, or children of U.S. citizens or permanent residents. About 26 percent of the million earned college degrees, slightly more than native-born Americans. However, 33 percent dropped out of high school, compared to 13 percent of natives. California receives the largest share of immigrants, both Latin American and Asian. Half of all illegal immigrants currently live there.

In response to concerns about illegal immigrants, Congress passed the 1986 Immigration Reform and Control Act. It grants amnesty to illegals residing in the United States before 1982, but punishes employers for hiring future illegals. Congress next passed the 1990 Immigration Act, which increased legal immigration to 700,000 annually and changed the distribution of visas. The government tripled to 140,000 annually the number of immigrants admitted for their special skills, while reducing unskilled immigration from 30,000 to 10,000.

Congress made few people happy. High-tech businesses want Congress to further ease immigration for skilled foreign workers. They argue America must take more advantage of the brain drain from other countries. Hotels, restaurants, and the garment industry decry the reduction of low-paid, low-skill immigrants. Unemployed Americans at all wage levels, rightly or wrongly, blame foreigners for taking their jobs.

According to a September 1993 *Time*/CNN poll, 60 percent of Americans favor changes in federal law to reduce legal immigration to the United States. Eighty-five percent favor such changes to reduce illegal immigration. But our 1,400-mile-long border with Mexico and the ease with which ships can arrive from Haiti and China make that task very difficult.

In the November 1994 election 59 percent of Californians voted for Proposition 187, dubbed "Save Our State" by its sponsors. This proposition sought to exclude all undocumented aliens from receiving any welfare services, nonemergency medical care, and schooling paid for by the state. Under the proposition, doctors and teachers would be required to report suspected illegals to state authorities and to the Immigration and Naturalization Service. Inspired by California's financial woes, Proposition 187 was intended to diminish that state's attractiveness to future undocumented aliens. Shortly after the election, opponents filed numerous lawsuits, claiming the proposition is unconstitutional and illegal. Judges immediately issued restraining orders blocking most of the proposition's measures.

Outlook

The future of the immigration issue rests with California's courts and the United States Supreme Court, which may take years to decide the constitutionality and legality of Proposition 187. The Republican-controlled Congress, responding to voter anger, will probably propose legislation to limit illegals. But since the Supreme Court has substantially protected the rights of illegal residents in earlier rulings, the anti-immigration movement may enjoy limited success.

President Clinton is taking several initiatives to control the flow of immigrants. The Immigration and Naturalization Service will expand and streamline its processing of up to one million immigrants claiming political asylum. Clinton also hopes to better patrol our border with Mexico by adding more than a thousand new agents in 1995. Clinton's immigration agreement with Cuba will probably control the flood of boat people from that nation.

The debate on welfare reform may put new pressure on curbing immigration. Some House members want to end the $4 billion paid annually in welfare and related payments to illegal immigrants. With an improving U.S. economy, proposals to radically slow immigration will likely fail. Too many American companies now require foreigners to fill positions for which Americans do not qualify.

Governing the
Government

42. Should There Be Term Limits for Politicians?

YES

Term limits reduce the power of special interests. Studies by such groups as Citizens for a Sound Economy and the National Taxpayers Union reveal that our legislators associate themselves with more special interest groups the longer they remain in office. Term limits might inspire legislators to protect the public interest rather than serve the monied interests.

Term limits encourage ability, not durability. The real power in Congress rests in the chairmanships of the most prestigious committees. Today these chairs belong to senators and representatives with the most seniority, not those with the most talent and vision. Without term limits, our legislators care more about protecting their government careers than confronting our most serious problems.

Term limits reduce wasteful spending. The favorite method for members of Congress to guarantee reelection is to send home pork-barrel projects. Without term limits Congress receives no incentive to cut pork.

Term limits make elections more competitive. Most elections to Congress and state legislatures merely perpetuate the status quo. Incumbent senators and representatives, with their free post office letter-stamping privileges, large staffs, unfair campaign finance laws, campaign contributions from lobbyists, and easy media access, enjoy a huge advantage over challengers.

Except for the extremely unusual 1994 election, turnover rates in the House have averaged only 5 to 10 percent per election. In 1988, only six of 405 incumbents running for relection lost.

The framers of the Constitution originally intended to have term limits for members of Congress. The Continental Congress, which preceded our present Congress, allowed delegates to serve for only three years. The framers believed limits would ensure a fresh supply of "citizen-legislators" who reflected their constituents' wishes. Although term limits were omitted from the final draft of our Constitution, many delegates assumed that limits would be voluntary.

N O

Why discard our most experienced and valuable legislators? Senators and representatives must cope with extremely complicated issues, legislation, and government bureaucracies. It takes many years to become competent in handling these complexities and the accompanying workload. Experienced legislators are strong assets we need to keep.

Term limits would only increase the power of the bureaucracy and special interests. New legislators are notoriously malleable and open to temptation. They need a quick introduction to the mechanics of government, the parliamentary and legal tricks, and the complex issues. The bureaucrats and special interests will gladly "help" these inexperienced legislators. We would end up with a government run by insider lobbyists and staffers, not by elected representatives of the people.

Lame duck representatives pay less attention to their constituents. Member of Congress who know they will not face the voters again have little incentive to follow their wishes.

Term limits encourage corruption. With only six or eight years in office, elected officials wishing to take personal advantage of their position will hurry to do so. In many southern states, which have limited governors to one or two terms since the end of the last century, corruption and self-interest have hardly been curbed.

Term limits are unconstitutional. The Constitution has only three requirements to serve as a representative in Congress: a person must be twenty-five years old, a U.S. citizen for at least seven years, and live in the state he or she will represent. The Constitution says nothing about term limits.

Citizens vote out unresponsive officials without needing term limits. The 1992 and 1994 elections demonstrate that the electorate can clean house without help. Nearly half the members of the Congress convened in January 1995 have been in office only since January 1993.

Background

Not since the tax protests of the 1970s has a populist issue swept so quickly into the political spotlight. Term limits could well become a fact of life by the end of this decade. It is an issue politicians find hateful but cannot ignore.

America's anger with its elected politicians exploded in the late 1980s and remains active in the mid-1990s. That anger expressed itself in the 19 million votes cast for Ross Perot in the 1992 presidential election and the massive defeat of congressional incumbents two years later. Voter disillusionment has also resulted in ballot initiatives for congressional term limits, which have been passed in a total of twenty-two states. Colorado started the trend in 1990 when 71 percent of its citizens voted for term limits in a referendum. According to recent polls, approximately 70 percent of Americans favor term limits nationwide.

American anger at Congress has been exacerbated by the recent flood of ethics violations, sex and drug scandals, the forced resignations of House Speaker Jim Wright and Democratic whip Tony Coelho, the House banking scandal, the savings and loan bailout, the Keating Five affair, and the large pay raises Congress voted itself. In the 1994 elections voter dissatisfaction with President Clinton, and a belief that Washington cannot solve major problems, resulted in a Republican takeover of Congress and the success of term limits referenda in seven states.

Traditionally, those working to institute term limits included angry citizens bent on vengeance against Congress, people who believe legislative careerism conflicts with the public good, Republicans hoping to dislodge the Democratic majority in the House, and pro-business conservatives with the same motive. Prominent Republicans in Congress have promised to introduce a congressional amendment calling for limits.

Some advocates believe term limits must accompany reforms in campaign finance laws. Since campaigns cost so much, only the wealthy or those heavily financed by special interests can win against incumbents. But if controls on the sources and amounts of campaign spending accompany term limits, neither party and no special interest group will garner an advantage.

Not surprisingly, many incumbents in Congress and state legislatures oppose limits. But few risk the self-serving image of speaking out forcefully on the issue. Former House Speaker Thomas S. Foley is a notable exception. In 1992 voters in Washington State approved a referendum to guarantee "a reasonable degree of rotation in office." The law limits senators to twelve years and House members to six years. Foley represented a congressional district in eastern Washington that voted against term limits 53 percent to 47 percent. Claiming to follow the will of his constituents, Foley filed a lawsuit in federal district court in Seattle arguing that term limits impose an additional qualification for members of Congress not cited by the Constitution. He then lost the 1994 election, partly due to the increasing popularity of term limits.

In February 1994 a federal district judge in Seattle ruled the state's new term limits law unconstitutional because it adds qualifications for congressional candidates beyond the three called for in the Constitution—citizenship, age, and residency. In March 1994 the Arkansas Supreme Court struck down that state's restrictions on incumbents. It ruled that term limits remove uniform qualifications for officeholders, creating imbalances among the states. In Arkansas, 60 percent of voters chose term limits.

Outlook

The constitutionality of term limits will probably be decided by the U.S. Supreme Court, which has agreed to review the Arkansas Supreme Court ruling. Will the Court find in favor of congressional term limits? In 1969, when the House tried to deny a member his seat due to misconduct, the Court allowed him to retain the seat because he met the three qualifications for the office. But since then the Court has become much more accepting of states' rights issues. Certain states have successfully circumvented the Constitution by banning certain offices, including membership in Congress, to convicted felons.

Aside from a Supreme Court ruling, the only other way term limits can become accepted law is through a constitutional amendment. Republicans in Congress—so long in the minority—were frequent supporters of term limits. It remains to be seen if Republicans—now in the majority and believing they can retain power in future elections—will aggressively push through a term limits amendment. In the meantime, signature drives continue nationwide to place term limit referenda on the ballots of additional states.

43. Should a Constitutional Amendment Mandate a Balanced Federal Budget?

YES

Federal deficits seriously harm our economy. According to the U.S. Chamber of Commerce, our federal deficit forces tax increases, reduces individual savings, makes private investment dollars more difficult to find, slows job growth, and hurts U.S. competitiveness abroad. Recent studies by the Congressional Budget Office and the General Accounting Office also point to the deficit as a very serious drag on our economy.

We cannot force future generations to pay for our fiscal irresponsibility. For more than twenty-five years neither the President nor Congress has managed to balance the budget. During the last decade in particular, the United States lived on a grand scale, borrowing money that our children and grandchildren must repay. By what right do we mortgage their future? It is economically and morally wrong to threaten their prosperity and lower their standard of living.

We must reduce our reliance on foreign investors. To support the U.S. government's lavish spending, we increasingly sell bonds to foreign interests. What happens if they suddenly lose confidence in the U.S. ability to pay these debts? It could create an economic catastrophe.

Paying interest on the debt wastes money. We have become the world's largest net debtor. In 1980 the national debt was $1 trillion. It now tops $4 trillion. The $294 billion in interest we paid in 1993 could have doubled our spending on poverty programs or increased spending on education eightfold.

Politicians lack the self-control to balance the budget. Citizens like receiving the benefits of public expenditures but hate paying taxes. Politicians who desire reelection try to satisfy their constituents with short-term rewards, sacrificing our long-term national interest. Our public officials prefer to please the public rather than to serve it. Only a constitutional amendment to balance the budget will make politicians responsible and accountable for their fiscal actions.

N O

The budget deficit is vastly overstated. Today's federal deficit is a smaller percentage of our national income than in any year from 1945 to 1960. We are not overspending today compared to the past. Some studies show that recent deficit figures of $200 billion to $300 billion per year are dramatically inflated because the government does not use standard business accounting procedures.

A forced balanced budget would harm the economy. The government must determine taxation and spending levels in response to business cycles and other economic trends. A budget amendment would hamper the government's flexibility in adjusting fiscal policy and managing the economy effectively.

Also, our federal budget acts as an *automatic* stabilizer to help the country out of recessions. In response to recession, U.S. government revenues spontaneously fall while spending grows, helping our economy back to health. An amendment would force the government to severely cut spending or raise taxes, either of which would further depress the economy.

The spending cuts would cause horrendous damage. To balance the budget would require military reductions that would seriously harm U.S. defense capabilities. Health research, programs for the disabled, prison-building, and veterans benefits would all require drastic cuts.

We should not force the judiciary to make fiscal and budgetary policy. Inevitably, disagreements about how to enforce balanced budgets or whose spending to cut would end up in federal courts. That would remove from Congress the constitutionally guaranteed power of the purse, designed to ensure they represent the people directly.

There is nothing wrong with responsible borrowing. A balanced-budget amendment would effectively stop the government from borrowing, but our capitalist system is based on it. Everyone borrows: businesses to buy new equipment, individuals to purchase a car or educate a child. Do we really want to deny government the opportunity to borrow money so it too can invest in future generations?

Background

For most of the nineteenth and into the early twentieth centuries the U.S. government generally experienced budget surpluses. Only during wartime did we experience deficits: half a million dollars during the Civil War and $23 million during World War I. But since 1931 the United States has experienced surpluses in only seven years.

All states except for Vermont currently have balanced-budget requirements. But these refer only to their operating budgets, not their total budgets. When a state needs to spend more than it receives in tax revenues it issues bonds, usually to finance construction of bridges, roads, and schools.

Congress attempted to reduce the federal deficit through the Gramm-Rudman-Hollings act, named after the three senators who sponsored it. The act intended to move the country toward a balanced budget by 1991 but became totally ineffective after Congress amended it during the 1980s.

Congress began considering balanced-budget amendments back in 1936. A constitutional amendment must first pass Congress with a two-thirds majority in both houses and then be submitted to the states for ratification. Unlike legislation such as the Gramm-Rudman-Hollings act, a constitutional amendment could not be reversed easily. In 1982 the Senate passed a balanced-budget amendment but the House did not. In 1986 the Senate came close again. The House came within only nine votes in 1992. Many thought that in 1994 it would finally pass. But both the Senate and House, owing in part to President Clinton's strong opposition, rejected a balanced-budget amendment yet again.

The staunchest supporters of the balanced-budget amendment have traditionally been Republicans and conservatives. Democrats, who usually wish to preserve spending on social programs that a balanced-budget amendment would surely slash, have generally voted against such an amendment. However, the liberal Senator Paul Simon (D-Illinois) led the 1994 effort to pass such an amendment.

Senator Simon's balanced-budget amendment, similar to the ones defeated in recent years, would have required a three-fifths "supermajority" in both houses of Congress to allow a spending increase over revenues, or any increase in the federal debt, except in wartime. A simple majority of fifty-one senators and 218 representatives would have been needed to raise taxes. Under existing law, a majority of just the members present and voting can approve tax increases. The amendment would have taken effect in 2001.

Aside from the efforts of Senator Simon and his colleagues, a grassroots movement to pass a balanced-budget amendment has been active since the mid-1970s. Those behind the movement hope to call a constitutional convention, the first since 1787, as allowed under Article V of the Constitution. Two-thirds of the states must request one before a convention is called. So far, thirty-two of the needed thirty-four states have passed resolutions demanding a convention to require a balanced budget. But in February 1993 the movement weakened somewhat when Michigan and New Jersey state legislators, realizing support for a convention had eroded in their states, decided to delay further consideration of the issue. Nationally, however, a February 1994 *Washington Post*/ABC poll showed that 77 percent of likely voters support a balanced-budget amendment to the Constitution.

Outlook

President Clinton believes that spending limits resulting from a balance-budget amendment would ruin cherished Democratic social programs and cause severe hardships to recipients. With budget deficits dropping—from $290 billion in 1992 to an expected $176 billion in 1995—Democrats believe the harsh medicine of such an amendment is no longer needed.

The Republican-controlled Congress, on the other hand, has made such an amendment one of its priorities. In fact, the first item in the Republicans' Contract with America, the Fiscal Responsibility Act, calls for a constitutional amendment requiring a balanced federal budget by 2002. Critics estimate such a goal will require $700 billion in spending cuts or new taxes. Republicans have yet to reveal how they expect to reach that goal.

44. Should Some Election Districts Be Redrawn to Guarantee African-American and Hispanic Majorities?

YES

Minorities are underrepresented at all levels of government. African-Americans constitute 12 percent of the population but hold only 8 percent of elected positions nationwide. Hispanics make up 8 percent of Americans but number only 2 percent of elected officials. Despite the election of seventeen new black lawmakers to Congress in 1992, blacks are still underrepresented in Congress and in other elected positions.

Our election laws must remedy past and present political discrimination. A vast majority of people tend to vote for candidates of their own race. But in the United States 51 percent of the voters wield 100 percent of the power. What results is not democracy for minorities, but tyranny over them. In effect the majority shut out the minority. Generally, blacks and Hispanics win elections only if they constitute a majority of voters.

Discrimination has always robbed minorities of electoral victories. Certain states have discriminated against African-American voters throughout history. For example, when the Voting Rights Act of 1965 forced Mississippi to register black voters, white politicians immediately reshaped local election districts to dilute the black vote among numerous white state legislators and members of Congress. As a result, even the heavily black Mississippi Delta did not elect a single black member to Congress. North Carolina, with a 22 percent black population, failed to elect a single black representative to Congress from the end of Reconstruction till 1992, when amendments to the Voting Rights Act created a black-majority district.

Race-conscious redistricting does not result in quotas. Some critics incorrectly claim that reshaping election districts resembles quotas and set-asides that will harm whites. Redistricting simply gives black candidates a fair chance in minority districts. Neither white voters nor candidates are denied equal opportunity on a statewide basis.

Fair redistricting does not guarantee the election of minorities. It only gives minorities a chance to elect representatives and legislators most likely to look after their best interests.

NO

Bizarrely shaped districts violate the Constitution's equal protection clause. Louisiana's Fourth Congressional District—four hundred miles long and only eighty feet wide at one point—looks like a giant letter Z. North Carolina's Twelfth District looks like a massive snake, at one point running along a highway. Voting districts are supposed to represent real geographic regions and communities, not special groups or factions. In June 1993 the Supreme Court correctly ruled that these districts were obviously designed only to create black majorities, violating the rights of white voters within them.

The Voting Rights Act perpetuates racial separatism. Many African-Americans do not wish to be segregated into electoral ghettos. Blacks do not all think alike, vote Democratic, or vote uniformly for black candidates. Blacks do not want more racial stereotyping or polarization. The Voting Rights Act has become a tool to further divide the races in American politics.

Racial redistricting ultimately hurts minority representation. By creating artificial districts, we put a cap on the number of African-American representatives. Although a handful of districts elect blacks, the neighboring districts then contain so few minorities that minority candidates are permanently shut out.

Minorities will gain more politically by creating alliances with whites and working together to solve mutual problems such as crime, unemployment, and poor education. White politicians who rely on a large minority vote for reelection are especially motivated to represent minority interests fairly.

At the same time, blacks *can* win elections with large white majorities, as witnessed by Governor L. Douglas Wilder's victory in Virginia. Prior to the 1992 reapportionment of election districts, 40 percent of black members of Congress came from districts in which blacks were the minority.

Redistricting creates racial quotas. Just as affirmative action relies on race and ethnicity to determine who gets jobs and who gets promoted, redistricting creates racial entitlements for voters. Such a system is fundamentally undemocratic.

Background

The term "gerrymander," in which politicians redraw election districts for their own benefit, was named in the early 1800s after Governor Elbridge Gerry of Massachusetts, who carved a salamander-shaped district for his party's political gain. Widely practiced and condemned through history, gerrymandering was for the first time viewed favorably in 1982 when amendments to the Voting Rights Act required over a dozen states notorious for racial discrimination to offer minorities a fair chance at electing representatives.

The Voting Rights Act of 1965 dramatically changed American society. In the first six years of its life, more blacks registered to vote in southern states than during the prior sixty-five years. The act quickly eliminated 75 percent of the gap between black and white registration rates.

In 1977 the Supreme Court ruled in *United Jewish Organizations* v. *Carey* that using race-conscious redistricting to comply with the Voting Rights Act is constitutional. The Court consistently let the Justice Department and individual states decide how to enforce the act. Since 1965 the act's influence has grown steadily as Congress and the courts allowed states to move beyond merely guaranteeing suffrage to every citizen and banning literacy tests to exclude black voters.

The 1982 amendment to the act requires states to redesign districts if, in the past, voting was polarized between whites and minorities, minorities usually lost, and residential patterns were distinct enough that black or Hispanic districts could be drawn. To allow minority candidates a fair chance at victory, some judges have required these states to configure the new districts with approximately 60 percent black voters. Since, on average, 5 percent fewer black voters register than whites and another 5 percent fewer turn out for elections, a 60 percent black district would give black candidates an equal opportunity. To comply with these laws, the first legally racially gerrymandered districts were drawn up in 1991, based on the 1990 census. The effort to increase minority representation in Congress certainly worked. In the 1992 election forty new black and Hispanic members were elected to Congress, bringing the total number to fifty-two. But when several states—including North Carolina, Louisiana, Georgia, and Texas—drew odd-shaped districts, white citizens and Republican politicians sued.

The first of these lawsuits against state governments reached the Supreme Court in 1993. Five white voters in North Carolina's Twelfth District sued that state for violating the Constitution's equal protection

202

clause. North Carolina's tortuously long, thin district was created by a judicial commission.

Justice Sandra Day O'Connor wrote for the majority that such districts violated principles of compactness and contiguousness. She questioned all racially inspired gerrymandering, cautioning that "even for remedial purposes, [it] may Balkanize us into competing racial factions" [and] . . . "bears an uncomfortable resemblance to political apartheid." O'Connor noted that while race may figure in redrawing districts, if race is the only factor, the injustice to white voters outweighs other considerations. She wrote that voters may challenge racial gerrymandering and remanded the case back to the North Carolina district court to determine if the election district must be redrawn.

Outlook

In the next few years, lawsuits against bizarrely shaped districts in other states should reach the Supreme Court. Until then we will not know if the Court will consistently rule against redistricting inspired by racial injustice. But in recent years the conservative Court has preferred not to actively correct historical wrongs. This traditionally conservative view treats all people equally, hoping inequality will correct itself over time. In contrast, liberals believe only active remedies for historical wrongs can result in a fair chance for minorities.

Some liberals, most noticeably Lani Guinier, President Clinton's one-time nominee for assistant attorney general, side with the conservatives, but for different reasons. Guinier believes racial gerrymandering will isolate blacks from whites and dilute their political strength. She has proposed radical alternative plans that include instituting minority veto power and giving minority voters a more heavily weighted vote to compensate for their small numbers. Given the rapidity with which President Clinton backed away from her nomination when the media dubbed her the "quota queen," radical ideas to achieve full minority representation seem far off.

Nature Versus Nurture

45. Is Homosexuality Genetic?

YES

A well-regarded study reveals a gay genetic marker. In July 1993 molecular geneticists at the National Cancer Institute (NCI) published a study showing that homosexuality can be genetically transmitted by the X chromosome from mothers to their sons. According to Dr. Dean Hamer, thirty-three of forty pairs of gay brothers whose blood he studied revealed a unique genetic marker on the X chromosome. Any male with this genetic marker has a 50 percent chance of being gay. In some extended families Dr. Hamer studied, a significant number of the men were gay going back several generations.

Recent studies reveal neurological differences in gays. Simon LeVay, a neuroscientist at the Salk Institute in La Jolla, California, studied the brains of forty-one cadavers, including nineteen homosexual men. The portion of the hypothalamus believed to control sexuality was less than half the size in the gay men than in the heterosexuals. This indicates that a fundamental genetic difference exists between men of differing sexual orientation.

Studies of twins indicate homosexuality runs in families. In 1992 scientists at Northwestern University released the results of a study conducted on a variety of twin and nontwin brothers. It showed that if one twin is gay, the other twin is three times more likely to also be gay if he is identical rather than fraternal. Fraternal twins are twice as likely to both be gay than two brothers, one of whom is adopted. Clearly, a direct correlation exists between the amount of genetic materials shared and the likelihood of a second brother also being gay. The correlation is stronger for the sisters of lesbians.

Homosexuality occurs consistently worldwide. A recent survey of various studies, by researchers Paul and Kirk Cameron, reveals that about one percent of people in the United States, France, Norway, and other nations are exclusively gay. How can you explain such consistency across various cultures except by genetics?

N O

Genes alone have never been proven to control human behavior directly. In recent years various laboratories claimed finding genes primarily responsible for causing alcoholism, manic depression, schizophrenia, and criminality. All these claims were retracted upon further study. The "evidence" for the X chromosome predisposing someone toward homosexuality may also be disproved.

The neurological studies contain serious flaws. LeVay studied the hypothalamus of gay men who died of AIDS, a disease known to affect brain tissue. What he discovered may be a result of the disease. Also, LeVay never interviewed the men. Who can say if they were really gay or bisexual?

Various parts of the brain change in response to a person's experience. For example, newly blind people who learn to read Braille show growth in the portion of the brain that controls the reading finger. Many scientists believe the small hypothalami LeVay found may be the *result* of a homosexual lifestyle, not the cause of it.

The twins studies also contain flaws. The 1992 Northwestern study used some twins who grew up together. Their common environment, *not* genetics, likely caused the high incidence of homosexuality among siblings. Of twins where only one is gay, the other usually measures at the opposite end of the straight-to-gay sliding scale. If genetics predetermines behavior, how could identical twins raised in the same house turn out so dramatically different?

We are biologically heterosexual. Human beings procreate in male-female pairs. We are anatomically designed to mate with a member of the opposite sex. To say homosexuality is genetic goes against everything we know about biology and evolution.

Environmental factors lead to homosexuality. Psychologists believe most men become gay because of absent, distant, or detached fathers and controlling, overpossessive mothers. Environmental and cultural influences—not preordained genetics—determine a person's sexual preferences.

Background

The debate on whether homosexuality is genetic updates the "nature versus nurture" controversy but with politically charged stakes. The gay community is deeply divided over the issue. Some hope scientists will prove a biological root of homosexuality. Others fear a possible eugenics program and other consequences if gay embryos can be identified.

The first group has always argued that homosexuality is not a lifestyle they chose, but rather a deeply rooted biological fact. Many knew they were gay from a very early age. In the 1980s the term "sexual orientation" largely replaced "sexual preference," implying an innate nature to sexuality. Some gays believe that if homosexuality is predetermined, the animosity and homophobia against them may die. You cannot blame someone, they argue, for fulfilling his genetic destiny. A genetic cause removes all moral objections to homosexuality. Some parents, who feel guilty or embarrassed about their homosexual children, will have no reason to. If being gay is like being left-handed, then no one can blame herself, neither gays nor their parents.

If homosexuality is deemed medically "immutable" and "natural," gays could also gain civil rights protections granted to other minorities. For example, gays who sue for violations of constitutional rights do not benefit from being designated a suspect class. Members of a suspect class must be politically weak and have suffered unfair discrimination in the past. To correct historical wrongs, courts favor people of such a class. A biological basis for homosexuality would strengthen the legal arguments for gay rights laws. Gays could join other groups who receive protections based on such fixed characteristics as skin color, national origin, and ethnicity.

Despite all these potential social and political benefits, a significant number of gays fear this research. The possible discovery of a gene marker for homosexuality by Dr. Dean Hamer at the National Cancer Institute raises another group of issues. If scientists develop an inexpensive blood test for homosexuality, will some parents abort gay fetuses? Such an option could lead to eugenics programs against homosexuals much like the one attempted by the Nazis. If someone finds a medical "cure" will parents simply ask the doctor to change their child into a genetic heterosexual? If so, the homosexual population could also disappear.

Some gays feel angry and demeaned by this research. Searching for a biological cause of homosexuality, they argue, implies it is either a disease or a deviation from the norm. Many lesbians, whose sexuality has been largely ignored by geneticists, define their sexual orientation as a feminist matter of choice. A biological cause of homosexuality probably interests them less than it does gay men.

Outlook

Research into the origins of homosexuality continues on several fronts. Simon LeVay is now comparing gays and straights using magnetic resonance imaging (MRI) technology. By studying the hypothalami of living AIDS-free people, he hopes to duplicate the results of his cadaver studies. But LeVay's results will be analyzed carefully. Since he believes that finding genetic differences will improve the lives of homosexuals, his work draws special scrutiny from scientists and anti-gay activists.

Dean Hamer at the NCI is trying to duplicate his genetic marker results by testing a different group of gay brothers. He hopes to identify the exact gene responsible for homosexuality, rather than merely the approximate location on the X chromosome he found in his first experiment. Hamer also hopes to find a gene pattern common to lesbians.

Many scientists who study the nature versus nurture controversy believe an interplay between genetic and environmental factors may predispose someone toward certain behaviors. In other words, we are not programmed to follow a genetic destiny, although certain paths seem more likely than others. Even if Hamer's future genetic studies prove that some men are born homosexual, a majority of scientists will still argue that our upbringing, environment, and culture remain the stronger influences on a person's likely behavior and choices in life.

46. Should Adopted Children Be Returned If Their Biological Parents Want Them?

YES

The law supports rights of birth parents. Federal law and the law in most states are very clear. Unless a child is abused, neglected, or abandoned, birth parents usually get custodial rights. In some states, birth parents may request their adoptive children back up to six months after birth.

The courts recognize the powerful, primordial attachment between a biological mother and her child. Humans are fundamentally biological creatures. The courts cannot and should not engage in social engineering. Even if the adoptive home can better provide for the child economically, the bond between biological parent and child should always take precedence.

Switching homes does not ultimately harm young children. If the adoptive home and the subsequent home of biological parents both provide a secure, loving environment, most children adapt well. Most biological parents wish their children back because the parents' improved health or economic situation allows it. The birth parents profoundly want them. These children are not headed for an uncaring, impersonal foster home system.

The stigma of adoption makes biological parents preferable. Many children who know they were adopted feel abandoned and rejected, missing a crucial part of themselves. They hunger for their genetic roots, as evidenced by the growing number of adoptees seeking to learn who their biological parents are.

Adoption is meant to serve the best interests of the child, not the interests of infertile couples.

Poor people have as much right to children as rich ones. The vast majority of parents who put a child up for adoption are poor, single young women. Often they feel forced into this decision by society or a fast-talking adoption lawyer. On the other hand, the vast majority of adoptive parents are well-off, better educated, and older. When it comes to children, the privileged have no right to take advantage of the poor.

N O

Biology does not make a family. Just contributing to a child's genetic makeup does not make you a parent. If the birth parent gives up a child, that should be the end of his or her claim. You cannot just show up later demanding custody. *Real* parents are those who love and care for a child, not those who cast him or her off at birth because the child is unwanted or inconvenient.

Ripping children from their home devastates them. Who will ever forget the 1993 television pictures of two-and-one-half-year-old Jessica DeBoer being taken away, screaming, from the only parents she had ever known? The courts forced the return of this adopted girl to her unfamiliar biological parents, even after she profoundly bonded with her loving, adoptive family.

Toddlers rely on familiarity for their well-being—their own room, the way a parent holds them, the usual kitchen smells. The loss of both adoptive parents and a home can create a type of psychological death in a child. Toddlers cannot possibly understand what is happening. Studies show that moving a child at this age can result in personality disorders and even reduced intellectual ability.

Children are not pieces of property, like furniture, to be won in a dispute. The courts must consider the best interests of the child, not simply the rights of parents. Courts must decide who are the "psychological" parents and stop treating children like slaves.

Adoptive parents need reassurance that their children cannot be taken away. How would you feel if a child came into your home, you loved him or her as one of your own, you fully bonded, and then some judge ordered the child removed? If adoptive parents cannot feel confident in the finality of their adoptions, the whole system will collapse. That means even more children will never find a loving home.

Background

In the last decade the U.S. adoption scene has changed considerably as a result of the shortage of available babies. Adoptions declined from nearly 90,000 per year in the 1970s to only 50,000 per year today. Many couples try to circumvent the long lines and rigid standards at official adoption agencies. Often they turn to intermediaries, such as lawyers, who privately negotiate an adoption before birth. In private adoptions, the birth mother often reviews résumés of many prospective adopters, unlike in former times when rigid barriers prevented birth mothers from learning about or finding their children after adoption.

In the vast majority of cases, neither the birth parents nor the adoptees search for one another. But the estimated 2 to 5 percent who do search are growing. Most states allow the birth mother between two weeks and six months to change her mind. Most states also require mandatory counseling to help women accept giving up a child. But what about the father? In some states the unmarried biological father can appear well after the private adoption, claim he never knew about the child, and attempt to gain custody.

The highly publicized case of Jessica DeBoer involved just such a scenario. When the baby's mother, Cara Clausen, gave the child up for adoption a few days after birth in Iowa, she claimed her boyfriend was the father. But when the real father, a prior boyfriend named Dan Schmidt, learned of the child's existence a few weeks later, he petitioned for custody of the baby. The adopting couple, the DeBoers of Michigan, were ordered by the Iowa courts to return the baby to the biological father. They refused, starting a two-year battle in the courts of both states that eventually resulted in Jessica's return to her biological parents, after the Supreme Court refused to hear the case. According to news reports a year after moving, the child appears to have adjusted well to her new life.

Until 1972 unwed biological fathers like Dan Schmidt had no constitutional rights to their children. A Supreme Court decision that year changed the situation. Some 460,000 foster children now await adoption. The courts still prefer a biological parent in all cases where he or she can properly care for the child. But children often suffer long waits while officials search for birth fathers or while biological parents try to stabilize their own lives.

To avoid the problem of unwed fathers, many adoption agencies no longer handle adoptions in which a woman refuses to name the father. In response, seven states have created registries for unwed fathers that inform them of adoption proceedings involving their children. But if the father fails to register, an adoption can progress without his knowledge or agreement.

The courts tend to favor biological parents over adoptive ones for young children. But in two recent cases, older children were allowed to "divorce" their biological parents on their own initiative. Thirteen-year-old foster child Gregory K got the parental rights of his deeply troubled mother terminated so his foster parents could adopt him. Kimberly Mays, a teen switched at birth, got court permission to stay with the man who raised her, denying her biological parents visitation or other rights. Later, however, she decided to live with her biological parents.

Outlook

In mid-1994 a case similar to Baby Jessica's received national attention. Many months after separating from his girlfriend, a Czech émigré living in Chicago learned she had borne his child and put the baby up for adoption. The Illinois Supreme Court eventually ruled that since the father had been denied a timely opportunity to press for the baby's return, the biological parents, who have since married, should get custody of the three-and-one-half-year-old boy. Bowing to public furor over the fate of the boy, known as "Baby Richard," the Illinois legislature passed an amendment to the state's adoption law requiring a special court hearing in cases such as this one. Since the U.S. Supreme Court has declined to hear the case, it will eventually be decided in the Illinois courts.

To avoid future contested adoptions, the National Conference of Commissioners on Uniform State Laws has drafted a model state adoption law. It clearly defines the procedures for each step in adoption, including consent in relinquishing a child, evaluation of adoptive parents, transfer of the child, and access to records. This law proposes that most adoptions become final after 120 hours. If the states adopt this law uniformity, it would greatly reduce contested adoptions.

Being Green

47. Will Rapid Population Growth Soon Lead to Environmental Catastrophe?

YES

World population is exploding. During 1994 alone, some 95 million human beings will join the 5.5 billion already inhabiting planet Earth. By the middle of the next century, the head count is expected to double, with most of the new arrivals residing in struggling Third World countries.

Too many people must compete for diminishing resources. Rapid population growth has already exhausted once-ample supplies of food, clean air, water, shelter, and fuel. The United Nations reports that nearly one-fourth of the world's major fishing zones are now over-fished. Unregulated deforestation continues at a breakneck pace, depleting soil fertility. Vast numbers of impoverished people increasingly strip our environment of precious natural resources and food.

Uncontrolled population growth will fragment society. To escape starvation, whole populations will crowd into cities whose infrastructures are already stretched to their limits. By 2010, more than half the inhabitants of Third World countries will reside in urban centers plagued by air pollution, fouled water, and inadequate sewage treatment. Such poverty can only lead to large-scale social unrest.

We are not investing in our overpopulated future. Despite pleas from the scientific community, the Reagan-Bush administrations denied funding increases for much-needed agricultural research, technology development, and population control through the distribution of contraceptives. Such inaction will cause environmental degradation in the short run and dramatic crop shortfalls in the long run.

Scientific innovation alone cannot save an overpopulated world. A report issued jointly by the U.S. National Academy of Sciences and the Royal Society of London indicates that new technologies will not remedy the world's population crisis. A doubling of the global population during the next century would require a five- to ten-fold increase in economic growth to meet the basic needs of most people. How can such an increase in economic activity occur without further draining valuable natural resources and endangering already-fragile ecosystems?

NO

Alarmists have always been wrong about impending crises. In 1970, Professor Paul Ehrlich of Stanford University predicted that during the 1980s, 4 billion would die of hunger, including 65 million Americans. His 1991 book, *Healing the Planet,* contains similar but no more believable predictions for widespread starvation in the next century.

According to University of Chicago agriculturalist D. Gale Johnson, the people of developing nations are better fed and enjoy a more secure food supply than at any time in the last two centuries.

Food production poses no problem. New farming techniques and strains of rice and grains will produce between 15 and 60 percent greater yields in the next few years alone. According to agronomist Paul E. Waggoner of the Connecticut Agricultural Experiment Station, these innovations will even enable the return of large tracts of land to nature, as in India where 100 million acres once under tillage have been spared.

Dramatic population increases will not degrade environmental quality. In the 1970s scientists worried that the Earth was cooling. Now they have noticed a warming trend, some say due to increases in greenhouse gases, including carbon dioxide. But these temperature changes probably result from natural fluctuations. A recent Gallup poll of global climate researchers revealed that only 17 percent believe global warming has started, 53 percent believe it has not, and 30 percent are not sure.

Environmentalists' hysteria about acid rain is also unfounded. According to the National Acid Precipitation Assessment Program, acid rain has *not* caused widespread damage to forests, crops, or human health. Predictions about DDT killing off the oceans and crop failure due to pollution blocking sunlight have also proven wrong.

Human resourcefulness and productivity will ensure the Earth's survival. Many experts foresee a brighter future in which technological innovations—such as new forms of alternative energy, recycling, building materials, and foods—will replace depleted resources and enable us to thrive.

Background

Prior to 1950 global population increased at a modest rate. Improvements in health care, sanitation, and food production since then have stimulated population growth dramatically. Today's population of 5.5 billion human beings will double within the next seventy years if current trends prevail.

Concern for the Earth's limitations first surfaced during the late eighteenth century when Thomas Malthus described our natural resources as finite and warned that uncontrolled population growth would result in devastating famine. Not until the population boom following World War II, however, did anxiety about the consequences of global overpopulation become broad-based. In 1960 the American Association for the Advancement of Science called for in-depth research into population-related problems. In 1968 biologist Paul Ehrlich wrote *The Population Bomb,* predicting widespread starvation and pollution due to overpopulation and calling for a worldwide effort to curb population growth.

During that same period the United Nations, supported by the United States and other industrialized countries, established the Fund for Population Activities (UNFPA) to oversee international family planning programs. In the 1980s, however, the Reagan-Bush administrations withdrew U.S. backing for UNFPA programs because they provide abortion services. As a result, many otherwise effective projects lost critical funding. President Bush further distanced himself and the United States from overpopulation and environmental issues when he declined to attend the 1992 Earth Summit in Rio de Janeiro. In 1993 the Clinton administration announced the resumption of U.S. funding for international family planning programs.

The proliferation of family planning services since the 1960s has produced some measurable benefits. Overall, fertility rates in developing nations have declined by a third. In countries such as Bangladesh, the use of contraceptives has doubled during the past decade. Fertility rates still remain high in much of sub-Sahara Africa, the Gaza Strip, and elsewhere in the Middle East. Despite efforts by the United Nations and other private organizations, the world population continues to rise because recent scientific and public health advancements have significantly reduced infant and child mortality, and because many world cultures see children as old-age insurance for enfeebled parents.

Historically, two factions have debated whether the Earth can sustain rapid population growth. One group, composed of biologists and ecologists, takes its lead from Malthus. These scientists predict dire consequences unless we curtail population growth. Opponents, primarily economists, contend that human inventiveness will overcome any shortages by raising crop yields and finding substitutes for diminishing resources.

Recently, a third group has entered the fray, arguing that although human ingenuity can probably sustain an expanding population, that ingenuity will be wasted unless the various segments of our global society cooperate. Affluent industrialized nations must assist less developed nations to acquire new technologies. Otherwise, those countries already struggling to survive will fall victim to economic ruin and social unrest.

Increasingly important in the population debate is the role of religion. The Roman Catholic Church, for example, does not recognize overpopulation as a problem and prohibits the use of artificial birth control. The church wields tremendous influence over its followers, particularly in the developing nations of Latin America where Catholicism is the predominant religion. Strong opposition by Vatican officials prevented the 1992 Earth Summit from issuing proposals to stabilize the world's population. The Vatican joined forces with Muslim fundamentalists during the 1994 International Conference on Population and Development in Cairo to battle proposals for spreading birth control.

Outlook

President Clinton and Vice President Albert Gore, although promising major changes in U.S. policies on environmental and population issues, have yet to follow through. Their emphasis on "sustainable development" promotes economic growth that will not overburden the Earth's capacity for waste disposal or exhaust essential resources.

Major population-control initiatives will most likely continue to come from the United Nations. By promoting education, health care, and economic measures, as well as controlled population growth, the United Nations hopes to encourage Third World countries to participate more fully in the global economy without further diminishing their environmental assets. However, it remains to be seen just how much U.S. funding will materialize for this cause and what impact it will have. Neither population control nor environmental protection are high priorities of the Republican-dominated Congress.

48. Should We Save Animals from Extinction at the Cost of American Jobs?

YES

The Earth's creatures are in crisis. We are destroying our environment at an unprecedented rate worldwide. Endangered species range from tiny plants that provide medicines on up to huge whales. Scientists estimate that owing to our devastation of habitats like the rain forest, we are losing animal, plant, and insect species at a rate of up to 27,000 per year worldwide. Twenty years ago the songbird population in the United States was twice as large. Twenty percent of freshwater fish worldwide face extinction today. Twenty percent of *all* plant and animal species could die out in the next thirty years. Where does this madness stop?

The Endangered Species Act rarely costs jobs. Of the 10,000 times a year the Fish and Wildlife Service must give permission or approval to a human development project, only twenty-five may harm an endangered species. Most of these cases are resolved without loss of jobs.

Environmental protection and sustainable development can actually promote job growth. According to the Environmental Protection Agency, the Clean Air Act alone will create 20,000 to 40,000 new jobs each year during the 1990s. By sustaining and regrowing such resources as fish and lumber, we can increase employment in these industries in the future. Furthermore, states that maintain their natural beauty and cleanliness attract many visitors; tourism jobs may offset those lost to environmental protection.

Without biodiversity we face extinction ourselves. We must learn to include environmentalism in our plans or we ourselves will die out someday. Since many species depend on others for food, killing one can have a domino effect. Humans face serious crop damage, floods, loss of medicines we extract from plants, and other calamities. We must balance the needs of the Earth with our own.

We must learn to share the Earth. Animals are as valuable as humans. Just like us, animals are unique, irreplaceable, and beautiful, and have just as much right to exist.

N O

Loss of species is often a natural phenomenon. Between 5 million and 100 million different species inhabit the Earth. Every century some species become extinct as a result of natural causes. Major geologic and other events have nearly destroyed all the Earth's species at least five times.

People are more important than a single species of birds. According to the Interior Department, 31,000 jobs in the Pacific Northwest will disappear over the next twenty-five years directly due to plans to protect the spotted owl. Overzealous environmental regulations harm other industries even more. According to the American Petroleum Industry, more than 400,000 American oil-industry jobs have already been lost in part because of environmental regulations. The loss of related jobs is even higher. For each offshore oil-drilling job lost, local economies lose an additional four onshore jobs. An estimated 700,000 new jobs will never be created because Congress rejected a proposal to permit oil drilling in Alaska's Arctic National Wildlife Refuge.

Yes, we should take reasonable measures to preserve endangered species. But the poverty and unemployment caused by environmentalism are at least as painful and devastating as pollution or a lost species. The Endangered Species Act never allows consideration of economic hardships when a species is listed as threatened or endangered.

Unreasonable regulations hamper U.S. competitiveness. Our lost jobs go directly overseas. Countries with less stringent environmental regulations are happy to employ their own people while American oil and forest workers suffer unemployment.

According to a recent poll, nearly three-quarters of industry leaders believe that their company's mandatory environmental programs hurt their competitiveness. That means manufacturing jobs also get transferred to other countries.

Regulations cost us a fortune. Unreasonable environmental regulations make everything more expensive. Americans will spend an extra $1.6 trillion in the 1990s to pay for products, services, and taxes inflated by environmental regulations.

Background

For many generations the American frontier mentality governed our use of land and natural resources. Industrialists and farmers took what they needed, then moved farther west. Saving the environment became a serious issue only twenty years ago. During these two decades many legislated and voluntary changes have reversed—or at least slowed—some pollution. But our ever-expanding agricultural and industrial activities exert new pressures on fragile ecosystems.

In the 1960s and 1970s, the United States took the lead worldwide in supporting environmentalism. Congress passed a series of measures to protect our water, air, and animal life, while our technological innovations reduced car and smokestack emissions and water pollution. But in the 1980s, while European Green parties were advancing stringent environmental regulations and while Japan produced the lowest-emission cars, the United States lagged behind. Environmentalism suffered as a result of the Reagan and Bush administrations' efforts to deregulate and boost the U.S. economy.

Typically, when recession and unemployment worsen, public support for conservation diminishes. In the early 1990s, as unemployment rates soared over 7 percent, the environmental lobby clashed with certain business lobbies, particularly those relying on natural resources. The highly publicized owls versus loggers battle took place in the Pacific Northwest after the Interior Department protected 6 million acres of old growth forest to save the northern spotted owl, an endangered species. In 1993, President Clinton worked out a compromise that somewhat reduced the protected acreage but failed to satisfy either loggers or conservationists. The next battles in the Northwest will be fought over salmon and other endangered fish.

In Florida, another state at the forefront of the jobs versus environment issue, farmers are fighting a proposal to flood 58 square miles of farmland surrounding the Everglades. The flooding would help filter phosphorus from farming runoff now emptying into the Everglades. Local agricultural firms believe 15,000 jobs will be lost.

These battles pit two powerful forces that find compelling reasons not to back down. The environmental lobby, including such organizations as the Sierra Club and the Wilderness Society, believe we cannot afford to lose a single additional species. By refusing to compromise, environmentalists hope to establish a mentality that conservation must always take precedence over other needs. On the other side, business interests represent workers whose livelihoods will disappear if environmental regulations force plants to shut down or end reclamation of natural resources. They feel equally compelled not to compromise.

But economic forces the government cannot control make a much bigger impact on employment than environmental policy. Continuing a long-term trend, many American jobs in manufacturing and farming are disappearing while jobs in service industries replace them. Improvements in automation, technological advances, and the lower wages of overseas workers account for most of the jobs lost. Environmental regulations do cause some unemployment, but many of these jobs would be lost anyway.

A March 1993 Gallup poll revealed that 85 percent of those surveyed in the United States and twenty-three other countries believe the loss of animal and plant species is very serious or somewhat serious. According to a March 1992 Roper poll, 58 percent of Americans believe that sacrifices of some economic growth and jobs are worth making to protect endangered species.

Outlook

Republican politicians have traditionally supported less environmental protection and government regulation than have Democrats. But the Republican-dominated Congress will probably pass legislation sponsoring the retraining of forestry workers and those in other industries displaced by environmental regulations.

Another way to moderate the loss of jobs is through tradable pollution credits. Companies with difficulties meeting environmental regulations can purchase credits from other firms that exceed regulations. Instead of simply closing a factory—or moving to a foreign country—the polluter can stay open but has a strong financial incentive to come into compliance. Florida's farmers near the Everglades may try such a system to prevent the flooding of their farms.

Foreign Despairs

49. Should We Use Protectionist Trade Policies to Help Shield U.S. Industries from Foreign Competition?

YES

We cannot afford to lose more American jobs. Almost every day we read about yet another American company laying off thousands of workers or moving its factories abroad. During the 1980s, 410,000 U.S. jobs in the automobile industry alone were permanently displaced—a direct result of imports of foreign cars and parts.

Free trade especially hurts low- and middle-income Americans. Current U.S. free trade policy and the North American Free Trade Agreement (NAFTA) unfairly protect industries employing highly skilled U.S. workers at the expense of industries that hire working-class people.

Foreign countries often use unfair trading practices. The nearly $100 billion annual U.S. trade deficit largely results from unfair foreign trading practices. Japan in particular protects its own industries by creating numerous roadblocks to American companies wishing to sell there. Japanese roadblocks include outright exclusion of some foreign products and services, government subsidies to Japanese companies, inadequate protection for foreign patents, and excessive red tape and bureaucratic rules for foreign firms. Companies from Japan and other countries also "dump" their products in the United States at below-cost prices, driving American firms out of business.

Protectionism is a fair and necessary form of retaliation. Why should we let other countries excessively protect *their* industries while we do so rarely? If we do not adequately intervene with our own trade, regulatory, and industrial policies, foreign countries will dictate the realities of international trade. We must compensate for and deter the unfair practices of foreign nations.

Even the threat of protectionism often gets results. The French in particular protect their agricultural industries. In 1992, when the French refused to adequately reduce the subsidy paid to their oilseed farmers, President Bush threatened them with a 200 percent duty on imported European white wines. It worked. The French lowered their subsidy to a rate acceptable to American trade negotiators.

N O

Protectionism only leads to destructive trade wars. If the United States raises protectionist barriers, other nations will do the same, restricting our own industries from selling goods abroad. If enough nations join the protectionist bandwagon, the world will suffer reduced economic activity, high unemployment, and even a worldwide depression.

Have we learned nothing from the past? In 1930 the United States passed the Hawley-Smoot Act, greatly raising tariffs on foreign goods. That helped trigger and extend the Great Depression.

Free trade increases U.S. competitiveness. Foreign competition forces American firms to create cheaper, better goods that can compete worldwide, not just domestically. Trade barriers would likely reduce sales in high-tech industries, where America's future lies.

Protectionism ultimately hurts the U.S. economy. For America to remain prosperous, inefficient factories and companies must close. Forestalling that reality with protectionism will only foster an inefficient economy. The hard-line protectionist policies of the former Eastern Bloc nations contributed substantially to creating their backward, uncompetitive factories, and to the economic decline of those countries.

Free trade benefits all consumers. Without tariffs and trade barriers, consumers pay less for many goods. This access to low-priced foreign products gives U.S. consumers more discretionary money to spend here at home. Because working-class people spend a greater percentage of their income on basic consumer goods, they especially gain from the lower prices resulting from free trade.

Our barriers to trade are already too high. U.S. tariffs on some goods—including clothes, shoes, and glassware—exceed those in the European Community. In addition, our already high customs duties inspire many nations to call *us* an unfair trading partner.

Protectionism has already failed. The U.S. steel industry has failed to turn profitable despite U.S. government coddling, which, most significantly, includes limits on imported steel.

Background

Many Americans believe that protectionism strengthens the U.S. economy and increases employment. But the vast majority of economists believe free trade is a better policy for all countries. They argue that the general public fails to understand the "principle of comparative advantage," introduced by English economist David Ricardo in 1817. Ricardo noted that both England and Portugal could produce cloth and wine, but England had a "comparative advantage" in producing cloth cheaply while Portugal's "comparative advantage" lay in producing inexpensive wine. Both countries, Ricardo showed, would benefit from exporting some of their inexpensive products while importing foreign products they found too expensive to produce themselves. Such specialization of labor created the most product, at the lowest prices, with the highest total employment. Throughout history, say many economists, strong special interests from inefficient or failing industries have convinced their governments to protect their companies with tariffs.

The United States has debated the free trade versus protectionism issue throughout the twentieth century. Most recently the North American Free Trade Agreement escalated into a major debate before its passage by Congress in November 1993. NAFTA is a trade pact by the United States, Mexico, and Canada that gradually eliminates tariffs and nontariff trade barriers between the three countries over the next fifteen years.

The debate over the United States joining NAFTA pitted President Clinton and most businesses against Ross Perot, labor unions, many farmers, environmentalists, and heads of low-tech industries expecting to lose business as a result of NAFTA. Finally, after making concessions to certain industries, Clinton gained the necessary congressional votes. Although most economists believe NAFTA will ultimately increase U.S. employment and strengthen the economy, certain labor-intensive industries such as winter fruits and vegetables, apparel, glassware, and ceramic tiles will probably suffer. However, businesses such as computers, financial services, and oil-production equipment are expected to gain.

Even more sweeping than NAFTA, a regional trading pact, is the General Agreement on Tariffs and Trade (GATT), a set of rules governing global commerce between nations that began in 1947. Because of cooperation between GATT member countries, tariffs since World War II have dropped from an average of 40 percent to 4.7 percent—a huge boon to world trade.

In December 1993 the GATT nations completed seven years of crisis-filled negotiations that eliminate tariffs on thousands of products. The 550-page pact resulting from this round of negotiations brings financial services, agriculture, and intellectual property like patents under GATT rules for the first time. Each of the 117 nations must now approve the pact.

Despite the free trade agreements facilitated by both NAFTA and GATT, the U.S. government may feel obliged to protect American industry as a result of our ever-widening trade deficit with Japan—$59.3 billion in 1993. For many years the Japanese have promised to promote imports to Japan, break down monopolies, deregulate various industries, and increase government spending on foreign products. The Clinton administration has attempted to apply "objective criteria" to monitor Japan's cooperation in opening its markets. The Japanese call that "numerical targeting" of specific goods, resulting in "managed trade," not free trade.

The United States came close to retaliating in February 1994. Japan's failure to open up its markets to U.S. cellular telephones led the Clinton administration to seriously consider sanctions, including special tariffs on Japanese goods. This trade crisis, like others before it, was avoided by additional Japanese concessions designed to reduce the trade deficit.

Outlook

Two trends seem likely for the future. Huge multilateral pacts like GATT will be increasingly difficult to negotiate. More bilateral or regional pacts like NAFTA will govern world trade. For example, the Japanese and their Pacific Rim neighbors may form a trading bloc to counteract NAFTA and the European Community.

The United States and Japan will continue to fight over opening Japan's markets. But neither side will risk a massive trade war because both have too much to lose.

50. Should We Curtail Trade with Countries That Violate Human Rights?

YES

The United States should not help sustain foreign regimes that flagrantly disregard basic rights. China in particular, one of America's largest trading partners, violated the basic human rights of its citizens long before and since the massacre of pro-democracy demonstrators at Tiananmen Square. China imprisons, tortures, and kills citizens for their nonviolent expression of political and religious beliefs.

China often exports goods made by political prisoners in forced labor camps. The United States cannot encourage and sustain foreign oppression by purchasing products made with illegal labor. U.S. companies with strong ethical guidelines, such as Levi Strauss and Timberland, have already started pulling out of China. Why can't the U.S. government demonstrate the same backbone?

Trade embargoes can generate change without military action. Countries like China and Indonesia, which ignore human rights pleas from other nations, will only respond to meaningful threats. With a widespread trade embargo, China and Indonesia would lose their export markets. The resulting economic hardship and unemployment would force changes in the human rights policies of these countries.

The South African trade embargo worked. When the world's nations united to cut off trade with South Africa, it hastened democratic reforms, substantially improved human rights, and ultimately led to majority rule. Why can't we help the people in other oppressed nations as well?

Only a country as powerful as the United States can protect the world's weak. The United States cannot support and condone these violations by continuing to trade freely and offer most-favored-nation status to these countries. To allow our pursuit of money to replace our protection of human rights is to lose our soul. We spent trillions of dollars during the cold war to export our values. Let's not now sacrifice these cherished values for cheap labor and export markets.

NO

Cutting trade will hurt the United States profoundly. U.S. exports of over $9 billion to China each year keep more than 165,000 Americans employed, especially in agriculture, aviation, and high technology. Can we really afford *not* to trade with China, soon to replace the United States as the world's largest economy? A drastic cut in trade would devastate our export industries.

Other alleged rights violators like Indonesia are also major markets for our products. If we alienate these people, the Japanese and Europeans will eagerly rush in to fill the vacuum and take our place.

Increased trade creates democratic changes in China. Because of trade, China's booming economy over the last decade has helped create a middle class with greater access to the Western media and information-disseminating machines like faxes, which spread new social and political views. Change in China must come from within—from the very people exposed to new ideas as a result of trade.

Threats to cut trade cause Chinese leaders to dig in their heels. China's arrogant and stubborn dictatorial rulers are only provoked by threats. What they perceive as U.S. bullying will not change their willingness to brutally crush dissent.

By *increasing* our trade and mutual trust we will increase their cooperation not only on human rights, but also on issues more crucial to our national interests such as nuclear proliferation and environmental conservation. To drastically cut trade would only drive the Chinese government further into the hands of hard-line Communists.

Asian peace and prosperity are essential to America's interests. Since World War II, Asian nations have lacked the unity and mutual cooperation we usually see in Europe. The potential for conflicts among Asian countries requires both the United States and China to pursue stability in the region. Chinese-American cooperation helps create that stability.

Background

One of the central foreign affairs debates during the cold war took place between humanitarians, who wanted the United States to isolate and punish dictatorships guilty of major human rights violations, and military advisors, who feared driving these countries into the Soviet camp. Today the debate is increasingly between humanitarians and U.S. business interests, who believe that demands for human rights are an impediment to U.S. foreign policy and economic growth.

President Jimmy Carter first made human rights a central issue in the 1970s. His view, that the United States should concern itself with how countries treat their citizens, was popular among U.S. citizens. Presidents Reagan and Bush deemphasized human rights as an official U.S. policy. These Republicans believed increased cooperation between the United States and countries like China would improve human rights in those nations.

Bill Clinton campaigned on a platform promising to expand U.S. protection of human rights worldwide and to expand U.S. exports. So far he has found that these moral and economic goals conflict. During his first year as president, in May 1993, Clinton was faced with granting China a continuation of its most-favored-nation (MFN) trading status. Each year China must satisfy the President and Congress that its human rights record merits MFN status, in which the United States accords most trading partners lower tariffs on goods imported into the United States. By revoking China's MFN status, Clinton would have effectively raised tariffs on Chinese goods from 8 to 40 percent on average, rendering Chinese goods prohibitively expensive and setting off a trade war. In May 1993 the United States did continue China's MFN status only after several months of tense relations. Clinton sent the Chinese a list of fourteen areas of concern that might prevent the renewal of MFN status in 1994, including weapons proliferation, trade barriers, and human rights violations.

During the first several months of 1994, lobbyists of large U.S. corporations bombarded the media with warnings against cutting MFN status to China. Top U.S. business executives describe China as the new engine for world economic growth. For example, only two of every hundred Chinese own a telephone. U.S. firms like AT&T are extremely eager to keep China, with a population of 1.1 billion, as a trading partner. If the United States were to discontinue MFN status, China would likely retaliate by canceling orders for Boeing airliners, General Electric generators, Caterpillar earthmovers, and products of other major U.S. companies.

Three prior secretaries of state and many other foreign policy experts also criticized the linkage of human rights to trade. They believe Clinton's policy would not succeed and ran counter to larger U.S. interests in China and elsewhere in Asia. Clinton policy analysts, however, argued that a tough, consistent policy would make the aging Chinese leadership concede. Since the Chinese sell 40 percent of their exports to the United States, they have strong economic and political reasons to maintain their MFN status.

In May 1994, Clinton again renewed MFN status for China. Taking the position held by Reagan and Bush, Clinton announced that the United States must "intensify and broaden its relations" with China in order to advance the cause of human rights.

Outlook

It is relatively easy for the United States to stop trade with small countries that violate their people's rights, like Western Sahara. But countries like China and Indonesia, with their huge potential marketplaces, present a difficult dilemma for the United States. The rights situation in China is certainly better today than when Nixon first visited in the early 1970s or when Carter normalized relations in the late 1970s. But images of the Tiananmen slaughter and continuing stories of dissidents in prison will continue to put pressure on the American President each spring when MFN status must be reviewed.

To increase the likelihood of protecting rights in China, the Clinton administration is working with major U.S. corporations to establish voluntary ethical guidelines for firms doing business with China. Such guidelines will probably require Chinese suppliers to meet certain criteria regarding worker compensation and health protection, and forbid the use of child labor and forced labor.

Bibliography

CRIME AND PUNISHMENT

PAGES 16–19

Baker, Peter. "The Many Pitfalls of Abolishing Parole." *The Washington Post* (Jan. 9, 1994), B1.

Bennett, William J. "Yes on 593: Three Strikes and You're Out." *The Seattle Times* (Sept. 20, 1993), B7.

Dolejsi, Ned. "No on 593: A Costly Scenario for Injustice." *The Seattle Times* (Sept. 19, 1993), B7.

Heymann, Philip B. "The Lock-'em-Up Debate." *The Washington Post* (Feb. 27, 1994), C1.

Lewis, Peter. "Three Strikes Initiative Gains Strength." *The Seattle Times* (Aug. 31, 1993), A1.

———. "Three Strikes Laws Have Struck Out Elsewhere." *The Seattle Times* (Sept. 30, 1993), A1.

Savage, David G. "Justices Uphold Sentencing Rules." *Los Angeles Times* (Jan. 19, 1989), 1.

Valbrun, Marjorie. "Controversy Swirls Over 3 Strikes." *The Philadelphia Inquirer* (Feb. 9, 1994), S1.

Zehren, Charles V. "NY Debates Locking Up Repeat Felons for Life." *Newsday* (Jan. 16, 1994), 19.

PAGES 20–23

Birnbaum, Jesse. "When Hate Makes a Fist." *Time* 141 (Apr. 26, 1993), 30–31.

Biskupic, Joan. "Hate Crime Laws Face Free-Speech Challenge." *The Washington Post* (Dec. 13, 1992), A10.

———. "Supreme Court Upholds Penalties in Hate Crimes." *The Washington Post* (June 12, 1993), A1.

Bradshaw, James. "Justices Uphold Ethnic Intimidation Law." *The Columbus Dispatch* (Jan. 13, 1994), 1C.

———. "Ohio's Justices Asked to Reinstate Hate-Crimes Law." *The Columbus Dispatch* (Sept. 12, 1993), 8D.

Gellman, Susan. "Sticks and Stones Can Put You in Jail, but Can Words Increase Your Sentence? Constitutional and Policy Dilemmas of Ethnic Intimidation Laws." *UCLA Law Review* 39 (Dec. 1991): 360.

"Hate Crimes Do More Harm." *The Washington Post* (June 22, 1993), A18.

Hentoff, Nat. "Beware of Stiffer Sentences for Thought Crimes." *The Washington Post* (June 19, 1993), A21.

Jost, Kenneth. "Hate Crimes." *CQ Researcher* 3 (Jan. 8, 1993): 3–23.

Smolla, Rodney A. *Free Speech in an Open Society.* New York: Alfred A. Knopf, 1992.

PAGES 24–27

Dority, Barbara. "Not in My Name." *Humanist* 53 (Mar./Apr. 1993): 36–37.

Foster, Carol D. *Capital Punishment: Cruel & Unusual.* Wylie, Texas: Information Plus, 1992.

Goldberg, Steven. "So What If the Death Penalty Deters?" *National Review* 41 (June 30, 1989): 42–44.

Greenhouse, Linda. "Death Penalty Is Renounced by Blackmun." *The New York Times* (Feb. 23, 1994), 1, 14.

Hertzberg, Hendrik. "Premeditated Execution." *Time* 139 (May 18, 1992): 49.

Nathanson, Stephan. *An Eye for an Eye?: The Morality of Punishing by Death.* Totowa, N.J.: Rowman and Littlefield, 1987.

Smolowe, Jill. "Race and the Death Penalty." *Time* 137 (Apr. 29, 1991): 68–69.

White, Welsh S. *The Death Penalty in the Nineties: An Examination of the Modern System of Capital Punishment.* Ann Arbor: University of Michigan Press, 1991.

PAGES 28–31

Benjamin, Daniel K., and Roger L. Miller. *Undoing Drugs: Beyond Legalization.* New York: Basic Books, 1991.

Boaz, David, ed. *The Crisis in Drug Prohibition.* Washington, D.C.: Cato Institute, 1990.

"Bring Drugs Within the Law." *The Economist* 327 (May 15, 1993): 13–14.

Courtwright, David T. "Should We Legalize Drugs? No." *American Heritage* 44 (Feb./Mar. 1993): 43, 53–56.

DiIulio, John J. "Cracking Down." *The New Republic* 208 (May 10, 1993): 53–57.

"Elders Reiterates Her Support for Study of Drug Legalization." *The Washington Post* (Jan. 15, 1994), A8.

Kane, Joseph P. "The Challenge of Legalizing Drugs." *America* 167 (Aug. 1, 1992): 61–63.

Lynch, Gerald W., and Roberta Blotner. "Legalizing Drugs Is Not the Solution." *America* 168 (Feb. 13, 1993): 7–9.

Nadelmann, Ethan A. "Should We Legalize Drugs? Yes." *American Heritage* 44 (Feb./Mar. 1993): 42, 44–48.

Roberts, Thomas B. "When the Drug War Hits the Fan." *Phi Delta Kappan* 73 (Sept. 1991): 58–61.

Wilson, Jerry V. "Our Wasteful War on Drugs." *The Washington Post* (Jan. 18, 1994), A19.

American Tort Reform Association. *Reform of the Law of Punitive Damages*. Washington, D.C.: American Tort Reform Association, 1994.

"Business Jury Awards Should Be More Just." *BusinessWeek* (Feb. 22, 1993), 130.

Gibson, W. David. "Tort Reform Having a New Day in Court." *Chemical Business* 15 (May 1993): 10–11.

Jost, Kenneth. "Too Many Lawsuits?" *CQ Researcher* 2 (May 22, 1992): 435–50.

Moss, Debra Cassens. "The Punitive Thunderbolt: How Much Should Courts Curb Extraordinary Awards?" *ABA Journal* 79 (May 1993): 88–92.

Mullins, Edward W., Jr. "Tort Reform Takes a Turn." *Risk Management* 39 (July 1992): 33–36.

Murphy, Betty Southard, Wayne E. Barlow, and D. Diane Hatch. "Supreme Court Refuses to Limit Punitive Damages." *Personnel Journal* 72 (Sept. 1993): 33.

Quayle, Danforth. "The Legal System's Impact on the American Economy." *Vital Speeches of the Day* 57 (Oct. 1, 1991): 738–41.

Riga, Peter. "Capping a Gusher: What Punitive Damages Cost." *Commonweal* 118 (Sept. 13, 1991): 502–504.

"Sue the Rascals." *The Economist* 326 (Feb. 13, 1993): 18–19.

"The Case for Mandatory Minimum Sentences." *The Washington Post* (June 30, 1992), A18.

Cohn, Gary. "More Judges Balking at Mandatory Drug Sentences." *The Philadelphia Inquirer* (June 30, 1993), A1.

"Mandatory Madness." *The Washington Post* (July 7, 1993), A20.

McCarthy, Colman. "Justice Mocked: The Farce of Mandatory Minimum Sentences." *The Washington Post* (Feb. 27, 1993), A23.

Meddis, Sam. "Reno Bumps Heads with the 'Get Tough' Movement." *USA Today* (Sept. 20, 1993), A7.

Potterton, Reg. "A Criminal System of Justice." *Playboy* 39 (Sept. 1992): 46–47.

Romley, Richard M. "Mandatory Sentencing: An Appraisal." *The Arizona Republic* (Aug. 11, 1991), C1.

Sturgill, Richard. "Mandatory Sentencing: Keep It." *The Phoenix Gazette* (Jan. 18, 1992), A17.

"Talk of the Town." *The New Yorker* 68 (Apr. 13, 1992): 27–28.

York, Michael. "Judge Rejects Federal Sentencing Guidelines." *The Washington Post* (Apr. 30, 1993), D5.

PAGES 40–43

Gibbs, Nancy. "Up in Arms." *Time* 142 (Dec. 20, 1993): 18–24.

Kates, Don B., and Patricia T. Harris. "How to Make Their Day: The Gun Control Lobby." *National Review* 43 (Oct. 21, 1991): 30–32.

Kleck, Gary. *Point Blank: Guns and Violence in America*. New York: Aldine de Gruyter, 1991.

Lacayo, Richard. "Beyond the Brady Bill." *Time* 142 (Dec. 20, 1993): 28–32.

McConnell, Joe. "Firearms: No Right Is an Island." *Whole Earth Review* (Winter 1992): 40–48.

Nisbet, Lee, ed. *The Gun Control Debate*. Buffalo: Prometheus Books, 1990.

Siegel, Mark A., ed. *Gun Control: Restricting Rights or Protecting People?* Wylie, Texas: Information Plus, 1989.

Sullum, Jacob. "Wait a Minute." *National Review* 46 (Feb. 7, 1994): 48–51.

Wirkin, Gordon. "Taking Aim at the Wrong Target." *U.S. News & World Report* 112 (June 1, 1992): 8–9.

PAGES 44–47

Aron, Charles J. "Women Battered by Life and Law Lose Twice." *The National Law Journal* 15 (July 19, 1993): 13.

"Battered Women: Murderers or Victims?" *The Economist* 326 (Jan. 16, 1993): 30–31.

Baum, Geraldine. "Should These Women Have Gone Free?" *Los Angeles Times* (Apr. 15, 1991), E1.

"The Commuted Sentences." *The Washington Post* (Mar. 20, 1991), A18.

"Compassion on a Case by Case Basis." *Los Angeles Times* (Jan. 18, 1993), B6.

D'Antonio, Michael. "Why She Shot Him." *McCall's* 119 (Oct. 1991): 32–37.

Madden, Alison M. "Clemency for Battered Women Who Kill Their Abusers." *Hastings Women's Law Journal* 4 (Winter 1993): 1–86.

Shen, Fern, and Howard Schneider. "Freedom in a Divided World." *The Washington Post* (Feb. 21, 1991), B1.

PAGES 48–51

"Abolish the Insanity Defense?" *U.S. News & World Report* 93 (July 5, 1982): 15.

Biskupic, Joan. "Insanity Defense: Not a Right in Montana Case." *The Washington Post* (Mar. 29, 1994), A3.

Brown, David. "Insanity Defense: Setting a Benchmark of Human Intellect and Will." *The Washington Post* (Jan. 27, 1992), A3.

Caplan, Lincoln. "Not So Nutty: The Post-Dahmer Insanity Defense." *The New Republic* 206 (Mar. 30, 1992): 18–20.

Rowe, Jonathan. "Why Liberals Should Hate the Insanity Defense." *The Washington Monthly* 16 (May 1984): 39–46.

Salholz, Eloise. "Insanity: A Defense of Last Resort." *Newsweek* 119 (Feb. 3, 1992): 49.

Simon, Rita J., and David E. Aaronson. *The Insanity Defense: A Critical Assessment of Law and Policy in the Post-Hinckley Era.* New York: Praeger, 1988.

PAGES 52–55

Clark, Charles S. "Prostitution." *CQ Researcher* 3 (June 11, 1993): 507–25.

"Condoms Required in Nevada Brothels." *San Francisco Chronicle* (Jan. 21, 1988), A6.

Decker, John F. *Prostitution: Regulation and Control.* Littleton, Colo.: F. B. Rothman, 1979.

DuPuis, Tomm. "Meanwhile, Back at the Brothel." *Cosmopolitan* 212 (Mar. 1992): 124–26.

"Holland Makes Prostitution Legal—Union Objects." *San Francisco Chronicle* (May 27, 1992), A10.

"Nevada's Legal Brothels AIDS-Free." *The Washington Post* (Nov. 3, 1987), A8.

Petersen, John R. "The High Cost of Sex Police." *Playboy* 35 (May 1988), 41.

Pillard, Ellen. "Rethinking Prostitution: A Case for Uniform Regulation." *Nevada Public Affairs Review* (Winter 1991): 45–49.

"San Francisco Considers a City-Run Brothel." *The New York Times* (Nov. 28, 1993), 44.

"Street Cleaning." *The Economist* 320 (Sept. 7, 1991): A28.

MEDICINE AND MORALS

PAGES 58–61

Bernards, Neal, ed. *Euthanasia: Opposing Viewpoints*. San Diego: Greenhaven, 1991.

Gibbs, Nancy. "Mercy's Friend or Foe?" *Time* 140 (Dec. 28, 1992): 36–37.

———. "Rx for Death." *Time* 141 (May 31, 1993): 34–40.

Morganthau, Tom. "Dr. Kevorkian's Death Wish." *Newsweek* 121 (Mar. 8, 1993): 46–48.

Pallone, Nathaniel J. "Costs and Benefits of Medicide." *Society* 29 (July/Aug. 1992): 34–36.

Shapiro, Joseph P. "Death on Trial: The Case of Dr. Kevorkian Obscures Critical Issues—and Dangers." *U.S. News & World Report* 116 (Apr. 25, 1994): 31–38.

Smith, Wesley J. "The Right to Die, the Power to Kill." *National Review* 46 (Apr. 4, 1994): 38–42.

Tong, Rosemarie. "Euthanasia in the 1990s: Dying a 'Good' Death." *Current* 354 (July/Aug. 1993): 27–33.

Worsnop, Richard L. "Assisted Suicide." *CQ Researcher* 2 (Feb. 21, 1992): 147–63.

PAGES 62–65

Cunningham, Mark. "The Abortion War." *National Review* 44 (Nov. 2, 1992): 42–48.

Gordon, Mary. "A Moral Choice." *The Atlantic* 265 (Apr. 1990): 78–88.

Lacayo, Richard. "Abortion: The Future Is Already Here." *Time* 139 (May 4, 1992): 26–30.

Lawton, Kim. "Twenty Years After Roe . . ." *Christianity Today* 37 (Jan. 11, 1993): 36–38.

Schwarz, Stephen. *The Moral Question of Abortion.* Chicago: Loyola University Press, 1990.

Sheler, Jeffery L. "The Theology of Abortion." *U.S. News & World Report* 112 (Mar. 9, 1992): 54–55.

Shettles, Landrum B., M.D., and David Rorvik. *Rites of Life.* Grand Rapids, Mich.: Zondervan, 1983.

Smolowe, Jill. "New, Improved and Ready for Battle." *Time* 141 (June 14, 1993): 48–51.

Van Biema, David. "But Will It End the Abortion Debate?" *Time* 141 (June 14, 1993): 52–54.

PAGES 66–69

Barnard, Neal D. "Product Testing on Animals." *The Animal's Agenda* 11 (Apr. 1991): 50–51.

Cowley, Geoffrey. "Of Pain and Progress." *Newsweek* 114 (Dec. 26, 1988): 12–13.

Hanson, Gayle. "Tactics Turn Rabid in Dissection War." *Insight* 7 (Sept. 23, 1991): 18–21.

Loeb, Jerod M. et al. "Human vs. Animal Rights." *The Journal of the American Medical Association* 262 (Nov. 17, 1989): 2716–20.

Siegal, Steve. "Animal Research Is Dangerous to Human Health." *Utne Reader* 10 (Sept./Oct. 1989): 47–49.

Trull, Frankie L. "Animal Research Is Critical to Continued Progress in Human Health." *USA Today* (Magazine) 116 (Mar. 1988): 52.

Williams, Jeanne, ed. *Animal Rights and Welfare?* New York: H. W. Wilson, 1991.

PAGES 70–73

AIDS Action Council. *Federal Spending on AIDS-Specific Programs.* Washington, D.C.: AIDS Action Council, 1994.

Bylinsky, Gene. "New Weapons Against AIDS." *Fortune* 126 (Nov. 30, 1992): 104–107.

Cimons, Marlene. "AIDS—A Funding Backlash." *Los Angeles Times* (June 18, 1990), A1.

————. "AIDS Research Funding Changes Proposed in Bill." *Los Angeles Times* (Feb. 9, 1993), A5.

Foreman, Christopher H., Jr. "The Fast Track: Federal Agencies and the Political Demand for AIDS Drugs." *Brookings Review* 9 (Spring 1991): 30–37.

Freundlich, Naomi. "No, Spending More on AIDS Isn't Unfair." *BusinessWeek* (Sept. 17, 1990), 97.

Goldstein, Amy. "Where AIDS and Money Cross Paths." *The Washington Post* (July 11, 1993), A1.

Kong, Dolores. "Clinton AIDS Leader Says Funding to Remain Tight." *The Boston Globe* (Aug. 27, 1993), 26.

Nulty, Peter. "Where All That AIDS Money Is Going." *Fortune* 129 (Feb. 7, 1994): 139–40.

Scrage, Michael. "Debate on AIDS Research Spending Should Focus on Broader Benefits." *The Washington Post* (Aug. 3, 1990), F3.

Viano, Emilio. "Health and Unequal Opportunity: The Battle for Federal Dollars." *USA Today* (Magazine) 122 (July 1993): 22–24.

PAGES 74–77

Armey, Richard K., and Newt Gingrich. "The Welfarization of Health Care." *National Review* 46 (Feb. 7, 1994): 53–56.

"The Birth of Universal Health, Inc." *The Economist* 330 (Mar. 26, 1994): 73–74.

Church, George J. "Oh Noooo!" *Time* 143 (Mar. 14, 1994): 34–35.

"Critical Lessons from the Health Reform Front." *The Washington Monthly* 26 (Mar. 1994): 19–21.

McCaughey, Elizabeth. "No Exit: What the Clinton Plan Will Do for You." *The New Republic* 210 (Feb. 7, 1994): 21–25.

Quinn, Jane Bryant. "Foes of Health Care Reform Spreading Disinformation." *The Washington Post* (Apr. 3, 1994), H3.

Rovner, Julie. "Winners and Losers in Health Care Reform." *The Washington Post* (June 21, 1993), A17.

"Small Business Becomes Powerful Foe of Health Care Proposals."
The New York Times (Apr. 26, 1994), A1, B8.

Thompson, Roger. "Small Firms' Stake in Health Reform." *Nation's Business* 81 (Nov. 1993): 18–28.

Trafford, Abigail. "U.S. Health Costs to Pass $1 Trillion in 1994." *The Washington Post* (Jan. 11, 1994), Z7.

Wilensky, Gail R. "Health Reform: What Will It Take to Pass?" *Health Affairs* 13 (Spring 1994): 179–91.

Zelman, Walter A. "The Rationale Behind the Clinton Health Care Reform Plan." *Health Affairs* 13 (Spring 1994): 9–29.

PAGES 78–81

Callahan, Daniel. "Perspective on Cloning: A Threat to Individual Uniqueness." *Los Angeles Times* (Nov. 12, 1993), B7.

Conley, John J. "Narcissus Cloned." *America* 170 (Feb. 12, 1994): 15–17.

Ehrenreich, Barbara. "The Economics of Cloning." *Time* 142 (Nov. 22, 1993): 86.

Elmer-Dewitt, Philip. "Cloning: Where Do We Draw the Line?" *Time* 142 (Nov. 8, 1993): 64–70.

Evers, Williamson M. "These Babies Don't Need Big Brother." *Los Angeles Times* (Nov. 29, 1993), B7.

Fackelmann, Kathy A. "Cloning Human Embryos: Exploring the Science of a Controversial Experiment." *Science News* 145 (Feb. 5, 1994): 92–94.

Kolberg, Rebecca. "Human Embryo Cloning Reported." *Science* 262 (Oct. 29, 1993): 652–53.

Nossal, G. J. V., and Ross L. Coppel. *Reshaping Life: Key Issues in Genetic Engineering*, 2d ed. Cambridge: Cambridge University Press, 1990.

Rollin, Bernard E. "The Frankenstein Thing: Ethical Issues in Genetic Engineering." *USA Today* (Magazine) 119 (Nov. 1990): 70–72.

Weiss, Rick. "The Ethics of Cloning: Who Decides?" *The Washington Post* (Nov. 15, 1993), Z12.

PAGES 82–85

Andrew, James H. "The Massachusetts Senate Approves Child-Abuse Bill." *The Christian Science Monitor* (Nov. 19, 1993), 4.

Bullis, Ronald K. "The Spiritual Healing 'Defense' in Criminal Prosecutions for Crimes Against Children." *Child Welfare* 70 (Sept./Oct. 1991): 541–55.

Colburn, Don. "In 7 Cases, 5 Convictions." *The Washington Post* (Sept. 25, 1990), Z17.

Goodrich, Lawrence J. "Florida Court Overturns Spiritual-Healing Case." *The Christian Science Monitor* (July 6, 1992), 8.

Jones, Tamara. "Prayers, Parent Duty: Child Deaths Put Faith on Trial." *Los Angeles Times* (June 27, 1989), 1.

Lyons, Stephen J. "Should Parents Be Punished for Using Prayer to Treat a Fatally Ill Child? No: Prayer Is Not a Crime." *ABA Journal* 78 (Mar. 1992): 39.

Manion, Maureen D. "Parental Religious Freedom, the Rights of Children, and the Role of the State." *Journal of Church and State* 34 (Winter 1992): 77–92.

Sitomer, Curtis J. "Prayer and Public Policy." *The Christian Science Monitor* (July 12, 1990): 13.

Skolnick, Andrew. "Religious Exemptions to Child Neglect Laws Still Being Passed Despite Convictions of Parents." *Journal of American Medical Association* 264 (Sept. 12, 1990): 1226, 1229, 1233.

Talbot, Nathan. "Spiritual Healing: Still in Court After Eight Decades." *Los Angeles Times* (May 1, 1988), 3.

———. "When Some Turn to Prayer." *The Washington Post* (Nov. 27, 1990), A21.

Tate, David A. "Should Parents Be Punished for Using Prayer to Treat a Fatally Ill Child? Yes: Parents Have a Duty." *ABA Journal* 78 (Mar. 1992): 38.

PAGES 86–89

Beardsley, Tim. "Blood Money: Critics Question High Pharmaceutical Profits." *Scientific American* 269 (Aug. 1993): 115–17.

Carey, John. "A Bitter Tonic for Drugmakers?" *BusinessWeek* (Mar. 8, 1993), 84–86.

———. "How Many Times Must a Patient Pay?" *BusinessWeek* (Feb. 1, 1993), 30–31.

Conlan, Michael F. "Eyes North: Should Canada's Price Control Plan Go South?" *Drug Topics* 137 (Apr. 5, 1993): 59.

Day, Kathleen. "Study Faults Drug Firms' Pricing Defense." *The Washington Post* (Feb. 26, 1993), A1.

Greenwald, John. "Ouch!" *Time* 141 (Mar. 8, 1993): 53–55.

Rich, Spencer. "Drug Price Review Board Is Proposed." *The Washington Post* (Feb. 11, 1993), B12.

"Should We Cap Prices of Prescription Drugs?" *The Washington Post* (July 27, 1993), Z14.

Sommer, Constance. "Drug Firms Post Excessive Gains, Congress Is Told." *Los Angeles Times* (Feb. 26, 1993), A18.

"Task Force May Call for Panel on Drug Prices." *Los Angeles Times* (May 17, 1993), A25.

Tully, Shawn. "Why Drug Prices Will Go Lower." *Fortune* 127 (May 3, 1993): 56–61.

PAGES 90–93

Battagliola, Monica. "The Results Are In: Drug Testing Saves Money." *Business & Health* 11 (Aug. 1993): 22–26.

Elmuti, Dean. "Effects of Drug-Testing Programme on Employee Attitudes, Productivity and Attendance Behavior." *International Journal of Manpower* 14, no. 5 (1993): 58–69.

Gray, George R., and Darrel R. Brown. "Issues in Drug Testing for the Private Sector." *HR Focus* 69 (Nov. 1992): 15.

Harris, Michael M., and Laura L. Heft. "Alcohol and Drug Use in the Workplace: Issues, Controversies, and Directions for Future Research." *Journal of Management* 18 (June 1992): 239–66.

MacDonald, Scott, Samantha Wells, and Richard Fry. "The Limitations of Drug Screening in the Workplace." *International Labour Review* 132, no. 1 (1993): 95–113.

Shaffer, Jay R., and Brian H. Kleiner. "Drug Testing in Organizations: Pro and Con." *Equal Opportunities International* 11, no. 2 (1992): 10–13.

Wall, Patricia. "Drug Testing in the Workplace: An Update." *Journal of Applied Business Research* 8 (Spring 1992): 127–32.

PAGES 96–99

Banks, Howard. "A Liberal Embraces the Supply-Side." *Forbes* 145 (Mar. 5, 1990): 86–88.

Byron, Christopher. "Cut and Run: Playing Politics with Taxes." *New York* 24 (Nov. 4, 1991): 20–22.

Levinson, Marc, and Rich Thomas. "Pandering for Votes." *Newsweek* 119 (Jan. 27, 1992): 41.

Lindsey, Lawrence B. "It's Time for Another Cut in Tax Rates." *Forbes* 145 (Mar. 5, 1990): 82–86.

"Lip-Flop." *The New Republic* 203 (July 23, 1990): 7–8.

McIntyre, Robert S. "The Populist Tax Act of 1989." *The Nation* 246 (Apr. 2, 1988): 445, 462–64.

Mufson, Steven. "Economists Take Dim View of Using Cuts to Stimulate the Economy." *The Washington Post* (Dec. 18, 1991), A18.

Perry, George L. "Should We Cut Taxes?" *Brookings Review* 10 (Winter 1992): 53.

Reaser, Alison Lynn. "Savings Will Be Loser from Higher Taxes." *ABA Banking Journal* 85 (Oct. 1993): 20–23.

Reinhardt, Uwe E. "Reaganomics, R.I.P.: The Returns Are in on the 'Supply-Side' Experiment." *The New Republic* 196 (Apr. 20, 1987): 24–26.

Spiers, Joseph. "Fixing the Economy: Let's Get Real About Taxes." *Fortune* 126 (Oct. 19, 1992): 78–81.

Stein, Herbert. "Myth and Math: How Cutting Taxes Trims the Truth." *The Washington Post* (Aug. 30, 1992), C1.

Steuerle, C. Eugene. *The Tax Decade: How Taxes Came to Dominate the Public Agenda*. Washington, D.C.: Urban Institute Press, 1992.

"Tax Cuts: An Idea Whose Time Has Gone." *BusinessWeek* (Oct. 28, 1991), 150.

Ture, Norman B. et al. "To Cut and to Please." *National Review* 44 (Aug. 31, 1992): 35–39.

Barone, Michael. "The Battle Over 'Losing Ground.' " *The Washington Post* (Apr. 3, 1985), A23.

Borger, Gloria. "Clinton's Hard Sell on Welfare." *U.S. News & World Report* 115 (July 19, 1993): 41.

Cloward, Richard A., and Frances Fox Piven. "A Class Analysis of Welfare." *Monthly Review* 44 (Feb. 1993): 25–31.

Mead, Lawrence M. *Beyond Entitlement: The Social Obligations of Citizenship.* New York: Free Press, 1986.

Offner, Paul. "Workfail: Waiting for Welfare Reform." *The New Republic* 207 (Dec. 28, 1992): 13–15.

Rich, Spencer. "Going to Bat for Nation's Welfare State." *The Washington Post* (Nov. 27, 1990), A19.

Sancton, Thomas. "How to Get America Off the Dole." *Time* 139 (May 25, 1992): 44–47.

Siegel, Fred. "Conservative Opportunism, Liberal Cowardice: The Racialization of American Politics." *Commonweal* 118 (Nov. 8, 1991): 642–47.

Taylor, Paul. "Welfare Policy's 'New Paternalism' Uses Benefits to Alter Recipients' Behavior." *The Washington Post* (June 8, 1991), A3.

Weidenbaum, Murray. "It's Up to Individuals to Fight the War on Poverty." *Los Angeles Times* (Sept. 23, 1990), D2.

Weiss, Michael D. "Reducing Poverty." *Current,* n. 348 (Dec. 1992): 14–19.

Goodgame, Dan. "Welfare for the Well-Off." *Time* 141 (Feb. 22, 1993): 36–38.

Kaus, Mickey. "Telling the Truth About Social Security." *The Washington Post* (Nov. 1, 1992), C3.

Mandel, Michael J. "From New Deal to Raw Deal." *BusinessWeek* (Apr. 5, 1993), 68–69.

Martz, Larry, and Rich Thomas. "Fixing Social Security." *Newsweek* 115 (May 7, 1990): 54–57.

Mufson, Steven. "Senators Differ on Deficit Cuts Involving Social Security Recipients." *The Washington Post* (Feb. 1, 1993), A4.

O'Lessker, Karl. "Demagoguing the Deficit." *The American Spectator* 25 (Dec. 1992): 54–56.

Pearlstein, Steven. "The Battle Over 'Generational Equity.' " *The Washington Post* (Feb. 17, 1993), F1.

Perez, Robert C., and Irene Hammerbacher. "Looking Towards a Sounder Social Security System." *Review of Business* 14 (Spring 1993): 30–34.

Porter, John. "Keeping Social Security Successful in the 21st Century." *USA Today* (Magazine) 120 (July 1991): 43–44.

Shapiro, Walter. "Their Turn to Pay?" *Time* 142 (Dec. 20, 1993): 36–37.

Smith, Lee. "The Tyranny of America's Old." *Fortune* 125 (Jan. 13, 1992): 68–72.

————. "The War Between the Generations." *Fortune* 116 (July 20, 1987): 78–81.

PAGES 108–111

Barrett, Wayne M. "Baseball's Fiscal Falsehoods." *USA Today* (Magazine) 120 (May 1992): 81.

Brunning, Fred. "The Millionaires of Mediocrity." *Maclean's* 103 (Jan. 8, 1990): 11.

"Flawed Diamonds." *The Economist* 327 (May 1, 1993): 98.

Harsham, Richard. "Grand Salaries Are Ruining the Grand Old Game." *The Christian Science Monitor* (Jan. 4, 1993), 19.

Henderson, Keith. "Sports 'Consumers' Cry Foul." *The Christian Science Monitor* (Feb. 26, 1993), 12.

Kirshenbaum, Jerry, ed. "Captivating." *Sports Illustrated* 77 (Dec. 21, 1992): 11.

Perry, George L. "Covering All the Economic Bases of Troubled Major League Baseball." *Los Angeles Times* (Jan. 10, 1993), D2.

Saporito, Bill. "The Owners' New Game Is Managing." *Fortune* 124 (July 1, 1991): 86–91.

Sell, Dave. "NHL on the Rise, but How High Can It Go?" *The Washington Post* (Jan. 23, 1994), D14.

Serwer, Andrew E. "How High?" *Sports Illustrated* 79 (Nov. 8, 1993): 88–91.

Sommers, Paul M., ed. *Diamonds Are Forever: The Business of Baseball.* Washington, D.C.: Brookings Institution, 1992.

Stone, Marvin. "Those High-Priced Athletes." *U.S. News & World Report* 93 (Oct. 4, 1982): 88.

Teitel, Jay. "Small Change." *Saturday Night* 105 (Oct. 1990): 71–76.

"Yastrzemski: Baseball's 'High Salaries Improve the Game.' " *U.S. News & World Report* 87 (Sept. 10, 1979): 74.

SCHOOLS AND RULES

PAGES 114–117

August, Diane, and Eugene E. Garcia. *Language Minority Education in the United States.* Springfield, Ill: Charles C. Thomas, 1988.

Bane, Nancy. " 'Official English': Fear or Foresight?" *America* 159 (Dec. 17, 1988): 515–16.

Carvajal, Doreen. "When Languages Collide." *Los Angeles Times* (Dec. 19, 1993), A1.

Chavez, Linda. "Why Bilingual Education Fails Hispanic Children." *McCall's* 118 (Mar. 1991): 59–60.

Cummins, Jim. "Bilingual Education and Politics." *Education Digest* 53 (Nov. 1987): 30–33.

Hayakawa, S. I. "Why English Should Be Our Official Language." *Education Digest* 52 (May 1987): 36–37.

Imhoff, Gary. "The Position of U.S. English on Bilingual Education." *The Annals of the American Academy of Political and Social Science* 508 (Mar. 1990): 48–61.

———, ed. *Learning in Two Languages.* New Brunswick, N.J.: Transaction, 1990.

Sanchez, Nicolas. "Bilingual Education: A Barrier to Achievement." *Education Digest* 53 (Dec. 1987): 42–43.

Seo, Diane. "It's All Spoken Here." *Los Angeles Times* (Apr. 18, 1993), 14.

Sundberg, Trudy J. "The Case Against Bilingualism." *English Journal* 77 (Mar. 1988): 16–17.

Worsnop, Richard L. "Bilingual Education." *CQ Researcher* 3 (Aug. 13, 1993): 699–717.

Alan Guttmacher Institute. *Teenage Sexual and Reproductive Behavior.* Facts in Brief. New York: Alan Guttmacher Institute, 1993.

Bethell, Tom. "A Girls' School in Baltimore." *The American Spectator* 26 (Feb. 1993): 17–18.

Chu, Henry. "Free Condoms Now Just a Fact of Life at High Schools." *Los Angeles Times* (July 6, 1993), B1.

Goldstein, Amy, and Paul W. Valentine. "For Teens, Norplant Is a Personal Issue." *The Washington Post* (Mar. 8, 1993), A1.

Kuharski, Mary Ann. "Teens Want, Need Chastity—Not Clinics." *St. Paul Pioneer Press Dispatch* (Jan. 21, 1987), 11A.

Reynolds, Jennifer Hincks, and Kris Keith, comps. *Condom Efficacy and Use Among Adolescents.* Washington, D.C.: Center for Population Options, 1993.

Weed, Stan E. "Curbing Births, Not Pregnancies." *The Wall Street Journal* (Oct. 14, 1986), 32.

Bernstein, David. "Why Johnny Can't Pray." *Reason* 23 (Feb. 1992): 56–58.

Biskupic, Joan. "Religious Access to Schools Widened." *The Washington Post* (June 8, 1993), A1.

Booth, William. "Bring Back School Prayer?" *The Washington Post* (Dec. 20, 1993), A1.

Conn, James J. "Graduation Prayers and the Establishment Clause." *America* 167 (Nov. 14, 1992): 380–82.

Cord, Robert L. "Church, State, and the Rehnquist Court." *National Review* 44 (Aug. 17, 1992): 35–37.

Doerr, Edd. "Freedom of Religion, Freedom from Religion." *Humanist* 53 (May/June 1993): 31–34.

Fenwick, Lynda Beck. *Should the Children Pray?: A Historical, Judicial, and Political Examination of Public School Prayer.* Waco, Texas: Baylor University Press, 1989.

Methvin, Eugene H. "Let Us Pray." *Reader's Digest* 141 (Nov. 1992): 75–79.

Novak, Michael. "Prayer in School: An Intolerant Supreme Court." *American Legion* 133 (Dec. 1992): 20–22.

PAGES 126–129

Gaff, Jerry G. "Beyond Politics: The Educational Issues Inherent in Multicultural Education." *Change* 24 (Jan./Feb. 1992): 31–32.

Gray, Paul. "Whose America?" *Time* 138 (July 8, 1991): 13–20.

Hassenger, Robert. "True Multiculturalism: Setting No Boundaries." *Commonweal* 119 (Apr. 10, 1992): 10–11.

Howe, Irving. "The Value of the Canon." *The New Republic* 204 (Feb. 18, 1991): 40–47.

Landers, Robert K. "Conflict Over Multicultural Education." *Editorial Research Reports* 1 (Nov. 30, 1990): 682–94.

Schlesinger, Arthur, Jr. "A Dissent on Multicultural Education." *Partisan Review* 58 (Fall 1991): 630–34.

————. *The Disuniting of America.* New York: W. W. Norton, 1992.

Smoler, Frederic. "What Should We Teach Our Children About American History?" *American Heritage* 43 (Feb./Mar. 1992): 45–52.

Stotsky, Sandra. "Academic vs. Ideological Multicultural Education in the Classroom." *The American School Board Journal* 178 (Oct. 1991): 26–28.

Woodward, C. Vann. "Equal but Separate." *The New Republic* 205 (July 15, 1991): 41–43.

PAGES 130–133

Banks, Sandy, and Dan Morain. "The Voucher Initiative: Savior or Fatal Blow?" *Los Angeles Times* (Oct. 31, 1993), A1.

Beiler, David. "The Great California School Voucher Massacre." *Campaigns & Elections* 15 (Dec. 1993/Jan. 1994): 60–61.

Bolger, Glen, and W. D. McInturff. "School Vouchers: A Republican Perspective." *Campaigns & Elections* 14 (Oct./Nov. 1993): 43–44.

"California's Schools: No Vouchers Yet." *The Economist* 329 (Nov. 6, 1993): 25.

"California's Schools: The Price of Choice." *The Economist* 329 (Oct. 9, 1993): 25–26.

Chavez, Stephanie, and Dan Morain. "In Wake of Defeat, Voucher Backers Vow a Stiffer Fight." *Los Angeles Times* (Nov. 4, 1993), A1.

Doerr, Edd. "The Head of the Hydra." *Humanist* 54 (Jan./Feb. 1994): 43–44.

Flanigan, James. "School Choice Campaign Goes Beyond the Election." *Los Angeles Times* (Oct. 24, 1993), D1.

Huston, William T. "Free-Enterprise Education." *Industry Week* 241 (June 1, 1992): 36.

Morais, Richard C. "A Revolution Betrayed." *Forbes* 152 (Dec. 20, 1993): 118–30.

Shanker, Albert. "America's Education Problems: Why Vouchers Are Not the Answer." *Survey of Business* 28 (Spring 1993): 28–31.

Shogren, Elizabeth. "A Chance to See Choice at Work." *Los Angeles Times* (Oct. 22, 1993); A1.

Shrag, Peter. "Bailing Out of Public Education: School Vouchers in California." *The Nation* 257 (Oct. 4, 1993): 351–54.

Yang, Frederick S. "School Vouchers: A Democratic Perspective." *Campaigns & Elections* 14 (Oct./Nov. 1993): 43–44.

PAGES 134–137

Barrett, Michael J. "Notes: The Newest Minority." *The Atlantic* 272 (July 1993): 22–25.

Colvin, Richard L. "School Finance: Equity Concerns in an Age of Reforms." *Educational Researcher* 18 (Jan./Feb. 1989): 11–15.

Curtis, Gregory. "School's Out." *Texas Monthly* 21 (June 1993): 7–10.

"Fairer Schooling in Michigan." *The New York Times* (Mar. 18, 1994), A28.

Kozol, Jonathan. *Savage Inequalities*. New York: Crown, 1991.

Lacayo, Richard. "School's Out—of Cash." *Time* 141 (Apr. 5, 1993): 34–35.

"Texas Schools: A Tale of Two Districts." *The Economist* 327 (May 29, 1993): 31–32.

Walters, Jonathan. "School Funding." *CQ Researcher* 3 (Aug. 27, 1993): 747–67.

PAGES 140–143

Brady, James. "No Job for a Woman." *American Legion* 136 (May 1994): 28–29.

Fields, Suzanne. "Why Women Shouldn't Get Wartime's License to Kill." *Insight* 8 (Dec. 7, 1992): 18–19.

Hackworth, David H. "War and the Second Sex." *Newsweek* 118 (Aug. 5, 1991): 24–28.

Holm, Jeanne. *Women in the Military: An Unfinished Revolution.* Novato, Calif.: Presidio Press, 1992.

Horowitz, David. "The Feminist Assault on the Military." *National Review* 44 (Oct. 5, 1992): 46–49.

Pine, Art. "Women Will Get Limited Combat Roles." *Los Angeles Times* (Jan. 14, 1994), A18.

Schmitt, Eric. "Army Allowing Women in 32,000 Combat Posts." *The New York Times* (July 28, 1994), A12.

———. "Pentagon Plans to Allow Combat Flights by Women." *The New York Times* (Apr. 28, 1993), A1.

PAGES 144–147

Akerman, Robert. "Old Principles Should Guide Our New Mission." *Atlanta Journal* (Apr. 13, 1992), A10.

"American Foreign Policy: Otherwise Engaged." *The Economist* 329 (Oct. 30, 1993): 21–24.

Carpenter, Ted Galen. *A Search for Enemies: America's Alliances After the Cold War.* Washington, D.C.: Cato Institute, 1992.

Cooper, Mary H. "Foreign Policy Burden." *CQ Researcher* 3 (Aug. 20, 1993): 723–43.

Forbes, Malcolm S., Jr. "Passivity Begets Not Peace but More Bloodshed." *Forbes* 152 (July 5, 1993): 25.

"How America Sees the World." *The Economist* 329 (Oct. 30, 1993): 15–16.

Judis, John B. "Clinton's Radical Failure: The Foreign Unpolicy." *The New Republic* 209 (July 12, 1993): 16–20.

Thomas, Evan et al. "Playing Globocop." *Newsweek* 121 (June 28, 1993): 20–24.

Tonelson, Alan. "Superpower Without a Sword." *Foreign Affairs* 72 (Summer 1993): 166–80.

PAGES 148–151

Braffman-Miller, Judith. "Swords into Plowshares: Military Conversion for the 1990s." *USA Today* (Magazine) 122 (Jan. 1994): 12–14.

Budiansky, Stephen, and Bruce B. Auster. "Missions Implausible." *U.S. News & World Report* 111 (Oct. 14, 1991): 24–31.

Daggett, Stephen. "How Much for Defence?" *Congressional Research Service Review* 13 (Apr./May 1992): 5–8.

Fessler, Pamela. "Hill Struggles to Assist Victims of Post-Cold War Budget Cuts." *Congressional Quarterly* 50 (Mar. 7, 1992): 542–45.

Isaacs, John. "Treading Water." *The Bulletin of the Atomic Scientists* 49 (June 1993): 3–5.

Levinson, Marc, and John Barry. "Defense: The Real Debate." *Newsweek* 118 (July 15, 1991): 34–36.

O'Rourke, Ronald. "Reducing the Size of the Military: How Large a Force Is Needed?" *Congressional Research Service Review* 13 (Apr./May 1992): 2–4.

Segal, David. "The Shell Game." *The Washington Monthly* 25 (July/Aug. 1993): 37–43.

Smith, Lee. "Coping with the Defense Build-Down." *Fortune* 125 (June 29, 1992): 88–93.

Weber, Vin. "Tactical Retreat." *National Review* 45 (May 10, 1993): 20–21.

Wiesner, Jerome B., Philip Morrison, and Kosta Tsipis. "Ending Overkill." *The Bulletin of the Atomic Scientists* 49 (Mar. 1993): 12–23.

PAGES 152–155

Bacevich, A. J. "Gays and Military Culture." *National Review* 45 (Apr. 26, 1993): 26–31.

Biskupic, Joan. "High Court Lifts Bar to Gay Ban." *The Washington Post* (Oct. 30, 1993), A1.

"The Case of the Gay Midshipman." *The Washington Post* (Nov. 26, 1989), W28.

"Clinton: Policy on Gays in Military Is 'Sensible Balance.'" *The Washington Post* (July 20, 1993), A12.

"Homosexuals in the Military: Dishonourable Discharges." *The Economist* 327 (June 26, 1993): 95–96.

Keen, Lisa. "The Fears Are Unjustified." *The Washington Post* (Jan. 31, 1993), C7.

"See You Later, Alligator." *National Review* 45 (June 7, 1993): 17.

Stedman, Craig W. "The Constitution, the Military, and Homosexuals: Should the Military's Policies Concerning Homosexuals Be Modified?" *Dickinson Law Review* 95 (Winter 1991): 321–52.

Thompson, Tracy. "Judge Backs Navy's Right to Oust Gay Midshipman." *The Washington Post* (Dec. 10, 1991), A4.

Wilkinson, Francis. "About Facing Chairman Nunn: Inside the Gay Lobby." *Rolling Stone,* no. 656 (May 13, 1993): 39–43.

Worsnop, Richard L. "Gay Rights." *CQ Researcher* 3 (Mar. 5, 1993): 195–212.

CULTURE WARS

PAGES 158–161

Bolton, Richard, ed. Introduction to *Culture Wars: Documents from the Recent Controversies in the Arts.* New York: New Press, 1992.

Brookman, Philip. Preface to *Culture Wars: Documents from the Recent Controversies in the Arts,* ed. Richard Bolton. New York: New Press, 1992.

Glueck, Grace. "Art on the Firing Line." *The New York Times* (July 9, 1989), H1.

Helms, Jesse. "It's the Job of Congress to Define What's Art." *USA Today* (Sept. 8, 1989), 12A.

Hughes, Robert. "A Loony Parody of Cultural Democracy." *Time* 134 (Aug. 14, 1989): 82.

Smith, Joshua P. "Why the Corcoran Made a Big Mistake." *The Washington Post* (June 18, 1989), G1.

Trescott, Jacqueline. "Arts Agency's Inviting Ways." *The Washington Post* (Feb. 5, 1994), G3.

U.S. Congress. Senate. Debate in Senate Over the NEA. *Congressional Record* (May 18, 1989), vol. 135, no. 64, S 5594.

PAGES 162–165

Alger, Dean E. *The Media and Politics.* Englewood Cliffs, N.J.: Prentice Hall, 1989.

Baker, Brent H. "Media's Liberal Slant on the News." *USA Today* (magazine) 118 (July 1989): 64–66.

Clark, Charles S. "Public Broadcasting." *CQ Researcher* 2 (Sept. 18, 1992): 811–28.

Henry, William A., III. "Are the Media Too Liberal?" *Time* 140 (Oct. 19, 1992): 46–47.

Kurtz, Howard. "President Without a Pundit." *The Washington Post* (Sept. 17, 1993), D2.

McCarthy, Colman. " 'MacNeil/Lehrer': FAIR Game." *The Washington Post* (June 3, 1990), F2.

Rusher, William A. "All the News That's Fit for Democrats." *National Review* 40 (Mar. 18, 1988): 32–33.

Shearer, Harry. "The Objectivity Diet." *Los Angeles Times* (Dec. 8, 1991), 14.

Willis, Jim. *The Shadow World: Life Between the News Media and Reality.* New York: Praeger, 1991.

PAGES 166–169

Bayles, Martha. "Fake Blood: Why Nothing Gets Done About Media Violence." *Brookings Review* 11 (Fall 1993): 20–23.

"Breaking the Addiction to TV Violence." *The Washington Post* (Nov. 1, 1993), A16.

Clark, Charles S. "TV Violence." *CQ Researcher* 3 (Mar. 26, 1993): 167–87.

"Despite Censorship Fears, Reno Says Government May Stop TV Violence." *The Houston Post* (Oct. 25, 1993), A8.

Edwards, Ellen. "Cable Leaders to Develop Violence Ratings." *The Washington Post* (Jan. 11, 1994), B1.

———. "Reno: End TV Violence." *The Washington Post* (Oct. 21, 1993), A1.

Fowles, Jib. *Why Viewers Watch: A Reappraisal of Television's Effects.* Newbury Park, Calif.: Sage, 1992.

Gerber, Eric. "Fighting Over TV Violence Settles Nothing." *The Houston Post* (Aug. 4, 1993), D1.

"Reno Softens Stance on TV Violence." *The Washington Post* (Mar. 24, 1994), C4.

Silver, Marc, Katherine T. Beddingfield, and Kenan Pollack. "Sex, Violence, and the Tube." *U.S. News & World Report* 115 (Sept. 20, 1993): 76–79.

"TV Violence and the Feds." *The Washington Post* (Oct. 23, 1993), A22.

PAGES 170–173

Dezell, Maureen. "Bundy's Revenge." *The New Republic* 206 (Mar. 9, 1992): 15–16.

Donnerstein, Edward I., and Daniel G. Linz. "The Question of Pornography." *Psychology Today* 20 (Dec. 1986): 56–59.

Echols, Alice. "Sex and the Single-Minded: The Dworkinization of Catharine MacKinnon." *Voice Literary Supplement* (Mar. 1994), 13–14.

Farrell, David. "The Insidious Impact of Pornography." *The Boston Globe* (June 17, 1985), 15.

Kurkjian, Stephen. "U.S. Panel Urges New Vigilance on Pornography." *The Boston Globe* (July 17, 1986), 1.

Kurtz, Howard. "The Pornography Panel's Controversial Last Days." *The Washington Post* (May 30, 1986), A13.

Melillo, Wendy. "Can Pornography Lead to Violence?" *The Washington Post* (July 21, 1992), Z10.

Nichols, Mark. "Viewers and Victims." *Maclean's* 106 (Oct. 11, 1993): 60.

Phillips, Frank, and Toni Locy. "Liability for Porno Producers Debated." *The Boston Globe* (Mar. 17, 1992), 20.

Stengel, Richard. "Sex Busters: A Meese Commission and the Supreme Court Echo a New Moral Militancy." *Time* 128 (July 21, 1986): 12–19.

Wolfe, Alan. "For Adult Users Only: The Dilemma of Violent Pornography." *The New Republic* 202 (Feb. 19, 1990): 27–31.

PAGES 174–177

Biskupic, Joan. "Ruling by Hawaii's Supreme Court Opens the Way to Gay Marriages." *The Washington Post* (May 7, 1993), A10.

Clark, Joe. "Rights, Privileges, and Gay Lovers." *The Advocate,* no. 597 (Feb. 25, 1992): 56–58.

Essoyan, Susan. "Hawaii Tries to Take a Stand Against Same-Sex Marriages." *Los Angeles Times* (Apr. 26, 1994), A5.

Gaines-Carter, Patrice. "Legal Snag Keeps Gays from Tying the Knot." *The Washington Post* (Dec. 6, 1990), C5.

Gross, Jane. "Hawaii's Pioneering Role on Gay Rights." *San Francisco Chronicle* (Apr. 25, 1994), A7.

Hartinger, Brent. "A Case for Gay Marriage: In Support of Loving and Monogamous Relationships." *Commonweal* 118 (Nov. 22, 1991): 681–83.

Isaacson, Walter. "Should Gays Have Marriage Rights?" *Time* 134 (Nov. 20, 1989): 101–102.

Leo, John. "Gay Rights, Gay Marriages." *U.S. News & World Report* 114 (May 24, 1993): 19.

Mitchell, Henry. "Gays and the State of Matrimony." *The Washington Post* (Jan. 11, 1991), D2.

O'Brien, Dennis. "Against Gay Marriage—I: What Heterosexuality Means." *Commonweal* 118 (Nov. 22, 1991): 684–85.

Sullivan, Andrew. "The Politics of Homosexuality: A New Case for a New Beginning." *The New Republic* 208 (May 10, 1993): 24–31.

PAGES 178–181

Brimelow, Peter. "Spiral of Silence." *Forbes* 149 (May 25, 1992): 76–77.

Forman, James, Jr. "Saving Affirmative Action." *The Nation* 253 (Dec. 9, 1991): 746–47.

Hall, Patrick A. "Against Our Best Interests: An Ambivalent View of Affirmative Action." *American Libraries* 22 (Oct. 1991): 898–901.

Henry, William A., III. "What Price Preference?" *Time* 138 (Sept. 30, 1991): 30–31.

Monroe, Sylvester. "Nothing Is Ever Simply Black and White." *Time* 138 (Aug. 12, 1991): 6–7.

Norris, Jeffrey A. *Corporate Affirmative Action Practices and the Civil Rights Act of 1991.* Washington, D.C.: Employment Policy Foundation, 1992.

"The Quota Question: Civil Rights." *The Economist* 321 (Nov. 30, 1991): 27–28.

Steinberg, Stephen. "Occupational Apartheid." *The Nation* 253 (Dec. 9, 1991): 744–46.

Weimer, George. "Quotas and Other Dumb Ideas." *Industry Week* 241 (Apr. 6, 1992): 86.

PAGES 182–185

Belsky, Jay. "The 'Effects' of Infant Day Care Reconsidered." *Early Childhood Research Quarterly* 3 (Sept. 1988): 235–72.

Caminiti, Susan. "Who's Minding America's Kids?" *Fortune* 126 (Aug. 10, 1992): 50–53.

Chapman, Fern Schumer. "Executive Guilt: Who's Taking Care of the Children?" *Fortune* 115 (Feb. 16, 1987): 30–37.

Hayes, Cheryl D., John L. Palmer, and Martha J. Zaslow, eds. *Who Cares for America's Children? Child Care Policy for the 1990s.* Washington, D.C.: National Academy of Sciences, 1990.

Labich, Kenneth. "Can Your Career Hurt Your Kids?" *Fortune* 123 (May 20, 1991): 38–44.

Shell, Ellen Ruppel. "Babes in Day Care: The Controversy Over Whether Nonmaternal Care Harms Infants." *The Atlantic* 262 (Aug. 1988): 73–74.

Wallis, Claudia. "The Child-Care Dilemma." *Time* 129 (June 22, 1987): 54–60.

———. "Is Day Care Bad for Babies?" *Time* 129 (June 22, 1987): 63.

Zinsmeister, Karl. "Brave New World: How Day Care Harms Children." *Policy Review* 44 (Spring 1988): 40.

"At America's Door." *The Economist* 328 (July 24, 1993): 11–12.

Conniff, Ruth. "The War on Aliens: The Right Calls the Shots." *The Progressive* 57 (Oct. 1993): 22–28.

Cooper, Mary H. "Immigration Reform." *CQ Researcher* 3 (Sept. 24, 1993): 843–63.

Fierman, Jaclyn. "Is Immigration Hurting the U.S.?" *Fortune* 128 (Aug. 9, 1993): 76–79.

Maital, Shlomo. "Out of the Melting Pot into the Fire." *Across the Board* 30 (Sept. 1993): 59–60.

Mandel, Michael J., and Christopher Farrell. "The Immigrants: How They're Helping to Revitalize the U.S. Economy." *BusinessWeek* (July 13, 1992), 114–22.

Moore, Stephen. "Mixed Blessings." *Across the Board* 28 (Mar. 1991): 45–49.

Solomon, Charlene Marmer. "Two Weaknesses in the U.S. Immigration System." *Personnel Journal* 72 (Feb. 1993): 60–61.

Suro, Roberto. "An Abundance of Asylum-Seekers." *The Washington Post* (Mar. 14, 1994), A1.

"They're Coming." *The Economist* 328 (July 24, 1993): 23–24.

GOVERNING THE GOVERNMENT

PAGES 192–195

Balz, Dan. "Term Limits Drive Dealt Sharp Blow." *The Washington Post* (Feb. 11, 1994), A1.

Benjamin, Gerald, and Michael J. Malbin, eds. *Limiting Legislative Terms.* Washington, D.C.: CQ Press, 1992.

Clancy, Paul. "Term-Limit Drive Continues." *Nation's Business* 80 (Nov. 1992): 34–37.

Clift, Eleanor. "Wild Pitch: George Will Strikes Out Against Term Limits." *The Washington Monthly* 24 (Nov. 1992): 48–50.

Coyne, James K., and John H. Fund. *Cleaning House: America's Campaign for Term Limits.* Washington, D.C.: Regnery Gateway, 1992.

Eastland, Terry. "The Limits of Term Limits." *Commentary* 95 (Feb. 1993): 53–55.

Egan, Timothy. "House Speaker and Ex-Attorney General Dueling Over Term Limits." *The New York Times* (July 29, 1993), A16.

Greider, William. "Should We Throw the Bums Out?" *Rolling Stone,* no. 648 (Jan. 21, 1993): 27–29.

Will, George F. "Scared to Death of Term Limits." *The Washington Post* (Jan. 16, 1994), C7.

PAGES 196–199

Byrd, Robert C. "A Hollow and Dangerous Promise." *The Washington Post* (Oct. 31, 1993), C7.

"The Case for a Balanced-Budget Amendment." *Nation's Business* 82 (Jan. 1994): 79.

Dewar, Helen, and Clay Chandler. "Imbalanced Balanced-Budget Hearings Offer Stark Views of Amendment." *The Washington Post* (Feb. 16, 1994), A8.

Eaton, William J. "Amendment to Balance Budget Fails in Senate." *Los Angeles Times* (Mar. 2, 1994), A1.

Fink, Richard H., and Jack C. High, eds. *A Nation in Debt: Economists Debate the Federal Budget Deficit.* Frederick, Md.: University Publications of America, 1987.

Morris, Charles R. "Deficit Figuring Doesn't Add Up." *The New York Times* (Feb. 12, 1989); 36.

"Not Insane—but Very Unbalanced." *Los Angeles Times* (Feb. 25, 1994), B6.

Pianin, Eric. "A Balanced Budget Amendment: The Dream and the Debate." *The Washington Post* (June 2, 1992), A17.

Simon, Paul. "A Tool to Force Officials to Do the Right Thing." *Los Angeles Times* (Feb. 25, 1994), B7.

"Why We Need the Balanced Budget Amendment." *The Washington Post* (Nov. 25, 1993), A30.

PAGES 200–203

"Back to the Ghetto?" *The Economist* 328 (July 10, 1993): 13–14.

Biskupic, Joan. "N.C. Case to Pose Test of Racial Redistricting." *The Washington Post* (Apr. 20, 1993), A4.

Broder, David S. "North Carolina's 12th." *The Washington Post* (July 7, 1993), A21.

Brownstein, Ronald. "Minority Quotas in Elections?" *Los Angeles Times* (Aug. 28, 1991), A1.

Cooper, Kenneth J. "Justice Dept. Moves to Defend Black-Majority Voting District." *The Washington Post* (Feb. 23, 1994), A11.

"Gerrymandering: Whither Shall It Wander?" *The Economist* 328 (July 10, 1993): 18–19.

Grofman, Bernie. "Race and Redistricting: No One Is Using the Voting Rights Act to 'Whiten' Majority Districts." *The Washington Post* (Oct. 21, 1991), A19.

Guinier, Lani. "Lani Guinier." *The New York Times Magazine* (Feb. 27, 1994), 42.

Lane, Charles. "Ghetto Chic: New York's Redistricting Mess." *The New Republic* 205 (Aug. 12, 1991): 14–16.

Meacham, John. "Voting Wrongs." *The Washington Monthly* 25 (Mar. 1993): 28–32.

Rosen, Jeffrey. "Gerrymandered." *The New Republic* 209 (Oct. 25, 1993): 12–13.

Terry, Gayle. "Perspective on Civil Rights: The True Concern Is Racial Justice." *Los Angeles Times* (July 27, 1993), B7.

Van Biema, David. "Snakes or Ladders?" *Time* 142 (July 12, 1993): 30–31.

NATURE VERSUS NURTURE

PAGES 206–209

Billings, Paul, and Jonathan Beckwith. "Born Gay?" *Technology Review* 96 (July 1993): 60–62.

Bull, Chris. "Mom's Fault." *The Advocate,* no. 636 (Aug. 24, 1993): 30–32.

Burr, Chandler. "Homosexuality and Biology." *The Atlantic* 271 (Mar. 1993): 47–65.

Gelman, David et al. "Born or Bred?" *Newsweek* 119 (Feb. 24, 1992): 46–53.

Horgan, John. "Eugenics Revisited." *Scientific American* 268 (June 1993): 123–31.

Rensberger, Boyce. "Study Links Genes to Homosexuality." *The Washington Post* (July 16, 1993), A1.

"Researcher Pledges to Protect Test for Genetic Pattern Linked to Gays." *The Washington Post* (Feb. 22, 1994), A4.

Rist, Darrell Yates. "Sex on the Brain: Are Homosexuals Born That Way?" *The Nation* 255 (Oct. 19, 1992): 424–27.

PAGES 210–213

Cowley, Geoffrey. "Who's Looking After the Interest of Children?" *Newsweek* 122 (Aug. 16, 1993): 54–55.

Franks, Lucinda. "The War for Baby Clausen: Annals of Law." *The New Yorker* 69 (Mar. 22, 1993): 56–73.

Gibbs, Nancy, Andrea Sachs, and Sophfronia Scott Gregory. "In Whose Best Interest?" *Time* 142 (July 19, 1993): 44–50.

Shapiro, Joseph P. "Bonds That Blood and Birth Cannot Assure." *U.S. News & World Report* 115 (Aug. 9, 1993): 12–13.

Taylor, John. "Biological Imperative." *New York* 26 (Aug. 16, 1993): 12–13.

Terry, Don. "Storm Rages in Chicago Over Revoked Adoption." *The New York Times* (July 15, 1994), A1.

Uniform Law Commissioners. *Uniform Adoption Act Ready for Final Approval.* Chicago: National Conference of Commissioners on Uniform State Laws, 1994.

Walsh, Edward. "Illinois Court Backs Biological Parents." *The Washington Post* (July 14, 1994), A3.

BEING GREEN

PAGES 216–219

Bailey, Ronald. *Eco-Scam: The False Prophets of Ecological Apocalypse.* New York: St. Martin's Press, 1993.

Brown, Lester R. "The World Transformed: Envisioning an Environmentally Safe Planet." *Futurist* 27 (May/June 1993): 16–21.

Cooper, Mary H. "Population Growth." *CQ Researcher* 3 (July 16, 1993): 603–20.

Gelbspan, Ross. "Racing to an Environmental Precipice." *The Boston Globe* (May 31, 1992), 1.

Hahn, Robert W. "Toward a New Environmental Paradigm." *Yale Law Review* 102 (May 1993): 1719–61.

McNamara, Robert S. "The Population Explosion." *Futurist* 26 (Nov./Dec. 1992): 9–13.

Revkin, Andrew. "Doomsayers (Again): We're Doomed and This Time They May Be Right as Global Population Zooms." *Newsday* (June 9, 1992), 89.

Stevens, William K. "Feeding a Booming Population Without Destroying the Planet." *The New York Times* (Apr. 5, 1994), C1, C8.

PAGES 220–223

Begley, Sharon et al. "The Birds and the Trees: Clinton Convenes a Summit on the Spotted Owl." *Newsweek* 121 (Apr. 5, 1993): 53–54.

Cooper, Mary H. "Jobs vs. Environment." *CQ Researcher* 2 (May 15, 1992): 411–31.

"Dying by the Thousands." *Scholastic Update* 125 (Apr. 16, 1993): 3–5.

Erickson, Deborah. "Sustainable Jobs." *Scientific American* 265 (Nov. 1991): 127–28.

Krug, Edward C. "Save the Planet, Sacrifice the People: The Environmental Party's Bid for Power." *Executive Speeches* 7 (Feb./Mar. 1993): 6–10.

Maucher, Helmut. "Industry and the Environment: The Views of an Industrialist." *Columbia Journal of World Business* 28 (Summer 1993): 6–10.

Rice, James Owen. "Where Many an Owl Is Spotted." *National Review* 44 (Mar. 2, 1992): 41–43.

Schiefelbein, Gregory. "Sustainable Development: Meeting Today's Needs, as Well as Tomorrow's." *Economic Development Review* 10 (Summer 1992): 13–15.

Warner, David. "Expanding the Wilderness." *Nation's Business* 81 (May 1993): 66–67.

PAGES 226–229

Behr, Peter. "117 Nations' Representatives Approve Historic Trade Pact." *The Washington Post* (Dec. 16, 1993), A41.

———. "Trade Pact Tackles a Sacred Cow: Farm Subsidies." *The Washington Post* (Dec. 16, 1993), B15.

Carey, Patricia M. "Trade War." *International Business* 6 (Nov. 1993): 62–68.

Dahl, David S. "Why Trade?" *Fedgazette* 5 (Oct. 1993): 2–3.

Dowd, Ann Reilly. "Let's Just Say Yes to NAFTA." *Fortune* 128 (Nov. 29, 1993): 108–109.

Krugman, Paul R. "Free Trade: A Loss of (Theoretical) Nerve? The Narrow and Broad Arguments for Free Trade." *AEA Papers and Proceedings* 83 (May 1993): 362–66.

Levinson, Marc. "America's Edge." *Newsweek* 119 (June 8, 1992): 40–43.

———. "The Trashing of Free Trade." *Newsweek* 122 (July 12, 1993): 42–45.

Marshall, Patrick G. "U.S. Trade Policy." *CQ Researcher* 3 (Jan. 29, 1993): 75–94.

Mollins, Carl. "Unfavorable Trade Winds: A Chronic Trade Surplus Adds to Tensions Between Japan and the United States." *Maclean's* 107 (Feb. 28, 1994): 36–38.

"The NAFTA Panic Attack." *U.S. News & World Report* 115 (Nov. 22, 1993): 22–24.

Orme, William A., Jr. "The NAFTA Debate: Myths Versus Facts—The Whole Truth About the Half-Truths." *Foreign Affairs* 72 (Nov./Dec. 1993): 2–12.

Rowen, Hobart. "GATT Accord: A Massive, but Maybe Moot, Success." *The Washington Post* (Dec. 19, 1993), H1.

PAGES 230–233

Awanohara, Susumu. "Hard Labour: Dispute Over Workers' Rights Sours U.S.-Indonesia Ties." *Far Eastern Economic Review* 156 (May 13, 1993): 13.

Baucus, Max. "Developing a China Policy." *China Business Review* 19 (Mar./Apr. 1992): 12–13.

Behr, Peter. "Offering China a Carrot on Trade." *The Washington Post* (Jan. 29, 1994), C1.

Brecher, Richard A. "A Pandora's Box?" *China Business Review* 20 (July/Aug. 1993): 6–9.

Friedman, Thomas L. "Trade vs. Human Rights." *The New York Times* (Feb. 6, 1994), A1, 10.

Goshko, John M. "Balancing Trade Pact and Human Rights in Mexico." *The Washington Post* (Jan. 30, 1994), A30.

Lippman, Thomas W., and Peter Behr. "U.S.-China Talks Set on Concerns Over Human Rights." *The Washington Post* (Jan. 13, 1994), A17.

McGrory, Mary. "Overrunning Human Rights." *The Washington Post* (June 15, 1993), A2.

Oberdorfer, Don. "Replaying the China Card." *The Washington Post* (Nov. 7, 1993), C3.